Silenced No More
Voices of 'Comfort Women'

By Sylvia S.J. Yu Friedman

SILENCED NO MORE: VOICES OF 'COMFORT WOMEN'

Freedom Campaign Publishers

ISBN: 978-154-987-9548

Acknowledgments

Almost 14 years later, after many hurdles and roadblocks and lugging boxes and suitcases full of documents and research from country to country as I moved around, it's surreal that this book is finally complete after beginning it in 2001. This book is to offer a voice for the voiceless victims of Imperial Japanese military sex slavery and to those suffering in the unbroken cycle of modern day slavery that continues to this day.

I want to give special thanks to the survivors for their courage in sharing their stories and thus exposing unspeakable horrors:

Kim Hak-Soon, Lee Young-Soo, Kim Soon-Duk, Hwang Geum-Joo, Kim Gun-Ja, Ji Dol-Yee, Kang Il-Chul, Bae Choon-Hee, Park Ok-Yeon, Moon Pil-Gi, Wan Ai-Hua, Yuan Zhu-Lin, Chen Lien-Hua, Ellen Van der Ploeg, Jan Ruff-O'Herne, Park Yong-Shim, Adela Reyes Barroquillo, Shim Dal-Yeon, Liu Haiyun, Li Jinyu, Wang E-hai, Liu Haiyu, Feng Nu-er, Yuan Gailian, Guo Fengying, Li Jine, Guo Maohai, Liu Fenghai, Qin Aizhen, Hao Gaiying, Hao Juxiang,

Hao Gaixiang, Bai Xiuying, Hao Yuelian, Li Gailan, Li Fulan, Li Ailian, Ren Lan-E, Zhao Zhilan, Zhao Lanying, Fan Lianhua.

I'm grateful to three former Japanese soldiers for their valuable time: Waichi Okumura, Tetsuro Takahashi, Yasuji Kaneko.

Thank you Jae Yu for the brilliant book cover design and Grace Kim for your professional editing.

Finally, my amazing parents and siblings— thank you for being my rock.

This book is dedicated to my extraordinary husband Matt Friedman. Your unwavering support for these women survivors and for their voices to be heard has inspired me to no end. I finished this book because of your inspiration and love.

Contents

Foreword

Dear Friends, Sisters, and Brothers,

"In times of war, it is always the women who have to pay the bill", says Ellen van der Ploeg, a Dutch survivor of Japanese military sex slavery, one of the women whose voices is heard, who are silenced no more, thanks to the work of Sylvia Yu Friedman.

It is an enormous honor and privilege for me to say some words and share some thoughts today, at the launch of the 'Healing River' film on 'comfort women' and the official launch of the book "Silenced No More: Voices of 'Comfort Women.'"

It is an honor because with the release of this book, Sylvia Yu Friedman not only made it possible for these silenced voices to be heard, with publishing this book, which is the result of many years of hard work and diligent research, of travels, deep emotions and shared pain, Sylvia marks a milestone in history.

And for several reasons.

First of all:

1. The voices we hear in this book are the voices of survivors of the Second World War, that ended, exactly this year 2015, 70 years ago. They are not young women and it is important that their stories are written down before it is too late. So that we can learn from them.

Because, as Ellen said, in times of war it is always the women who have to pay the bill.

2.   Secondly, if we look at history in general, the history of humankind and more, in particular, the history of women, we see that the history of women is a history of silence. Over the ages and until today, women are silenced. Women are not taken as seriously as men, women are underrepresented in all spheres of life, politics, academia, the private sector. Making women heard, as Sylvia does, is therefore basically a moral imperative issue.

3.   The third reason why Sylvia marks a milestone in history is because, in this year 2015, we not only celebrate the end of WWII, we also celebrate the 70 years of the United Nations, the organization of the international community, that was founded to keep world peace.

And today we see a world that is in more turmoil and confusion than ever before. A world in which the stories of these women, tell us what still is going on, in so many places. In Sudan, Burundi, Zimbabwe, or Guatemala, Honduras, in India, Myanmar, in refugee camps all over the world, from Darfur to today, also the borders of Hungary or France in Europe.

Because it is always women, -and girls I would add-, that pay the bill in times of war, as Ellen said. In situations of war and conflict women, female bodies are the frontline of war, since rape, mass rape, has become a mighty instrument, a powerful weapon of war, not only as a means to comfort the militaries, but also to morally breakdown societies, to demonstrate the weakness of the enemy, and to, by making women pregnant, ethnically cleanse a community.

"Has nothing been done?", one would ask? Has the international community not been able to give even the beginning of an answer in those 70 years?

There has been progress. In 2000, the Security Council of the UN adopted Resolution 1325, that states the disproportional impact of war on women and children. In this resolution also, women are not only seen as victims of war and conflict but also as indispensable parts of the solution. Without the voices of women, situations of conflict or war will not come to an end and peace treaties will not have a structural effect.

Also from national politics in various countries we have seen actions to improve the situation of women, to address their vulnerability in situations of conflict and, more specifically, the position of women and girls in Asia, - certainly in India and China-, has had political attention, as well as the situation of 'comfort women'.

In 2007, for instance, the parliaments of Canada, South Korea, Taiwan and the EU parliament passed resolutions that demand justice from the Japanese government for the military sex slavery survivors.

Back in 2009, when I was a member of parliament in the Netherlands we managed to get a resolution unanimously adopted, that said that recognizing the fate of the victims of the 'comfort women' system should remain part of the relations between the Netherlands and Japan and that the Dutch government should always continue to put pressure on Japan to offer a gesture towards the women who suffered.

A gesture, that could do justice to the comfort women and that could give them back, at least a little bit, of their human dignity. A gesture that could show respect to what is their right, their human right. To do justice would ask nothing more than for the perpetrators to recognize what has happened, nothing more than to admit that so many women have been wronged.

To do justice would be nothing more than just to say: "I am sorry".

But sorry still seems to be the hardest word as we have seen in the official speech of Japanese Prime Minister Abe at the commemoration of the end of the Second World War.

Fortunately, it is not only Prime Ministers, Heads of States, governments or politics alone that decide what happens in a country. Fortunately, there is civil society as the expression of what moves people in their day to day lives, in their family, community or social structures. These can be religious associations, trade unions or non-governmental organizations.

These institutions, of the people, should in any society be able to and thus be allowed to, play a decisive role. They should be recognized and taken seriously by any government, since they have proved to be a strong force, in bridging gaps, in promoting peace and mutual understanding.

Thanks to your work, Sylvia, thanks to all who have collaborated with you and surely thanks to all the women who let you break their silence, the voices of survivors of Japanese military forced prostitution can be heard.

And they have a strong appeal to us today, 70 years after the end of WWII, in our world where today millions of women still are victims of sexual violence and modern slavery, in which many women and girls do not seem to have the same human rights as men and boys but only serve to provide the men with what they want. In our world today in which countries like Syria and Iraq seem to be back in the dark ages, due to extremist groups, in a world in which IS, Islamic State proclaims that girls can marry at the age of 9 and that it is appropriate to abuse women and girls as sex slaves. In a world in which 223 girls can get kidnapped in Northern Nigeria and more than a year after that, their fate is still unknown, in this world, Sylvia, your book, makes a strong and timely appeal on all of us.

Because in times of war, it is always the women who have to pay the bill.

Because if we do not dare to face our history and finally listen to the voices of these women and girls, we will not be able to understand our present and if we do not understand our present, we will not be able to create a world that is free of slavery, of all forms of slavery and to give women and girls the human rights, that they are entitled to.

By Kathleen Ferrier

Kathleen is a former Member of Parliament in the Netherlands and involved in human rights issues. She has working experiences in Latin America, Europe and now Asia with migrant communities and related to human rights, international relations, cross-cultural communication and sustainable development issues.

Prologue

Bearing Witness to Historical Sex Trafficking

You may not know that the first mass trafficking of women and children since the transatlantic slave trade took place in Asia. From 1931, until the end of the war in 1945, it is estimated that somewhere between eighty thousand to four hundred thousand[1] women and children were trafficked into sex slavery camps throughout the Japanese Empire in the Pacific Theater. They were forced into this system for the sole purpose of satisfying the sexual needs of Japanese soldiers, and to prevent the soldiers from raping the local women. This was done to reduce hostility in occupied areas, stop the spreading of venereal disease and to avert potential espionage. There were more than one thousand military-run rape camps called "comfort stations" in China alone. Some call it the largest trafficking case of women and minors known in modern history— in this case the perpetrators were in fact the Imperial Japanese government and military.

The United Nations defines "trafficking in persons" as the recruitment, transportation, transfer, harboring or receipt of persons, by means of the threat or use of force or other forms of coercion, of abduction, of fraud, of deception, of the abuse of power or of the giving or receiving of payments or benefits to achieve the consent of a person having control over another person, for the purpose of exploitation[2]. Human trafficking is the modern-day slave trade. Most victims of trafficking are impoverished and come from vulnerable and at-risk populations such as migrants, runaways, refugees, and marginalized groups. Today, nearly thirty-six million[3] people are suffering in slavery, and half of these slaves are exploited in forced labor and sex slavery in Asia.

Similar to the strategies of today's traffickers, these victims were "conscripted" through deception with promise of jobs, physical force, coercion, kidnapping, and often sold as merchandise to keep the Imperial Japanese Military "comfort stations" running. Collaborators and brokers from their native countries often assisted the Japanese military. Many of the victims were taken on military vehicles and boats and were often gang-raped by the soldiers on board. Girls, as young as eleven years old, were forced into the rape stations on the frontlines of war and attacked by up to sixty soldiers a day in military brothels.[4]

After fifty years of silence, dozens of elderly women began to speak out about their experiences as sex slaves in the Imperial Japanese Military-run sex slavery system. In response, the Japanese government denied their direct involvement in running military sex slavery[5]. Some government officials call these women voluntary prostitutes.

This story broadened for me as I researched further and learned that these women and children (including Dutch women from prisoner of war camps) were forced and trafficked into military comfort stations all over China, Indonesia (formerly the Dutch East Indies, then a colony of the Netherlands), the Philippines, East Timor, Singapore, France's former colony in Vietnam, Cambodia, Laos, and other occupied territories that became part of the Japanese Empire during World War II. As Japan expanded militarily, the need for more war time sex slaves dramatically increased.

Today, there are less than two hundred known Japanese military sex slave survivors from East Asia and the Netherlands who have gone public with their testimonies. They are in their seventies and eighties. In Korea alone, less than one hundred women are alive out of the two hundred twenty-three former sex slaves who came forward to testify publicly of their enslavement.[6] In mainland China, less than a hundred known survivors are still living. The numbers of survivors are dwindling in Taiwan, the Philippines, the Netherlands, Indonesia, and so on. It is suspected that hundreds more will never emerge from the shadows to testify.

The military sexual slavery issue and the denials made by the Japanese government propelled me onto a journey of meeting these women, to document their stories. It has also led me to take several trips to Washington, D.C., Seoul, Shanghai, Tokyo, and The Hague so that I could meet Japanese military "comfort women" survivors. I wanted to know how these women were able to survive these experiences. Since 2001, I have listened to survivors, activists, and academics speak out on the state of Japan's continual cover-up, historical amnesia, and evasion of legal and moral responsibility for these human rights violations. From each survivor, I learned something different, but there were striking similarities in all of their experiences.

I was keen to find more of these women survivors and wanted to know why this issue, even with its horrific and calculated large scale, government-approved trafficking of women from different nations into rape camps, was not taught or researched and written extensively, like the Holocaust was. We need more voices to speak out on these very real crimes against humanity committed against these women by the Imperial Japanese Military. Even generations later in China and Korea, hatred for the Japanese runs deep, although the Japanese themselves cannot understand why they are hated and mistrusted.

As I remember the wrinkled faces of the women I have met who have survived Imperial Japanese military sex slavery, I am astounded by their resilience. I mourn for the lost youth and innocence of these women. Yet the testimonies of survivors are stories of incredible hope. These are women who have broken every barrier– culture, personal shame, rejection, oppression, trauma, and fear of oppressors– to speak out against human rights violations. And they have found their voices and raised awareness around the world of sexual enslavement and sexual violence in armed conflict. Their story of overcoming hardships has become an inspiring and redemptive legacy to help end the current cycle of sexual slavery of women and children today.

It is important we learn from and record this significant part of history. Former German President Richard von Weizsaecker's father was sentenced at the Nuremberg Trials at the end of World War II to seven years in jail for complicity in Nazi war crimes. Soon after taking office, he made history as the first German president to make a state visit to Israel. He laid a wreath at the Holocaust memorial in Jerusalem with tears in his eyes. In a separate speech at Parliament to mark the fortieth anniversary of Hitler's defeat, Von Weizsaecker stated, "All of us, guilty or innocent, young or old, must accept the past. It is not a question of overcoming the past because that is impossible. It cannot be altered later or undone. But those who close their eyes to the past become blind to the present."

Chapter 1

"The 'comfort women' issue is not yesterday's problem. It is today's and, if it is not dealt with now, it will be tomorrow's problem as well. A multitude of vital US interests are served by a definitive resolution of this moral issue still troubling the governments and peoples of Asia. It is also good for our very close ally Japan, as its government seeks long-overdue recognition of Japan's sixty-year history of constructive, responsible, and resolutely peaceful membership in the modern world community."
~ Mindy L. Kotler, Director of Asia Policy Point, a Washington, D.C.

Meeting Kim Soon-Duk

In July of 2001, I made a spur-of-the-moment decision to fly into Washington, D.C. from Victoria, BC to interview an eighty-year-old Imperial Japanese Military sex slavery survivor named Kim Soon-Duk. She was traveling all the way from her home in a suburb near Seoul, Korea as part of her quest for justice. A much anticipated resolution, which called on the Japanese government to give an official apology to former military sex slaves,[7] would be introduced by the late Democratic Representative of Illinois, Congressman Lane Evans. Surrounded by human rights activists, fellow congressmen, government aides, and journalists, the congressman was to introduce H.Con.Res.195, a resolution that called on Japan to issue a clear and unambiguous apology and provide compensation to former survivors as well as properly educate the youth generation of Japan's historical sexual slavery in militarism.

In DC, the activists from Korea were all gathered in the State Department Building. They had come to exercise their efforts in utilizing all available channels to place pressure on the Japanese government. They wanted an apology issued to the survivors and admission for moral and legal responsibility for Japan's involvement in trafficking women and girls for its military.

Kim Soon-Duk, or Kim *halmoni* (*grandma*),[1] as her supporters called her, appeared shortly. She was

---

[1] Korean activists affectionately refer to these survivors as *halmoni* even though many of these women never married or had families of their own. It is customary to call senior Koreans grandma or grandpa.

extremely petite, and wore a pink jacket over a silk *hanbok* (*traditional Korean dress*) and *gomoo shinbal* (*traditional Korean rubber shoes*). More than half a dozen photographers were gathered all around her clicking away furiously. Her eyes darted around the room and did not rest very long on anyone. As she settled into her seat, her shoulders seemed to straighten with a certain determination, and she appeared very comfortable in the spotlight. She reminded me of a Holocaust survivor who bore witness of a time, decades ago, of how ordinary humans could plumb the depths of depravity. It was imperative that this important piece of history would not be lost with her passing, as time was running out for any of these survivors to stand for and receive justice in their lifetime. When it was Kim's time to speak, she walked up to the podium and began telling her story with a raw child-like simplicity that seemed out of place with the formal nature of the State Department Room.

When she was sixteen, the Japanese people came to her village and told her that she would work as a temporary nurse in Japan. They selected one girl from each family in her village. Then, Kim found herself on a boat with fifty other girls between the ages of fifteen and seventeen. They consoled each other with stories of their families while they battled seasickness.

They ended up in Shanghai, China and were taken to a military brothel where they were immediately separated and placed into individual rooms with thin partitions. But no one informed them of what was to happen. Kim recalled seeing a long line of Japanese soldiers outside of the rooms. One after the other in a steady succession, the men raped the girls. Some screamed and fainted, some cried, while some girls tried to run away. Those who ran were caught and killed to intimidate the remaining young women.

Kim began three years as a sex slave servicing Japanese soldiers. She was raped a countless number of times, along with the other girls, while being subjected to the most abhorrent living conditions. Many girls committed suicide. Kim also tried three times.

"Every single day, the war soldiers lined up," she said. "There were so many, we couldn't count them. I was very sick. I couldn't sit down. I was bleeding so badly. When the military moved, we all moved with them. I wanted to die. The shock was so much, it is beyond words."

She had no idea where she was in China and had no means to return to Korea. All she could do to survive was to think of returning back to her home in Korea. When one high-ranking Japanese officer treated her with a special kindness, she appealed to him to allow her to return back to Korea. Later, he was able to obtain permission for her and three other young women to return to Korea in 1940. Kim was sent back home to Korea due to medical problems. Too ashamed to return to her family home, she migrated to Seoul instead where she worked as a maid and in other odd jobs. She was never able to marry legally as she was unable to overcome her feelings of shame and impurity, believing that her experiences were too much for a man to be able to accept and love her unconditionally. The cultural ethos demanded that brides were virgins when they married or else great shame would befall oneself and one's family honor. She concluded her testimony by calling on the government of Japan to sincerely apologize to all survivors and issue reparations.

During our one-on-one interview after the press conference, she disclosed what she wanted most at this point in her life. "I want the Japanese government to apologize first and make reparations to us," her voice drifted. "That's all I want. And that this kind of inhumane history of sex slavery would never be repeated," she said.

"Are you hopeful in receiving an apology in your lifetime?" I asked.

"We have to see. We don't know until we try," she said.

When she was young and living in a remote village, she had dreams of going to a big city and attending a big school. As a young girl, she had worn her long hair in a braid and had shoes made of straw. She had two older brothers and one older sister but was closest to her mom and younger sister. Her family endured hardships under Japanese colonial rule. They, as Koreans, were forced to change their names to Japanese ones. They were not allowed to speak in the Korean language. The soldiers confiscated their metal kitchen utensils and dishes to make weapons for their military supply. Her father, a distinguished man of customs and discipline always wore an immaculate white outfit, the traditional outfit of the day. He was mocked by the Japanese. They shot at his clothes with a black ink gun. Shortly thereafter, Kim and her family moved to another village to avoid the persecution.

In 1992, Kim came forward to testify of her ordeal in Japanese military sex slavery after hearing in 1991 of Kim Hak-Soon's public testimony. Kim was not legally married to the man she lived with. Now dead, he never knew of what she called her "shameful experience" neither did their three children, until almost ten years ago. She waited for her husband to die before she went forward. Three months after his death, she asked her cousin and niece if she should testify of her experience in sexual slavery. Both told her to keep her secret. She testified anyway, which infuriated them for making her past known to the public.

Slavery has had long-lasting effects on Kim's body. She suffers physically and mentally every day, and when she thinks of the past, she is unable to sleep. "I am still suffering today. If I hadn't been taken, I would have led a happy life with my family members," she laments. "I'm separated from my family now. They finally got to know the truth, and it was a big shock to them. They couldn't imagine that such a thing could happen to me." She still has nightmares. One reoccurring nightmare is of detached soldiers' legs chasing her, and just like many other survivors, she suffers from insomnia.

Kim does not harbor any prejudice towards the Japanese today. "We have to recognize in Japan today, there are many good citizens. I do not hate the younger generation," she says.

Because many Korean elders continue to harbor ill feelings towards the Japanese even generations after World War II, her response is an anomalous one. She hopes that the next generation in Korea will be smart and bright enough to keep their country free of foreign invasions and to keep the country's independence.

On a personal level, reconciliation with the Japanese takes place regularly at the residence where Kim lives called House of Sharing, a care facility for survivors of Japanese military sex slavery. Hyejin, a Buddhist monk and the Executive Director of the House of Sharing, shared that about one hundred fifty Japanese visitors come to visit Kim and the other survivors every month. Many of them bear gifts and offer tearful apologies on behalf of the Japanese government. One Japanese young woman volunteered for a year as a caretaker and cook at the home.

Kim said of the Japanese visitors, "They say they can't make up for what their grandfathers did, but they want to try and ease our burdens. We cry together, sing together and drink together."[8] I asked her if she believed she would be healed by an apology from the Japanese government. "Yes, we can only get healing if we solve this problem," she said. "Solving the problem means the Japanese government issuing an official apology as well as just compensation. There are also, of course, many other problems to be solved between the two countries, including island problems and territorial disputes."

When asked if she had ever been in love before, Kim briefly mentioned her relationship with a high-ranking Japanese officer. When pressed for more details, the confession of her love for the officer emerged and how kindly he treated her during the extended times she stayed with him. It seemed as though she had suffered from Stockholm Syndrome.[9] Kim had even looked for this general and longed to reunite with him during her trip to bear witness in Tokyo for the Women's International War Crimes Tribunal for the Trial of Japan's Military Sexual Slavery[10] on December 8, 2000. Her need to be loved is universal. Her yearnings are very much the same as women around the world, generations later. Even in the midst of being abducted and forced into sexual slavery, she has longed to be cherished and desired.

Kim has also become one of the few celebrated visual artists as a survivor, and her work depicts her pain far deeper than her words. One painting titled *Kidnapped* is of a young girl with terror stricken eyes as a Japanese soldier's hand is grabbing her tiny hand and taking her away from Korea. She has experienced some healing through her artwork. "I feel better when I do art exhibitions," she said. An art teacher taught Kim and the other survivors at their home how to paint, in the hopes that it would release some of their pain.

Kim has hosted a traveling art exhibit of her work entitled the *Quest for Justice: The Story of Korean*

Comfort Women as Told through Their Art in several cities in the US and in fifty venues across Japan.[11] It has featured the artwork of fellow survivors Kim Bok-Dong, the late Lee Yong-Nyeo, and the late Kang Duk-Kyung. In one of the paintings, a closed bud of a flower rests against a young girl's cheek. This bud never bloomed, a symbol that represents her stolen youth. In *At That Time, at That Place* Kim painted a naked girl hiding her face in a fetal position as three Japanese soldiers hover menacingly against a dark background. She said it depicted her first rape in Shanghai by a Japanese soldier who had stood in a long line-up.

Lastly, Kim described a day in her life at her home, the House of Sharing, near Seoul. She moved in when the home was opened by Buddhist supporters in 1992. Most of the women who reside at the facility had come from mainland China, where they were stuck— with no way of returning home to Korea after the war ended. "I do some farming, and I talk to guests. Sometimes I seek out doctors for medical care," she concluded.

In May of 1993, Kim and the other survivors began receiving monthly financial subsidies from the Korean government after a piece of legislation called Social Security Law for the Comfort Women of the Japanese Military during the Japanese Colonial Rule[12] was passed. This policy ensured that each survivor would be paid a one-time payment of five million won (equivalent to four thousand six hundred thirty-one US dollars), as well as a monthly allowance of one hundred fifty thousand won (approx. one hundred thirty-nine US dollars). Other security measures include a monthly assistance of 10kg of rice, 2.5kg of barley, twenty thousand won (nineteen US dollars) for food, fifteen thousand won (fourteen US dollars) for fuel, free medical insurance, and renting priority for government housing. The Korean Council for the Women Drafted for the Military Sexual Slavery by Japan was instrumental in lobbying for this government support and considered it a "sign of strong national sympathy towards the survivors."[13]

A year before this D.C. press conference, the US State Department went out of its way to file a formal request to dismiss the military comfort women lawsuit. They ignored the plight of these women even though they had endorsed The Victims of Trafficking and Violence

Prevention Act of 2000 (TVPA),[14] which declared that sexual slavery and trafficking of women and children are abhorrent to the principles on which the United States was founded. The TVPA is considered the most important piece of US legislation on trafficking because it defined it as "the recruitment, harboring, transportation, provision or obtaining of a person for the purpose of a commercial sex act" and led to the creation of an inter-agency task force to combat human trafficking.

On September 18, 2000, Kim and fourteen other survivors from Korea, Taiwan, and the Philippines filed a class action lawsuit in the US District Court in Washington, D.C., using the Alien Tort Claims Act of 1787[15]. Under this act, former members of the Japanese military and government, who were involved in the sexual slavery system, could be prosecuted. This filing was an unprecedented lawsuit in the United States after lawsuits in Japan launched by former military sex slaves were unsuccessful in achieving justice. It was the first ever US court case involving military sexual slavery, where Japan was a defendant.

Filing a lawsuit in Washington, D.C. brought some level of healing for Kim because it opened up an opportunity for her to speak out publicly and take action after more than more than fifty years of internal shame, inaction, and silence. But much to the surprise of human rights activists and former sex slavery survivors, the US responded to these lawsuits with objections and echoed the Japanese government's claim that all reparations issues had been settled in the 1951 San Francisco Peace Treaty[16] and other related treaties.

Barry Fisher, the former lead counsel for one of the comfort women lawsuits in the US, acknowledged the double standard on the American stance on comfort women. He attributes racism as the main factor for why the mostly Asian victims of Japanese war crimes have not received compensation and support on the same level as Holocaust victims. "The US championed the rights of European victims and helped them achieve multi-million dollar settlements in recent cases against companies that profited from slave labor in areas controlled by the Third Reich," he said. "The US State Department has even employed a full-time Holocaust case ambassador."[17] But it seems, according to Fisher, the US has been actively thwarting efforts on seeking justice for the former Japanese military sex slavery despite the fact that there is no statute of limitations on war crimes or crimes against humanity. Fisher said it was blatant discrimination towards the Asian victims[18] and that after Kim Soon-Duk filed the class-action lawsuit in September 2000, the US government filed a formal request to even dismiss the case because Japan has "sovereign immunity"[19]. The US government egregiously failed to help the survivors find a resolution with Japan.

Former victims of military sexual slavery are legally entitled to compensation, and as the comfort women system was in violation of international laws and agreements at that time, these women are no exception. The state of Japan, however, has refused to pay direct compensation to the former comfort women by saying all claims were settled by the San Francisco Peace Treaty, bilateral treaties, and other relevant treaties and agreements between Japan and South Korea, Indonesia, China, and the United States[20]. The Japanese government alleges that these women have no right to compensation because any individual claims these women had, were fully satisfied by peace treaties and agreements between Japan and other nations at the end of World War II.[21]

But not all of these treaties included provisions that waived individual claims by citizens of those countries against Japan. The 1965 Bilateral Treaty[22] between South Korea and Japan did not relinquish the individual rights of the Korean citizens arising from any violations of international law, and there were no terms such as crimes or violation of international law, in the so-called waiver provisions in the treaty or other agreements between South Korea and Japan.[23]

Chapter 2

Awakening: Meeting Survivors and Activists

"You may choose to look the other way but you can never say again that you did not know." ~ William Wilberforce

In 1999, early on in my exploration of Japanese war crimes, I met up with several people in the Chinese community in Vancouver who became important sources by pointing me to contacts and conferences. I was invited on a trip to China in 2004 to document the testimonies of survivors of Japanese military sex slavery, the Rape of Nanking (Nanjing),[24] and biological warfare conducted by the Imperial Japanese military's Unit 731[25], a biological and chemical warfare unit that carried out gruesome secret medical experiments on humans including Allied prisoners-of-war. The military-run experiments were considered some of the worst human rights violations in history.

I attended another conference in September of 2001, which was to be held in San Francisco and called "50 Years of Denial: Japan and its Wartime Responsibilities." It was being organized by Asian American leaders in the Bay Area, which included members of the Rape of Nanking Redress Coalition[26] and members of the Asian American Studies program at the University of California at Berkeley. Kim Soon-Duk and Ni Cuiping, a survivor of the Nanking massacre, were slated to be the main speakers. The gathering would be a bold protest that drew activists, lawyers, and survivors from all over the world to zero in on Japan's refusal to admit wartime atrocities. The conference would aim to challenge the fiftieth anniversary of the 1951 San Francisco Peace Treaty between Japan and the United States and denounce the official celebratory conference hosted by both the

Japanese and US governments. Over the years, Japanese officials had resorted to using the treaty for validation that all claims regarding the war, including personal lawsuits filed, were settled by compensation.

The organizers of "50 Years of Denial" declared that the treaty was unjust and that it overlooked the sex slaves who suffered at the hands of the Imperial Japanese Military. Conference organizers demanded an official apology and individual compensation for war victims, sex slaves and forced laborers from the Japanese government as the treaty made reparations between the nations and on governmental levels, but no direct apology or compensation was given to the individual victims.

Before the conference, Kim waited with her hands folded in front of herself, wearing her traditional Korean *hanbok*. She stood in the crowd, remaining close to her supporters. Among them was a grey-haired gentleman, Koken Tsuchiya, a lawyer from Japan, as well as Ni Cuiping, a petite seventy-two-year-old woman with short grey hair who was a little girl when the Japanese military invaded her hometown of Nanking in 1937. Very few survivors from the Rape of Nanking had ever testified in North America, so to hear Ni speak at the conference was a once-in-a-lifetime opportunity.

Ni shared her story for the first time in more than fifty years. As she began to speak, the entire room became silent. At one point, she pulled her shirt down to show a deep scar from a gunshot wound in the shoulder. She had witnessed the murder of seven of her own family members and relatives in 1937. Japanese soldiers first killed her father, who was washing vegetables, by shooting him three times. Then they killed her mother and grandfather. Then Ni was shot. She also witnessed the soldiers killing her uncle, two aunts, and one of their unborn children. Narrowly, Ni escaped with her life after being shot and left for dead. Her surviving family members had to flee to the countryside outside Nanking when the military invaded and began murdering hundreds of thousands of people.

Ni swore that although it had been more than fifty years since the war ended, she would continue to speak out against the Japanese government's denial of war history. She wept as she spoke. "I'm a witness to the

Nanking massacre. I'll never allow the Japanese government to deny history. As a witness, I will testify to the last breath of my life," she vowed.

Both elderly women, Ni and Kim, had traveled all the way from China and Korea, respectively, to demand nothing less than a sincere official government apology and reparations from the state of Japan before they die. Many survivors had passed away within the last five years which made their struggle especially urgent.

Since meeting Kim, I have begun to comprehend the sense of urgency the activists have in giving a voice to the dwindling numbers of elderly victims. Most of the survivors of Japanese military sex slavery are in their seventies and eighties. Time is running out as they await a long overdue apology from the government of Japan, an apology that would bring some healing.

The only new piece of information Kim shared during her testimony that was left out in D.C. was that she and the women were placed in and raped in "small tents."[27] The other women had fainted and struggled violently as they were raped: "Every single day, the war soldiers lined up. There were so many, we couldn't count them. Many girls committed suicide. I wanted to die. The shock was so much, it was beyond words," she reiterated.

After the press conference, these two women had to share their testimonies again in a larger venue of about a thousand people. Kim was nervous to speak after Ni Cuiping. She wanted to do a good job of testifying and felt her speaking ability was not as powerful as Ni's.

Her anxieties turned out to be unnecessary. When she spoke, men and women dabbed at their eyes with tissues as they were so moved by her testimony.

Meeting Hwang Geum-Joo

A few years after the San Francisco conference, in March of 2003, I attended another conference called 'Preventing Crimes against Humanity' at the University of British Columbia in Vancouver. Hwang Geum-Joo, another sex slavery survivor, was to speak at one of the seminars.

Before the conference started, Hwang stood outside of the main hall. She looked out of place in her traditional blue and white *hanbok,* rubber shoes, and her peppery hair pulled back into a tight bun. Hwang was on the panel of a seminar session at the conference along with Mee-Hyang Yoon, the Secretary General of the Korean Council for the Women Drafted for Military Sexual Slavery by Japan[28], and with a representative from the International Labor Organization (ILO), a United Nations organization that globally advocates for the labor rights of workers. Hwang had also been involved in the first lawsuit, the same as Kim Soon-Duk, in a US district court on behalf of military sex slave survivors.

Hwang Geum-Joo, as a young girl, was sent away to work for a family. When she was twenty-years-old, her father fell ill and the family became destitute. Hwang volunteered to work in a military supply factory, believing she was going to make a lot of money for her family. Instead of being employed in a factory, she was placed in a comfort station in what was then known as Manchuria, now referred to as Northeast China.

"The Japanese dragged us away during the annexation of Korea, and we had to obey. All high school boys were forced to join the Japanese military and were conscripted as soldiers. Unmarried young women were forced into sex slavery, including myself. The comfort women in the military unit were not treated as human beings. We were beaten almost every day. I was particularly rebellious and earned more beatings than the other girls. Even now, my ears go fuzzy sometimes, and I can't hear for long periods of time. I have magnetic strips attached to my knees and hips. If I take these off for a bath and forget to put them back on, my knees and hips swell up, and I am unable to sit down."

She had been forced to get a 606 injection, which was filled with a serum known as No. 606. This serum was being used for sterilization and was commonly used on the girls and women in the military sex slavery system.

When asked if she could, one day, forgive the Japanese military and government for the suffering she had to endure. She responded emphatically, "I cannot forgive the Japanese."

On the day Hwang was to return to Korea, I gave her a hug goodbye. It was apparent she was not used to being hugged, but she smiled sweetly anyway.

The case *Hwang Geum Joo et al. v. Japan* filed in 2000, was filed in the US because the lawsuits in Japan had failed to bring justice in the form of legal acknowledgement of the government's role and responsibility in organizing the military sex slavery system and compensation from the government to the survivors. The women testified on their rapes and forced sexual slavery as part of a wider human trafficking operation that it is commonly referred to as, "state-sanctioned rape and enslavement."[29] The lawsuit against the government of Japan states that the women "have never received compensation from Japan for their suffering."[30] And that Japan "committed, conspired to commit, furthered, and aided and abetted others who committed war crimes and crimes against humanity…and it enslaved female civilians under its control,"[31] violating international law. Due to the countless rapes these women had to endure for years on a daily basis, they suffered "serious health effects as a result, including permanent damage to their reproductive organs and urinary tracts from violent physical abuse and sexually transmitted diseases."[32]

Those who survived their unimaginable experiences have had to endure "lives of isolation and societal rejection, compounded by deeply instilled feelings of guilt and shame. Many are ostracized. Many are living in extremely poverty and suffer from severe physical and psychological problems. Many could not marry and also found themselves unable to bear children. Many suffer from sexually transmitted diseases contracted during their servitude and from drug addictions related to their wartime experiences. Sleep disorders, like insomnia and fearful nightmares, are common."[33]

The women, in the lawsuit, demanded the Japanese government admit that it violated international treaties and laws and prohibitions against enforced sex slavery, rape, and prostitution. The Japanese government responded by saying that the US courts lacked jurisdiction because of sovereign immunity under US law. The court confirmed sovereign immunity and eventually dismissed the case saying Japan's post-war treaties absolved it of all legal action by individual victims of war crimes. The verdict was deeply discouraging to survivors and activists.

Many of these survivors, especially the ones who did not have children, want to donate their financial inheritance to leave as a legacy in a museum dedicated to their struggle for justice. Typically, in the Korean culture, people think of their children as their legacy, but most of these survivors were unable to marry and have children. Hwang Geum-Joo has donated millions of Korean won.

"At first, when they passed away in their sixties, the funerals were large and many people lined up to honor them. Now they are dying in their seventies and eighties, and they don't have families. We arrange funerals," Mee-Hyang Yoon says. "We worry that the grandmas are dying off before they hear an apology from Japan. The grandmas who are living worry they'll die before an apology. They don't like hearing about their friends dying. Grandmas feel, if they don't receive an apology, they want to leave something behind as in the museum. We want to establish the museum before the grandmas die."

Chapter 3

"Justice is a conscience, not a personal conscience but the conscience of the whole of humanity. Those who clearly recognize the voice of their own conscience usually recognize the voice of justice."
~ Nobel Laureate Alexander Solzhenitsyn

Modern Day Repercussions

"Down with Japan! Down with Japan!" There were shouts and shrieks coming from the streets. Hundreds of people held up placards, Chinese flags, and other paraphernalia. Some had Japan's flag with an X mark on it. There was a synchronized cacophony of high-pitched voices and angry words. During the China Riots of 2005, the Chinese were incensed at the Japanese government's stance on its wartime past.

It was spring of 2005 and I had been living in Beijing, China for about a year. In the days that followed this protest, angry crowds threw rocks and bottles at the Japanese embassy, trashing Japanese cars, and chanting slurs. Young people were spewing venomous words everywhere. The protests, which lasted several days in China and across East Asia, were the culmination of a cyber phenomenon: a petition circulated to oppose allowing Japan the privilege of veto power with the United Nations. Marching protestors were calling on Beijing to block Japan from gaining a seat on the United Nations Security Council. In the span of just a few weeks, more than thirty million had signed the petition aimed at UN member countries, leaders, and ambassadors before the vote was taken.

A crowd of six thousand people marched towards the Japanese Embassy from the university area in Beijing's Haidian District. They smashed the windows of the Japanese ambassador's residence. Later that weekend, twenty thousand rioters in Shanghai went on a rampage and targeted Japanese noodle restaurants and turned over Japanese cars.[34] The Japanese government called in the

Chinese ambassador and demanded an apology, compensation, and protection for its nationals living in China. A Japanese embassy spokesperson stated that Chinese police stood by and did nothing while people threw rocks. The scene of streets filled with hundreds of soldiers wearing masks and shields and carrying submachine guns, as well as an equal number of police officers and curious onlookers, was surreal. Analysts have speculated the Chinese government allowed the protest to take place in order to stir up nationalism and divert attention from pressing domestic matters.

What have really infuriated the Koreans and Chinese is the Japanese government's multiple cover-up attempts of military sex slavery and their accusations that these elderly women volunteered to prostitute themselves. Furthermore, the prime minister of Japan, Junichiro Koizumi, had insulted the nation of China with repeated visits to the Yasukuni shrine where Japanese war criminals were honored. Due to the Japanese government's severe lack in effort and refusal in issuing a proper and sincere apology at the end of the World War II, people have been unable to let go of their bitterness over

Japanese war crimes committed before and during the war, even more than sixty years later. The resentment and hatred towards the Japanese, seems to unify the entire nation of China with an intense vitriol that runs deep. Many Chinese, generations after World War II has ended, have expressed anger over the cruelty of the Japanese soldiers, who murdered pregnant women and mutilated and murdered countless during their invasions of China.

The people's actions and raw emotions symbolize so much—the distrust that nations have towards Japan, the lack of true peace in the region, which is linked to the Japanese government's refusal to sincerely apologize to the formerly occupied countries and people groups affected, and a younger generation in China that is not willing to forget nor forgive what the Japanese military have done. These are young Chinese who have not experienced war firsthand but have watched countless movies and learned of military sex slavery and the Rape of Nanking in school.

These riots confirm that racial discrimination towards the Japanese still exists because of unresolved war crime issues like the sex slavery system, and that this racist attitude is generational. While there may not be outright hatred towards the Japanese, many elder Koreans subtly protest and boycott Japanese electronics and cars. There is something that haunts and taints the Koreans' perceptions of the Japanese. Perhaps that something is pain, unresolved historical pain. It has been passed on from generation to generation.

Breaking the Veil of Silence

When the nation of Japan surrendered to the Allied Forces on August 15, 1945, news traveled slowly around the vast Japanese occupied regions from northern China, known as Manchuria, to Myanmar in the west, to the Pacific Islands in the south. For many areas, the war continued to wage. When the war finally caught up to them, all the bombing stopped, military men dropped their arms, tanks rolled to a halt, and weary feet began to walk home.

In the aftermath, there was a special remnant of women left behind: survivors of sex slavery. They walked home from the frontlines where they were stationed with the Japanese military. For some, the journey home took months. They crossed over numerous borders and changing terrain, and hitching rides on boats to go back to their native countries. Many women chose to stay behind and piece their shattered lives back together in a foreign land. Physical and psychological scars marked their bodies and souls. Their lives were almost forgotten even after the Allied Forces interviewed some of the women for an official report. The women were listed on military lists as if they were mere supplies. Their shared experiences were fading into oblivion, until one day, decades later, an elderly Korean woman decided to unburden herself of a secret that she had kept hidden for fifty years.

On August 14, 1991, in Seoul, Korea, a slight pepper-haired, sixty-eight-year-old Korean woman in a white traditional *hanbok* was the featured speaker at a press conference. Her name was Kim Hak-Soon. If you had seen her on a street somewhere any other day, you would not have looked twice. But this time, there was a brooding intensity in her wrinkled face and hollow eyes that belied her ordinary appearance. At this event, Kim did something completely out of character for women in her culture. She testified tearfully, that as a sixteen-year-old, she was sold into sex slavery to the Japanese military. Japanese ultranationalists, conservatives, called her and others like her voluntary prostitutes when they bore witness in the media about being forced into sexual servitude for the Japanese military. She refuted that she was a willing prostitute.

Recounting how that impacted her for the rest of her life, Kim bore witness to an atrocity in her life and in history that was not as well-known as the Holocaust, yet has left a gaping wound in Asia that still festers many generations later. Her haunting eyes and her visage of mournfulness has become the symbol and rallying cry of the growing women's movement in Korea. This movement brought the issue of Japanese military sex slavery to the forefront by bringing it to the international area through raising awareness through the United Nations and international media.

Several months earlier, Kim happened to watch on the news that the Japanese government denied forcing young

Korean women to be sex slaves. The Japanese government dismissed their military sexual slavery system as a group of volunteers who were getting paid for prostitution. She knew it was a lie. "How did I become a public witness? When I read newspapers and watched the news, Japan kept denying the truth. They took us forcibly, put us directly in the military compound, and turned us into comfort women."[35]

Outraged, Kim decided to break the silence. More than anything, she wanted a clear apology from the Japanese emperor. "For these fifty years, I have lived by bearing and again bearing the unbearable. For fifty years, I carried a heavy pain, and I kept thinking in my heart about telling people about my experiences someday. As I try to speak now, my heart pounds against my chest because what happened in the past is something extremely unconscionable. Why does the Japanese government deny its knowledge of the comfort women system? I was forced to be a comfort woman, and I'm here, alive."[36]

Like many modern-day trafficking victims, Kim Hak-Soon was fatherless and came from an impoverished family. She was born into poverty in 1924 in Manchuria. It was a time of political instability in Korea under Japanese colonial rule. Her parents had fled to China after the infamous massacre on March 1, 1919, known as the March 1st Movement.[37] More than two million Koreans protested for independence from Japan in a peaceful movement involving more than fifteen hundred demonstrations. Many unarmed civilians were gunned down or imprisoned without trial and tortured.

Kim returned to Korea with her mother after her father passed away, and everyone around her seemed to think that she had been born under a curse. Her father had died because of her bad luck, they whispered. Because of such superstitions, she became a scapegoat for all of her family's misfortune. After her mother remarried, her stepfather adopted her at the age of fourteen. She wasn't very happy with her new family dynamic and ran away from home often. Instead of ensuring his stepdaughter's marriage prospects, Kim's stepfather sealed her fate as an "entertainer." He sent her to a *gisaeng* (*entertainer*) school for female entertainers who were taught the styles of Japanese geisha music and dance. After graduating at sixteen, Kim was taken to Manchuria to earn money as *gisaengs* along with her stepsister.

Her stepfather sold her and her stepsister to the Japanese military stationed in Manchuria. After being sold by her stepfather, she was deceived into thinking she was to entertain the soldiers with dancing and singing after her stepfather had sold them to the Japanese military as if they were cattle. This transaction delivered her to the frontlines of battle in Northeastern China where at least three hundred soldiers were stationed. With the troops and military barracks stationed nearby, Kim and her stepsister were taken to a large, empty house and for a period of four to five months, Japanese soldiers repeatedly raped her. Confined to a tiny room, like thousands of other women forced into military brothels or rape stations, she was beaten and violated over and over again.

The only relief she had was the presence of three older Korean girls at the house. She did not know their Korean names, as they were forced to go by their given Japanese names of Miyako, Sadako and Sijiae. Kim was the youngest one at sixteen; the oldest, Sijiae, was twenty-two years old and was in charge. In this cold, deserted house, Kim was confined to a bed and forced to endure visits by Japanese soldiers all the time. The soldiers even gave her a Japanese name. All of the Korean women were required to speak Japanese and entertain the men with Japanese songs. The soldiers referred to the Korean women as *chosenppi* (*Korean vagina*) or other racially charged, derogatory Japanese terms. By day, on meager food rations, the girls were forced to run errands, deliver ammunitions, cook, do laundry, and work as nurses to tend to injured soldiers. In the evenings, they were confined in their rooms to serve as sex slaves. Even at the slightest protest, Kim and the others were beaten and dragged around by their hair.

One day, the long curse over her life seemed to end. She escaped from her nightmare of a situation with the help of a Korean man who ran a pawnshop in Shanghai's French concession. It was an unlikely war romance. They were married in Shanghai, and by the end of the war, she bore a son and a daughter.

Eventually, she and her family made their way back to Korea. Life, she recalled, was filled with misery and tragic accidents. Her husband made a living as a military supplier for some time. After the Korean war ended in 1953, he died in an accident leaving her a widow. Then, her daughter died of cholera, and her son drowned in a swimming accident when he was only ten years old.

Years later, alone, with her secret past as a Japanese military sex slave locked in an internal vault, she hesitantly considered revealing her experiences. One small step away from life on the streets, Kim eked out a living as a housemaid or peddler, and at one point, a sock vendor on the harsh streets of Seoul. Her experiences in the Japanese military rape camp continue to haunt her. She reflected on the impact of her experience in the Japanese military brothel: "I was born as a woman but never lived as a woman...I suffer from a bitterness I do not know how to overcome. I only want to ask the Japanese government not to go to war again. I feel sick when I am close to a man. Not just Japanese men but all men—even my own husband, who saved me from the brothel—have made me feel this way. I shiver when I see the Japanese flag. Because it carried that flag, I hated the airplane I took to come to Japan. I've continued disclosing the facts...Why should I feel ashamed? I should not have to feel ashamed."[38]

"This pain is *han*,"[39] she says. *Han* is a Korean word that sums up everything from inconsolable woe to a profound sadness that is common in the souls of Korean people due to centuries of oppression from many military invasions. "From the time when I was little, what the Japanese inflicted on me— that's what makes knots in my chest and that *han*— how can it be untied? You can't untie it. Then, all the time when I have been fighting in the open since 1991, this knot of *han* has become even tighter. It is so completely blocked now that I can hardly breathe. That's my trouble."[40]

The Japanese government's initial reaction to Kim Hak-Soon's testimony in 1991 was to deny that it helped organize a system that coerced and enslaved hundreds of thousands of women and girls. They continued to refuse to take legal and moral responsibility for what happened to these women by stating that there was no documentation that proved who was responsible. Instead, they blamed private brothel owners and civilian profiteers as the ones who recruited the women and ran rape camps known as comfort stations.[41] The Japanese government consistently denies the testimonies of these surviving women.

Kim's courage in testifying, using her real name, had an unexpected ripple effect. It released hundreds of other survivors to talk about their long-held secrets. A hotline was even opened up by activists, and as a result, hundreds of women were able to identify themselves as survivors. In total, two hundred twelve elderly women in Korea have contacted the hotline, but according to activists, there are many more that have chosen to remain silent. This triggered the Korean government, which had been silent on Japanese military sex slavery, even during the negotiations with the Japanese government for the Korea-Japan bilateral treaty in 1965 that settled war issues, to eventually begin giving these women a monthly welfare allowance.

Aside from a few court cases after the war and mention of rape in war, no one from the Imperial Japanese Military was prosecuted and punished during the post-World War II International Military Tribunal for the Far East (IMTFE)[42], for the organized Japanese military sex slavery that Kim testified about. Compare that with how Nazis are hunted down by Israelis. The US State Department has a department dedicated to Holocaust issues. Was there not evidence of the Japanese military sex slavery system and how it was planned and carried out by the Japanese military and approved by the government of the day? Emperor Hirohito was considered the head of the military and government and was responsible for the policy of this sex slavery system. And yet he was set free at the end of the war and remains unpunished.[43]

Kim Hak-Soon took another step that was also out-of-the-ordinary: she took legal action against the Japanese government. It was utterly out of character for her— a woman in a Confucian or shame-based Korean society— to take such action. If a Korean woman had been sexually violated, it was considered better for her to kill oneself than live to tell about it. But Kim felt she had no family members to shame anymore. Her husband and children had died long ago. She did not have any living relatives. In Asian culture, one is not only bringing shame to oneself when sharing about potentially embarrassing experiences, but this shame is taken on collectively as a family unit.

In December of 1991, with the help of women's rights activists, Kim and two other former South Korean sex slaves of the Japanese military filed a lawsuit in the Tokyo District Court. Many refer to this lawsuit as the breaking of fifty years of silence. The women demanded an official apology and compensation from the Japanese government. They also sought a thorough investigation of their cases, a revision of Japanese school textbooks to identify this Japanese military sex slavery issue as part of the colonial oppression of the Korean people, and a memorial museum to be built so that the younger generations would learn of military sex slavery.[44]

After Kim Hak-Soon filed the lawsuit, Chief Cabinet Secretary Kato Koichi said at a press conference on December 6, 1991 that comfort stations had indeed existed, but no evidence could be linked to prove involvement by the government in recruitment.[45] The Japanese government held their ground despite other survivors who came forward to bear witness. They said the military comfort women system was the work of private entrepreneurs, and the women were prostitutes.[46]

The lawsuit filed was eventually dismissed on March 26, 2001. Presiding Judge Shoichi Maruyama admitted the plaintiffs had suffered but stated that individual victims' claims for damages against the victimizer country were not thought to be acceptable under international law. He said that individuals could not be compensated for wartime damages because the redress issue was settled by a 1965 bilateral agreement between Japan and South Korea.

This was a huge blow to the survivors and their supporters. The lawsuit also had a different unexpected impact on the Japanese public: it shocked them, causing them to face the reality of military comfort women and their war history for the first time in decades.

Until then, it had just been a topic that was written about in books and portrayed in theater productions.[47]

Yoshimi Yoshiaki

As a young man, Dr. Yoshimi Yoshiaki, a distinguished professor of Japanese modern history at Chuo University in Tokyo, had heard of the military comfort women. Then one day, he watched Kim Hak-Soon's testimony on the news and remembered that he had actually found documents related to military comfort women in the Self Defense Force Library in Tokyo.[48] These papers stated the Japanese military was involved in implementing and managing military brothels or comfort stations, and high-ranking military officers were involved. He decided to publicize his findings. In 1992, Yoshimi's documents were publicized in the national newspaper Asahi Shimbun. After the documents were published, Yoshimi immediately became a target for harassment and death threats by right-wingers for years thereafter.

Japanese nationalists insist the women were voluntary prostitutes, not sex slaves. Nationalist politicians were also in an uproar. Prime Minister Shinzo Abe, then a young largely unknown lawmaker from the ruling Liberal Democratic Party, led lobbying efforts to cancel the 1993 admission of the government's role in running military brothels, or comfort stations and forcing women and girls into sex slavery. It was the Chief Cabinet Secretary Yohei Kono who issued the acknowledgment that became known as the Kono Statement.

The government of Japan changed their stance and stopped their claim that only private businessmen were in charge of the military comfort women system. But they still did not take legal or moral responsibility for trafficking girls and women into military sex slavery.

Yoshimi Yoshiaki, and other historians have sifted through and gathered five hundred twenty-nine documents since 1993, including some from Japan's Defense Ministry that has evidence that the Japanese military and government trafficked girls and women from Asia into sexual slavery.[49] On June 2, 2014, five former survivors from Indonesia, the Philippines, and South Korea handed over some of these official documents to the Japanese government along with those collected from around the world.[50] The documents show the women were forced against their will into sex slavery. The survivors and their supporters demanded Prime Minister

Shinzo Abe formally apologize and admit that Japan's government and military implemented the sex slavery system of comfort women stations and that the women were forced into it. They also called for a full disclosure of all official government records about the comfort women system and asked that the government conduct an investigation into the issue.

Abe said Japan will not revise the Kono Statement, the apology in 1993, but that the study that led to the apology is being reviewed.

Pae Pong-Gi, the Little Known Survivor

What's little known is that Kim Hak-Soon was not the first to go public with her story. There was another survivor who bore witness to Japanese military sex slavery more than ten years prior to Kim Hak-Soon. In 1979, the same year Margaret Thatcher became the first woman in history in the UK to be elected Prime Minister, Pae Pong-Gi was featured in a few documentary films made by a Japanese filmmaker and a Korean filmmaker in 1991.[51]

The discovery of Pae fueled the feminist movement in Korea and Japan and gave them concrete evidence even though rumors about the Japanese military comfort women system had been circulating for decades before Kim Hak-Soon went public in 1991. After the war ended in 1945, stories of traumatized Korean women in the countryside obsessively washing themselves, in an effort to wash off the rapes, haunted Dr. Yun Chung-Ok, a university professor at Ewha Women's University, who opened a hotline and the NGO, the Korean Council for Women Drafted for Sexual Slavery by Japan to help survivors of Imperial Japanese military sex slavery. Knowledge of military comfort women was widespread through novels, movies and Kako Senda's book *Jugun Ianfu (Military Comfort Women)* that came out in 1973.

Pae Pong-Gi was married and twenty-nine years old when she was deceived and trafficked into sex slavery on Okinawa's Tokashiki Island in 1944. A woman had promised Pae a job where "if you open your mouth a banana falls into it." This was common bait for women living in hunger and poverty, and this lure of a job opportunity utilizing food under false pretenses is still used by traffickers today. When Pae and four other Koreans arrived in Okinawa, they were immediately taken to a Japanese military brothel.

A local Japanese women's association protested but were told the brothel "was intended for the women's own protection" against their own Japanese military.[52] By the end of World War II, only Pae and another sex slave survived the war on the island of Okinawa. She chose not to return to South Korea.

After the war, Pae had very few options for work as an illegal alien. Subsequently, she merely switched sides, from being forced to serving Japanese soldiers to working as a prostitute for American soldiers, out of desperation. She began to work in military brothels for the American military base that moved in after Japan surrendered to the Allies. She also worked in bars and sold black market American goods that US troops in Okinawa gave her. Though she entered a relocation camp for refugees including comfort women and slave labor victims and prisoners of war in Ishikawa, a prefecture of Japan on Honshu Island, after the war ended, she did not attempt to return home to Korea. She felt "abandoned in a strange country" and died there in 1991.[53] Her plight as a sex slave for both the Japanese military and American Occupation forces highlights the commonality and tragedy of sexual violence committed against women within militarism.

In May of 1990, during Korean President Roh Tae-Woo's visit to Japan, Korean women's rights groups demanded an apology and compensation from the Japanese government for implementing the volunteer corps, known as *jungshindae*, which refers to the Korean men and women who were forced into slave and sexual labor by the colonial Japanese government.

In the following month, on June 6th, the Japanese government again refused to acknowledge state or military involvement in a weak statement at the House of Councillors, the upper house of the National Diet[54] of Japan: "In regard to comfort women… it appears that the persons thus treated were led around by civilian operators following the military forces. We consider it impossible for us to investigate and make a definitive statement as regards the actual conditions pertaining to this practice."[55]

Catalyst to an International Women's Movement

Kim Hak-Soon's story has had a global effect and spurred other silent comfort women survivors to come forward in nations like the Netherlands, the Philippines, and China. Prominent activists such as Jan Ruff-O'Herne, a remarkable Dutch woman living in Australia who speaks on forgiving the Japanese, have emerged. Ruff-O'Herne was twenty-one when she was taken from a Japanese prisoner-of-war camp and forced into a military rape station in 1942. She kept it a secret for fifty years until she finally felt it was time to share her story. Among the survivors, she became one of the only voices to champion the need to forgive and initiate reconciliation with the Japanese.

Numerous activists like Ruff-O'Herne have sought out international forums to raise awareness around the world. The comfort women issue was first raised at the United Nations Commission on Human Rights, in 1992 by Japanese human rights lawyer Etsuro Totsuka. Later, public hearings were held in Tokyo and at the Vienna World Conference on Human Rights in 1993.[56]

The most exhaustive acknowledgment by the Japanese government on its involvement in the military sex slavery system came in 1993 when the issue was investigated by the United Nations. In one report, the Japanese government shared its findings from an investigation and used a lot of euphemisms stating that the military was involved in recruiting "in some areas" and that the women "lived in misery at the comfort stations under a coercive atmosphere" and that this "severely injured the honor and dignity of many women."[57]

Women's rights activists were outraged by their ambiguity. They stated that these statements "conceal the direct and utter brutality to which the Japanese military knowingly and intentionally subjected the comfort women as an integral part of its war effort."[58]

Chapter 4

The House of Sharing

In the summer of 2004, I set out for a long trip to Asia to speak with survivors, activists, lawyers, and writers. One of the activists, Yoon Mee-Hyang, the Secretary General of the most prominent activist organization in Korea that provided care for survivors, was engaged in legal battles for justice for these women. Yoon had short hair and a tough style of speaking. She had become involved in activism for Japanese military sex slaves after Kim Hak-Soon had testified in the media. An active participant in student democracy protests in Korea during the 1980s, Yoon graduated from college a few years before the 1988 Olympics, which were held in South Korea, and during a new surge of women's rights activities centered on raising awareness about sex tourism and prostitution during the sporting event.

When Yoon read Kim Hak-Soon's story in the newspaper, she was shocked and in disbelief at the Japanese military's recruitment of underage girls like Kim, who was sixteen at the time she was enslaved. "That newspaper article brought back childhood memories of hearing stories of a neighboring grandma who ran away from Japanese officials to escape being a military comfort woman. One of my aunts married hastily to run away from a similar situation. They were trying to recruit many young women. My aunt told me stories from her childhood and said she married fast so she wouldn't become a *jungshindae*. Another woman of marrying age in the neighborhood ran away to escape being a *jungshindae*."

Yoon joined The Korean Council for Women Drafted for Sexual Slavery by Japan in 1992, and after a five-year break, she returned in 2002 and remains at the helm today. With fatigue in her eyes, she expresses how tired the grandmas are and how disappointed they are to not receive an apology from the state of Japan yet. "As we approach the sixtieth anniversary of the end of World War II, we feel frustrated with both the Japanese and

Korean governments. After all the research we've done, we've received affirming judgments from international bodies like the UN that affirmed Japanese military sex slavery has occurred and that the Japanese government must redress the historic injustice," she said. "Although we want an apology before the sixtieth anniversary, we realize it will not come to pass, therefore we want the fight to continue as a legacy to the younger generation. We know that we won't win an apology anytime soon and wars will always occur."

But Yoon is happy with the symbolic victory in the change of the public's perception of women's issues in Korea and how the struggle of the aging Japanese military sex slavery survivors became part of the larger tapestry of the democracy and peace movement. The Korean Council also works with the United Nations and other international organizations on issues of human rights violations and sexual violence against women and children of war in places like Iraq and Afghanistan. "Military comfort women could've been easily buried in history because it was something Koreans did not want to face or discuss. This issue has become a larger movement for democracy and the women's rights movement," she says.

Yoon believes, without doubt, that the saddest part of the Japanese military sex slavery system is the group of Korean survivors living in China who are said to have lived and are living in worse conditions than any of the survivors in Korea. Because of the short duration since relations had normalized between China and Korea after the war had ended, the Korean women could not return to Korea so easily. It has been a long process for the Korean women in China to regain their Korean citizenship. In order for them to receive the financial support from the Korean government, they need to become Korean citizens. "They are always near the comfort stations. The memory of what they endured is always near. They can't return home to Korea. They're forced to live in a foreign land where they endured such atrocities," said Yoon. "And after they've endured it all, they were still not allowed to return to their homeland. It is a double whammy."

Yoon blames the United States for failing to conduct a thorough investigation of what happened to these women, even though they knew about it. "With Germany there were tribunals and judgments for Nazi war criminals and a lot of information was unearthed about what really happened during the Holocaust. The Americans deliberately buried the Japanese role in Korea," she said. "And it is only recently, that in Korea, we've been able to take a step back and look at history including military sex slavery. Initially after the war, Koreans had to deal with hardships of the Korean War and other economic difficulties and the fight for democracy. It was the same in China. All these events prohibited the Korean people from completing a thorough investigation of Japan's colonial role in Korea and war crimes."

There are many questions surrounding how much more the Korean Council can do to help the Korean survivors living in China. When asked if she would consider helping North Korean refugee women who are raped and trafficked into sex slavery in China, she admits the thought has never crossed her mind. "One of my hopes is to continue the fight for the Korean women in China," she says.

Their Twilight Years

In September of 2004, my friend Helen and I traveled for two hours, south of Seoul, by subway, bus, and taxi to The House of Sharing, the home that was set up by Buddhist organizations specifically for impoverished Imperial Japanese military sex slavery survivors who were previously stranded in China. The House of Sharing was founded a year after Kim Hak-Soon testified. The taxi carried us up a winding road on a hill where driveways of homes had sedans and chicken coops, and trees with rich green leaves leaned against the skyline. The home consisted of two dormitories for the survivors with a few spaces for overnight guests, a temple, and an office building with a lounge. In the front, there was a haunting statue of a young girl with her hair pulled back in a bun, wearing a traditional *hanbok*.

Beside the residences for the elderly women was the History Museum of Japanese Military Comfort Women, which was established on August 14, 1998. The museum consisted of two floors with five different sections depicting various experiences of the military sex slaves and multimedia presentations of survivors' testimonies. In the "experience room", one could stand in a creepy model of a bare room in a comfort station. There were nine women in their late seventies and eighties living at the House of Sharing. While I was there, I learned some sad news that earlier in the year, Kim Soon-Duk had passed away, the first survivor I had met in Washington, DC. She was eighty-three at the time of her death.

One volunteer at the House of Sharing stated that the *halmonis* feel like "animals in a zoo" and are very disappointed that visitors who had promised to return, never followed through. Their morale is low as they are aging. They hear the same questions all the time. Visitors are free to knock on any survivor's door and make small talk, and people expect them to confess their entire life stories. At the same time, the staff members actually encourage people to ask the elderly women questions so that their repressed pain is relieved. The volunteers also jokingly say that the house should be called "House of Quarrels and Lack of Peace" because these *halmonis* have stubborn streaks and are not afraid to voice their opinions.

One of the caregivers, Ms. Sohn, explained that the *halmonis* forget people easily, so it is like starting over all the time. She listens to the same stories. "Yes grandma. Yes grandma," she says, mimicking her responses to them. The *halmonis* pinch her and hit her in a strange kind of affectionate way when she reacts like this.

One woman was nicknamed the *ghost grandma* because of her habit of appearing suddenly and seemingly out of nowhere. Her name was Ji Dol-Yee, 82, and she was quite striking with her snow white hair and powdery white skin. She had Alzheimer's Disease. Ji *halmoni* only conversed in Mandarin, which was the language she inherited when she was stuck in China after the war ended. She ended up marrying a Chinese man, and her daughter and son continue to live in China today. Ji's children come to visit her from time to time and ask for some support from her government financial aid that is given to all comfort women survivors. Another *halmoni* at the house, Bae Choon-Hee, had an identity crisis and wished she were Japanese. She married a Chinese man after the war ended, and her son and daughter lived in China as well. And yet another grandma, seventy-nine-year-old Kang Il-Chul, was very warm for a few days, but that did not last for long. She stopped talking and avoided my eyes. It was as if I had literally stopped existing in her world. Once, as I snapped a photo of her at a group event when the women were taking a day trip to the city, she blocked her face with a piece of paper. Perhaps she was tired of being documented by strangers.

Later one evening in the TV viewing area, I brought a bag of scarves with me to give to the grandmas. "Please choose one for yourself," I said aloud. About seven grandmas dove into the pile of scarves to choose a color. One grandma whined that another grandma stole the pink scarf from her while she was deciding between two colors. I tied a scarf around one grandma. "Look in the mirror," I said.

"Why should I? I'm too old," Bae Choon-Hee, the eighty-year-old grandma said. She had heavy turquoise eye shadow and her eyes were rimmed with heavy black eyeliner. She had on a brown wig, too.

"You have pretty eyes," I told her.

"You're lying!" Bae cried and said a word in Japanese that sounded like it would be censored on TV.

Her flash of anger hinted at a troubled soul. I felt too shy to ask if she felt healed of her trauma.

Then a sad video about lost love came on the television. Another one was about a love triangle. Some *halmonis* began tearing. They were all riveted. They were intriguing for their simplicity and girlishness that had been somehow preserved after all these years. We watched a drama and the news in silence. Kang *halmoni* was interested in the news. "Canada needs to know about the comfort women issue," she said.

Kim Gun-Ja was the first grandma at the house with whom I felt a connection. At dusk, we walked down a twisting road as the sun was setting. She was wearing a dark track jacket and had a blue and turquoise scarf tied closely around her neck. Her leather shoes were striped with light brown, olive and white. Kim has a bad back and walks in a stooped, very slow manner using a cane.

When asked about her past, she started to open up. "I'm a Catholic," was all she said at first. "Do you know why we grandmothers live together?" She asked slyly. "Do you know what happened to us?"

"Yes, I've heard," I said gently. "We wanted to see you *halmonis*."

"I left China when I was twenty-years-old. It took me one month to get back to Korea. I took the train, and I walked a lot during that month. A few years later, the Korean War began. Then, someone I loved died, so a Catholic person visited me regularly to give me support. In 1996, I realized that Catholicism was the way to heaven. I used to be a Buddhist before I converted. I have peace now, and I don't feel sad. Kim Soon-Duk died, and I'm not afraid. She lived right beside me. My will to live is strong.

"There are two other Catholics and one churchgoer at this house. The Catholic Church is thirty minutes away. I don't want to be bedridden, and that's why I walk every night. Another grandma asks others to help her, give her meals. She just looks to see if anyone will help. The Chinese grandma has dementia. Says her husband wants to take her while she's watching TV. I had a man she loved but he took drugs and died. That's why I never married."

"I was also orphaned. I had no parents to arrange my marriage. That's what they did back then. My two other sisters and I were orphaned. My dad died when I was ten years old, and at sixteen, my mom died. I had an operation on my leg. I have arthritis. I had a thyroid operation that's why I sweat so much. I can't go anywhere because my health is weak. Other grandmas went to a day trip. They also went to China. I couldn't go. They're going to Japan."

I asked, "Why are they going to Japan?"

She responded in a fiery way, "To fight of course! You'll meet other grandmas tonight. Say hi and give them gifts. They'll be happy."

Kim suspected that her foster father, a policeman, sold her to a Korean broker for money or promotion[59]at the age of seventeen. A Korean man had rounded up many Korean girls and women for the Japanese traffickers, and they were taken by train to Manchuria. There she was raped by "cruel and violent" Japanese soldiers every day for three years. She was severely battered and lost hearing in one ear. Kim's heart and life were shattered, and after the war ended, she could not marry. She lived in poverty until she moved to the House of Sharing. She cannot forgive the Japanese soldiers and has a deep hatred for current Japanese politicians. Like the others, she also wants an official apology and compensation. "Otherwise, I will not be able to close my eyes when I die," she said.[60]

Hwang Geum-Joo and the late Kim Soon-Duk had been slightly more open to talking with strangers. One of the activists later explained why the grandmas at the House of Sharing were so reticent when it came to newcomers: they did not want to become attached to people.

The grandmothers woke up every morning at dawn. No one indulges in sleep at the House of Sharing. Many sounds are made in the morning. Windows open. Water splashes onto the ground in a nearby bathroom in staccato procession. The morning air is crisp and chilly enough for layers and layers of clothes. Helen and I stayed in one of the rooms on the bottom floor. We got up and folded up our musty bedding every morning. The faded flower print blanket, in the guest room, nor the cover for the thin mattresses, smelled as if it hadn't been washed in years. A few cockroaches crawled on the wall.

One morning, one of the grandmas walked into our room suddenly. It was Kim Gun-Ja. "The others are angry that you haven't returned two of the mugs," she says smugly and quickly walked out. We had taken mugs into our room for a drink of water the night before. That morning, the missing cups were the biggest controversy to hit the home. It was as if we had stolen a family heirloom from the grandmothers themselves. Apparently, they counted them every morning and were quite perturbed they found something missing. They also reprimanded us for missing breakfast. I profusely apologized to each of them.

When Kang *halmoni*, shared on her life in China after she was "freed from hell," she was quite animated and spoke with passion. "Seven years ago, I came here. I was living in China before then. I had married a North Korean man who died during the Chinese war, during the Communist takeover in 1949. I had a hard time with my mother-in-law. I hate North Koreans and I hate the Japanese. I worked as a support staff person at an eye and ear clinic, not as a nurse but I did similar work. I can speak Mandarin fluently. I can turn it on at-will. I have two sons, two granddaughters, and two grandsons. My sons both work in companies in China. I went to Full Gospel Church and became a Christian when I was seventy-three years old. I like Pastor Yong-Gi Cho (former pastor of the largest church in the world called the Korean Full Gospel church)."

Many photos of herself adorned her room, along with a picture of Jesus with a scripture verse beneath it. The most striking one of all was a large, recent photograph of her standing prettily in a wedding dress holding a bouquet of scarlet roses. Her large red lips, the most prominent feature on her face, stood out. She had taken that photograph recently because she had never had a formal wedding. Noticeably, she did not have a husband in the photograph, and perhaps it is to show she does not need a man or does not want one. Many survivors have expressed their hatred for men and sex. More than anything she had shared, this photo brought a deep sense of loss. She still longed to have a real wedding ceremony and to wear pretty things such as a beautiful white gown.

Her youth had been stolen from her, and she was trying to claim it back through a solitary wedding photograph.

I offered her a scarf and tiger balm cream. "Please choose one," I said.

Gifts had to be distributed fairly among the grandmas. She chose the Tiger Balm cream and put her index finger to her lips. "Shhh. I won't tell the others," she said as she revealed a bruise and a band aid on the back of her left knee where she would apply it.

"Do you pray," I asked, looking around at the many Christian pictures.

"Yes." She closed her eyes and folded her hands in front of her. With a low hushed voice she prayed: "Why, O God was Korea under Japanese oppression for thirty-five years? And why were we taken and made to suffer so much? God why did you allow me to be a *wianbu* (*sex slave*)? We still suffer and hurt. Why? God, in scripture, you said you bring justice. I know you will bring justice to this situation. I trust you and put my faith in you. Because we are poor and pitiful--that's why this young woman came here. Thank you for this day trip celebrating ancient Korean history and culture." Then she prayed the Apostles Creed.

She put her finger to her lips again and said "shhhh." That was the last time Kang *halmoni* would say a word to me. The next day after what I thought was a bond we shared, Kang ignored me. Even as I approached her and said hello in the dining area, she hurried past me. Later, Yoon Mee-Hyang stated that Kang had been more affected by trauma than the others.

Then there was Bae *halmoni*. She explained how beautiful Japan was. Bae's dramatic appearance and edgy personality stood out. She had lived in Japan as a stage singer for thirty years and sounded like a native speaker. She sang haunting songs for everyone in the house that seemed almost comical at times in an overly dramatic way.

One night after a shower, I used a blow dryer on low mode in my room for five minutes at midnight. I thought the grandmas wouldn't be able to hear it, but Park Ok-Yeon *halmoni* burst into the room. She complained to her friends the next morning that I was blow-drying until one in the morning, which was clearly a humorous exaggeration.

Moon Pil-Gi *halmoni* was the sweetest and the most gentle. We did not press her for much detail on her experiences in the beginning. She invited us to her room where we ended up talking. Moon was forced to quit school early because her father felt it was a waste to educate girls. That was the Confucian mindset of that time. When Moon was just fifteen, a Korean man lured her with prospects of an education and earning lots of money in 1942. Shortly thereafter, she was taken by train to northeastern China and forced into a rape station. It was painful for her to re-tell her story to us as we cried and held hands together. She said of her abuse in the comfort station:

They tried to rape me. They were forcing me. They were treating me as a slave and they kicked me [and] hit me when I was not very good to them. And also they...burned my skin...There was a red, burning, scorching, iron bar, and you know I have a scar, still underneath my arm.

Moon said mostly soldiers raped her and that the military comfort stations were surrounded by the barbed wires and she was under guard constantly, fearful of being killed if she escaped. She was forced to stay at this station until the end of the war. As most of the survivors have attested to, she also complained of sleep disorders and terrible nightmares. The suffering continues as none of these women have received closure of any kind.

A few days later, the *halmonis* went out for their weekly demonstration in front of the Japanese Embassy. They sat in chairs and wore bright yellow vests with printed banners and sashes demanding an apology and compensation from the Japanese government. Seventy people attended the weekly Wednesday demonstration— the majority of them were Japanese tourists. Younger activists gave impassioned speeches with the aid of a megaphone. I gave a short speech on how the Japanese government must stop treating these elderly survivors as violent protesters by having armed guards stationed in front of the embassy, but instead they should apologize sincerely and bring closure to them. I urged the twenty-five Japanese tourists in the crowd to go back to Japan and tell others the truth about Japanese military sex slavery and this chapter of history.

This weekly event was launched on January 8, 1992 and more than fifty groups, mostly women's groups affiliated with the Korean Council, organized it. Several activists and these survivors have resolved to rally every Wednesday until the Japanese government officially apologizes and grants compensation to survivors. The women have been fighting for justice for nineteen years, in more than a thousand protests, through all seasons of rain, freezing temperatures, and oppressive heat. The survivors feel energized by speaking about their experiences with younger people after weekly demonstrations in front of the Japanese embassy. Some healing has come to those who have spoken out while many others still prefer to remain anonymous and silent in order to protect their reputations and families.

When it was time for us to depart the House of Sharing, Moon grandma cried, and so did we, as we said our goodbyes. Although a few of the grandmas were charismatic and open to strangers, most of them had been cagey and standoffish. This was most likely the outcome of the long-term impact of their experiences. The grandmas were tired. They were aging. Morale was low.

Bonding with Hwang Geum-Joo

After I left the House of Sharing, I stayed at another house in Seoul sponsored by The Korean Council. That's where I got to know Hwang Geum-Joo better. At first, eighty-four-year-old Hwang, did not remember me from our Vancouver meeting; then her memory was jogged. She was wearing shimmering copper-gold pants that flared out and narrowed at the ankles, with a denim button-down shirt. She donned a beige embroidered vest on top of her ensemble. Her black and white hair was tucked in a bun. Her feet were tiny.

"I have no uterus," Hwang confessed with a flippancy one would expect from someone who was discussing the weather. She is a straight-shooter and does not mince words or waste time when it comes to sharing her opinions. She has rough hands and is tough as nails. "That Kim Dae Jung[61]... he promised that the first thing he would do as president was to resolve the comfort women issue. That son of a bitch didn't do anything. I had lunch with him. He promised," she spat out.

Though she shared her story of being raped by up to forty men a day, she never seemed depressed about her life. She said that she even forgives the Japanese and does not blame the younger generation for what she experienced. While her story seemed rehearsed at times, it was still fresh as yesterday listening to her recount travels to different countries to bear witness.

"I've had operations on my uterus and for my missing bone in my back. I've met so many people who call me *halmoni*," she said. "They all know me. I've traveled to so many cities and I wear my *hanbok*. People go crazy over my dress. I once touched Abraham Lincoln's statue in Washington, D.C. No one else could. Just me." She beamed as she spoke of meeting President Bill Clinton and shaking his hand. She also brought up the topic of sex when she spoke of the impact of her sex slavery ordeal. She has remained afraid of men.

Hwang has not had a mother figure since she was sixteen years old, yet she is surprisingly very nurturing despite her rough edges. A lot of these elderly survivors are unusually tough and resilient. Out of the hundreds of thousands of military sex slaves, only a small fraction of them have survived their ordeals. Hwang was the only one, out of the girls at her station, who attempted to go back to Korea.

"I walked; it took four months to get to Seoul and I traveled with other refugees. I wore a soldier's uniform. I begged for food and slept on the streets. It was a very painful time," she said. "When I returned, I learned my father had passed away. I had no desire to go home. I did not try to find my family. I couldn't tell anyone what happened as I was so ashamed, but when I saw Kim Hak-Soon's public interview, I decided to come out, too."

Following the Korean War, Hwang halmoni continued to endure sharp pain and discomfort as a result of contracting a venereal disease from being subjugated to forced sex labor. She remained single and adopted three orphans, one of whom died as a child. Hwang raised and supported her son and daughter through school by running a small restaurant near Seoul University. Today, her children have families of their own and still visit her.

The other activists have grown very close with her. Beneath her gruff exterior, she has a soft heart and a lot of *jeong*[62] *(kindred love)*.

I met an activist of renown, Professor Yun Chung-Ok, at the rest center for survivors in Seoul called *Shim Toh* (*resting place*) that is run by the Korean Council for Women Drafted for Sexual Slavery by Japan. Yun was one of the key leaders who helped launch the movement for justice for Imperial Japanese Military sex slaves in Korea. She is tiny and has short, old-fashioned styled, wavy, peppered hair and is quietly charismatic. She, herself, was almost conscripted into sex slavery, but her parents helped her hide. After the war ended, she heard haunting stories of former comfort women in the countryside: these traumatized and mentally unstable women were constantly washing themselves to rid the stain of repeated rapes. Years later, she became angered after hearing the grandmas' stories. She could not stop thinking about the women who never returned after the war. With a passion that belies her composed demeanor, she states that she cannot forget the images of the Japanese soldiers lined up with their pants partially down while the women lay exposed on their beds.

Another survivor, Lee Young-Soo, is known as the fashionable grandma and has been described as very smart, a natural politician, warm, and childlike. We met at the home for survivors in Seoul in 2004. Her mother protected her after she returned home after the war. By 2007, Lee had morphed into a type of superstar spokeswoman, touring the United States and speaking before politicians about the resolutions that call on the Japanese government to issue an unequivocal apology and compensation to military sex slaves.

Lee was born in 1928 in Daegu, South Korea. Her impoverished family of nine, including her grandparents, lived in a cramped home. She only had one year of formal education, but her ability to grasp complex information and communicate it in an eloquent way is an innate talent. At the age of fifteen, she was drafted into the "Voluntary Corps." In the fall of 1944, when she turned sixteen, she was lured away into military sex slavery with her friend

Kim Pun-San. On the way to a Taiwanese rape station, she was beaten and tortured.

"It was my first ride on a train, and I vomited. I called for my mother because I was sick. The Japanese soldier came, pulled on my ponytail, and banged my head on the floor. He did this to the other girls too," she recalled. "And to this day, I still hear a noise ringing in my head. I told the older girls I missed my parents and wanted to go home. I longed to see my mother. That's what I said. And the Japanese soldiers hit me again because he said I was using Korean. The older women advised me to use actions rather than words."

Before they were ordered on to the boat, Lee knelt down and desperately prayed to God for help. "As I was praying a Japanese soldier came and kicked me. He followed us all the time. When he kicked me as I was praying and weeping, if my friend hadn't caught me, I would've fallen over into the water," she said.

On the boat ride to Taiwan, Lee was raped for the first time, and the attacks continued until she could no longer walk properly once she had to disembark from the ship. Lee almost died after a bombing of the underground shelter she and the other women and comfort station proprietor took refuge in. She lost consciousness after she was struck in the head. They were soon moved to another bomb shelter where she was forced to serve soldiers. She caught a venereal disease and was given injections of Serum 606.

Despite the harsh conditions, Lee made it home to her family. She lived with her mother for the rest of her life. Her mother died when Lee was forty-eight years old.

Lee has managed to eke out a living through sales work. She hikes at 6 a.m. every day and maintains a wide circle of friends in different parts of the world. An avid shopper, Lee's wardrobe is now filled with expensive and beautiful clothing.

When asked if her *han* has been eased at all, Lee says, "I meet a lot of young people but I can't ask young people to relieve my *han*. The Japanese government has to resolve my *han*. If I have *han* or nurture it, it ruins my health. So in some ways I don't want to resolve my *han* for the younger generation. It is a fighting strength. Some *han* is released by talking to people or going to protests and seeing many younger people," she said. "When I speak with young people like you, my *han* is released a little. I believe it'll be healed by the younger generation to continue the fight for justice and by the legacy we leave. I don't think it'll be released while I'm alive. There has been a hint of relief through the Korean government as they are trying, to some degree, to resolve the redress issue with the Japanese government. But the Japanese government has not done anything to relieve the pain."

It is clear to see that these elderly women, who have survived, want nothing more than an apology before they die. The survivors are like pine trees in Korea, known as the *sonamu*. The *sonamu* is unusually tough and its leaves remain rich green throughout all seasons, through harsh winds, sun and blustery monsoons, sprouting up in impossibly craggy landscapes, and because of its resilience it carries great significance as a national symbol of the Korean people who have endured attacks from invading forces over the centuries. Ever unchanging, the pine's roots wind deep into the earth and give it strength. The survivors' strong will to live is like these pine trees. They are dignified, immensely strong, and stately. The reality is that they may never receive the long-awaited apology from the Japanese government that they want to hear. As they have shared their painful stories with the world and each other, they have also raised global awareness on the horrors of sex trafficking and sexual violence against women and children in war zones, and they have shown the world that these crimes against them must not be tolerated or ignored.

The women's rights and human rights movement that was birthed out of the struggle for justice for Japanese military sex slaves has had enormous international impact. The peak of this came through the activists' hard work in promoting the non-binding resolutions that were passed in several countries, including the United States, which called on the nation of Japan to issue a clear apology and take on moral and legal responsibility for its direct involvement in planning and implementing the military sex slavery system.

There must be an awakening to the plight of the suffering through our own sufferings. Before we can see and feel another's wounds, perhaps we have to be faced with the reality of our own poverty. These women have experienced so much pain. We are at risk of forgetting this is a human rights issue with great political implications in East Asia. There is a need for reconciliation between Japan and her neighbors. We are also at risk of turning a blind eye to the modern day sex trafficking and slavery. We are at risk of ignoring them and callously moving on with our lives.

Chapter 5

Wartime Sex Slaves in China

In summer of 2004, the same year I visited the survivors in Seoul, I was invited to join a research tour to several cities and villages in China. I helped document interviews with academics, as well as survivors who bore witness to the effects of sex slavery, biological warfare, and other hardships inflicted by the Japanese military during World War II. It was an introduction to the hall of suffering from the Japanese invasion era in China, the forgotten Asian Holocaust.

The aim of the study tour was to deepen the teachers' understanding of the Asia Pacific War from 1931 to 1945 and to give them a firsthand look at the impact of the war on the Chinese people by meeting survivors of Japanese military war crimes, hearing their testimonies and dialoguing with experts involved in redress work for victims. The one person I was looking forward to meeting most was Wan Ai Hua, another woman who had survived Imperial Japanese military sex slavery.

Shanghai, the first stop in the tour, and other parts of China, were much more modern than expected. There were mega malls, highways filled with sleek cars and steel towers. The vibe in the cities was decidedly electric, as if the possibilities were endless in this 'new' China.

The countryside appeared to be circa 1970. There were many elderly people who had been affected by biological warfare chemicals that the Japanese military had unleashed against civilians in the villages. As a result, the infected, bleeding sores on their bodies – a constant source of pain and a reeking of rotten flesh – prevented them from getting married and from working. With their families earning meager wages of about three hundred Chinese yuan (fifty US dollars) per month, they had been unable to afford proper health care after the dismantling of the commune system in the late 1970s. Their plight was heartrending. But even more tragic was that their circumstances, like the military sex slaves in China, were relatively unknown. The Chinese Comfort Women Research Center at Shanghai Normal University is the only academic center in China that is dedicated to the research of Japanese Imperial military sex slavery.

A dozen teachers and three of the group's translators sat around a wooden table in the informal lecture room while a dozen others sat in the chairs by the wall. One of the most active scholars in China who researches military comfort women is Professor Su Zhi Liang. He has a round face and a semi-permanent serious expression on his face. Su established the comfort women research center in 1999 and has compiled oral accounts from survivors, photos, and archival evidence and co-wrote a book in 2013 called *Chinese Comfort Women*. He has organized several international conferences on the issue. Through Su, monthly support is given to elderly survivors who have made their testimonies public, and at the time, he kept in touch with about forty-five women.

Professor Su helped facilitate the first ever talk of this kind at Shanghai Normal University: a Japanese Imperial military comfort woman survivor bearing witness to a Canadian delegation of teachers. Su summed up one telling character trait of Wan Ai Hua. "She's very brave. She's now fighting in court against the Japanese government. Her health is not so good right now. In her condition, she insisted to fly in and meet Canadian teachers to tell of her experience." Su explained that Wan became involved in the fight for redress in 1992 when a teacher approached Wan after reading a newspaper article of an international lawsuit for Japanese military comfort women in Tokyo. He knew Wan's story and encouraged her to bear witness. They contacted the overseas Chinese association in Japan and made arrangements for her to travel to Tokyo.

Wan was the first Chinese survivor to testify of her experience in China. When this tiny woman walked in, her head was held high, and her steps were very sure and brisk. She had a bright smile, but her eyes were flitting in several directions at once. For a seventy-six-year-old woman, Wan looked considerably young; her pretty face had few lines. She had that all-too-human drive to be understood for the truth of her experiences. Survivors like Wan deserve to have their stories told to as many people who will listen to the universal lessons they can pass on.

"This is my second time in Shanghai. I'm very delighted to meet you people in Shanghai," Wan said in a high voice. "Today I'm going to tell my personal story. I'm coming here as a witness." "The Japanese government came to our village. They murdered many people, they set homes on fire, and up until now, they refuse to admit their mistakes. In China, during the Japanese invasion, the Imperial Japanese military raped, killed, and committed crimes against Chinese people. I have personally witnessed the Japanese soldiers using a sword to kill a baby by throwing it up in the air. Some people were thrown into wells that the soldiers covered with stones thereafter. I hope you young people will remember this piece of history—the crimes the Japanese military committed—and make sure the Japanese government will bear their war responsibility and own up to their crimes.

"In October 2003, I went to Japan to give witness in court, but the government still refused to admit their crimes. They supplied all guns, tanks, and planes for the war, but how come they refuse to admit their mistake during the war? It is just unreasonable and ridiculous they still refuse to admit their mistakes. The fault should be borne by the government. I think all the names of the victims should be given to the Japanese government. We called the soldiers Japanese devils because their human rights violations were really heinous.

"In 1992, I came forward and bore witness to these atrocities and to tell how wicked they were and my hatred for them. I was born in Mongolia and grew up in the province of Shanxi. I was sold by child traffickers living in the province of Shanxi, and I became a child bride. I was only four years old. My family was able to sell me at a higher price, as I was taller than children the same age, so I was sold for the price of an eight-year-old."

Wan never saw her parents again after she was sold. She was raised by her husband's family. Wan's fate was common at that time. Daughters were not as valued, and poor families sold their young daughters as child brides to other families who would raise the girl for their son, a child husband. Child brides and the bride trafficking cycle continues today as Chinese and North Korean refugee women, as well as women from other nations, are trafficked and sold as brides for poor farmers in China.

At the age of thirteen, Wan joined a Chinese communist party but kept her identity as a Communist member a secret. She said that Deng Xiaoping, the politician most famous for reforming China's economy, was stationed in her area. Wan was a dynamic and brave mobilizer for the communists as the lead organizer to supply the military with food, and she was the chairman of one of their societies. Two years later, she was captured by the Japanese military and was tortured in order to extract names of other Communist party members. "Since I had joined the communists, I could not disclose the identities of the other members," Wan's voice trembled as she teared up. "The Japanese soldiers beat me, tortured me, and raped me." The pain in her voice made it clear that she was re-living the torture.

"The atrocities the Japanese military has committed are unmentionable. They must bear responsibility and apologize to us. The first time I was captured, it was at Quinwixu, where the Japanese soldiers had bunkers. I was kept in a cave under the houses. During the period of my capture, the Japanese soldiers raped me during the day and at night. Whenever they were not doing sweeping, invasive operations, they would come and rape me four to five times a day. At that time, I was the only one who was kept inside the cave, and they tortured me until I spelled out the names of the other Communist Party members. They did not give me food or drink." Wan broke down and cried for a couple of minutes. "You, young people, you cannot imagine what I've gone through. When I tell you these things I feel ashamed."

Professor Su reached out his hand and told her in a low tone that it was not her fault. A hush fell over the room; everyone was quieted by Wan's vulnerability.

After a short break, Wan felt the need to move forward with her story. Professor Su gently prompted her memory. "Actually," he says, "Madame was captured three times, and escaped each time. The first time she fled, she forced open the bars of the window and escaped when the guards weren't there."

"Yes, my first capture happened in spring when I was fifteen years old. The second time when I was captured, it was summertime, and I was in a locked room. I tried to lift the door and crawled out under the door. At the time I was captured a second time, I could not recall how long I was kept as a prisoner. The third time it happened during the winter in December. Soldiers from two different bases surrounded our village and got me a third time. They tortured and beat me up because I was a member of the Communist Party. They beat my chest and back. I was originally 1.6 meters in height. After all the torture," she said as she stood up to show us her curved back. "I could not stand up. My posture was ruined. You notice my two ears. My right ear lobe is partially missing because it was torn off by the Japanese soldiers. On the third time, I was beaten so much, I passed out and they dumped me as a dead person in the river. There was no way I could escape because they beat me unconscious. Fortunately, I was saved by a man who got me out of the river. This man's father knew me when I was first captured, and he took me back home. Now you've heard some of my story. How do you feel about the atrocities committed by Japanese soldiers?"

The morning was emotionally charged with Wan Ai Hua's story, which illustrated powerfully how ordinary people – the Japanese soldiers – could commit the most horrible human rights abuses. She emphasized that she was bearing witness for students to learn universal lessons from the evil of sex slavery that she has experienced. "I hope you young people will remember this piece of history and the crimes the Japanese committed," she concluded.

Many cried. People were moved by her story. She was seventy-six years old yet feisty and courageous. At this age, she was engaged in a legal battle against the Japanese government and has traveled to Tokyo to give testimony several times. Her haunting eyes easily water upon mention of the rapes, yet she has a fiery spirit in a petite frame. Due to shame, she had been silent for fifty years. She never married nor had children, but she has an adopted daughter whom she lives with. Ultimately, she was able to survive after finding someone else who was more in need than herself.

"I felt other people despised me because of the torture I went through," she says. "After all my sufferings, I had this will to live and to carry on, especially after I adopted my daughter. She gave me another reason to live. I survived by begging and taking lowly jobs. I learned Chinese medicine and massage in order to survive," she said. "I hope we won't have to starve, beg, or have a poor life again. I want a better livelihood for all people in China. And I hope that the Japanese military won't rise up again and invade China." She explained that the Chinese government does not directly support the survivors' quest for redress. She truly hopes the Chinese government will take better care of their livelihoods in the future.

It is clear that she has become more resolved in her fight for justice from the Japanese government after meeting other victims and sharing about their experiences. "We have talked as fellow victims of sexual atrocities. Hand in hand we resolved to expose the atrocities committed by the Japanese soldiers," she says. "Until they make reparations and apologize, we will continue the struggle against the Japanese government."

This trembling, elderly Chinese woman fights every day to take down the Japanese government. Wan boldly declared in communist era terms, "I would like to continue to fight and make resistance against the Japanese government as long as they do not admit their war responsibility and apologize. I will continue my resistance. Since 1992, when I attended the international forum, I have been to Japan six times to bear witness. I did all of this to show my determination in demanding that the state of Japan face up to war crimes and apologize. I hope that you will not forget this chapter of history."

Wan, like Hwang Geum-Joo, was also part of a lawsuit against the government of Japan. Her first lawsuit was filed in Tokyo in 1998. They lost. The judge did not dispute the evidence but said the crime was committed by individual soldiers more than twenty years ago, which exceeds the statutes of limitations of time and therefore releases the government of responsibility for crimes committed by individuals. She explained that besides the testimony of the witnesses themselves, they had side evidence to support their case. During that era, blankets were rare. When she escaped the first time, she took from the cave where the Japanese soldiers held her captive, a neighbor's blanket that was stolen by Japanese soldiers when they looted her home and village. Wan returned it to the owner, and Su was able to track down the owner of the blanket, Ho Dai-fu, to confirm Wan's story of escape. The blanket had a special pattern and therefore, it was evidence that Wan had indeed, been captured by Japanese soldiers who had looted Ho's village.

It is incredible that the western world is largely in the dark about what happened to thousands of women like Wan, and she's one of a handful who survived the ordeal and was in good health to engage in the struggle for justice.

Wan, aged 84, passed away on September 4, 2013 in Taiyuan, Shanxi, China.

China's Significance in the Movement

Professor Su believes the redress movement for Imperial Japanese Military war crimes is gaining new momentum in China as more new archival documents are uncovered and more survivors are speaking out in their old age and joining class action lawsuits in Japanese courts. He has stated that for the Asian peoples, the issue of the military comfort women and the atrocities committed by the military is their 'Holocaust,' comparable to the genocidal massacre of six million Jewish people by the Nazis.

"The public, more and more, is demanding redress. The Chinese government has clearly expressed it has only given up the state's right to compensation, and the people have rights as individuals to claim damages and reparations from the Japanese government," Professor Su said. "We're seeing a new era as far as the redress movement goes inside China."

He explains that in 1918, the powers of the world decided to interfere in the Russian Revolution, and at that time, Japan sent seven military divisions that moved in to the northeastern part of China and into Siberia until 1922. The Imperial Japanese military was troubled to find that among seven divisions, one division had been affected with venereal diseases due to the soldiers raping the local women. In the early twentieth century, STDs were difficult to treat. The Imperial Japanese military needed to prevent the spreading of STDs among its soldiers, but instead of disciplining their soldiers on sexual violence, they decided to provide sexual services to their soldiers. In 1931, the first comfort women stations in the world were set up in Shanghai.

The setting up of rape stations, or comfort stations, in Shanghai, was considered the first stage in the development of the sex slavery system, according to Professor Su. The first comfort stations were started in Shanghai because it was the main port for the third fleet of Japanese Marines and the official headquarters of their navy. Six thousand soldiers were stationed in Shanghai on a regular basis. The naval ministry initially set up four comfort stations to provide sexual services to the marines.

In a photograph Professor Su presented, one of the red brick houses, which was used as a station, had several windows and was surrounded by trees. It was situated in the district of Pukow in the northeastern part of Shanghai. There were five distinct buildings with two levels each. The second floor connected all five buildings. A yellow circle served as a dancing floor in the open air. You could see a special garage for officers' vehicles. War carvings of Mount Fuji were on the inside of the building. This former comfort station is a residence today. Professor Su says these houses may one day be "regretfully" demolished. "I'm trying to raise consciousness among the public to raise more awareness about the fate of these houses. I think it is important to preserve these comfort stations," he explained.

The second stage of the military sexual slavery system was enforced in 1932. When the Japanese military invaded Shanghai, Okamura, the Commander-in-Chief, organized a group of Japanese prostitutes to be sent to Shanghai to serve soldiers during the military operation. This is the first time the euphemism "comfort women" was used. After the Shanghai invasion, the Japanese women were sent back to Japan.

The third stage began in 1937. Professor Su pointed to a famous black and white photo of two military comfort women as he explains: two Korean women are laughing and walking; one woman is carrying luggage on her head as they cross the Yellow River. In 1964, an American military photographer discovered the photo and was surprised to know Korean women were in the frontlines in China.

In one photo taken by a Japanese soldier, about half a dozen, smiling Japanese soldiers are lined up as they stand in front of a comfort station. Another document shows the ratio of military comfort women to soldiers: 1:29 or 1:33. For every three hundred ninety soldiers, the military assigned ten comfort women because they did not want to spend too much money on food and transportation for the women. This was carefully calculated since fewer women meant the soldiers' needs would not be met.

Professor Su shared about the plight of the survivors' impoverished lives as he elaborated on how he tracked down and met with each woman. In Henan province, Su met a woman who was known during China's Cultural

Revolution as the "white haired girl." She was a military sex slave and managed to run away to the mountains. She lived in constant fear of people and made her home in a hole in the ground, surviving on wild fruits. She almost died from heat exhaustion before a young farmer found her and treated her. She recuperated after three years. The farmer wanted to marry her, but his parents forbade it, so the couple went to the mountains to live, and they had three children. He died in the 1960s from exhaustion due to physical labor. She died in January of 2004.

In Toronto, at a conference on Japanese war crimes, Professor Su met another former military comfort woman from Wuhan named Yuan Zhulin. She had been married to a local man with a baby daughter at the time the Japanese military invaded Wuhan. She was eighteen years old. The Japanese took her and she was raped repeatedly daily, often throughout the night. Su said he could see the suffering in her eyes. She had been deemed more beautiful than the other women and therefore served the officers as a sex slave instead of the soldiers. An officer named Nishiyama fell in love with her and visited her frequently. Nishiyama hated Japanese Imperialism.

They lived together for a time but he disappeared when the war ended. Penniless, she returned to Wuhan soon after. She adopted a baby girl. During the 1950s, this woman's mother foolishly told others that her daughter had been a comfort woman. The Chinese police learned of this and accused her of being a spy for the Japanese. She was sent to a prison labor camp run by the Communist government. At the end of the Cultural Revolution, she was freed from the camp, and she lived the rest of her life with her adopted daughter in Wuhan. Her first daughter had died while she was in the comfort station.

According to Professor Su's research, more than four hundred thousand young women were forced into sexual slavery, and of this number, more than two hundred thousand women were from China. He has discovered that the Imperial Japanese military invaded more than twenty provinces in China, and wherever they invaded, they set up comfort stations, particularly in the very northern and southern parts of China and in Shanghai. The Japanese soldiers ended up poisoning or shooting many of the women. Later, the Chinese military discovered their bodies and buried "the bodies of the miserable women."

Among the comfort women lawsuit cases in Japanese courts, there are cases that involve a woman from Taiwan who is suing the Japanese government as well as three other Chinese survivors, including Wan Ai Hua. In order for peace to be maintained in East Asia, Su expresses that Japan must deal with this chapter of history, as Germany has, through reparations, official apologies, passed laws, and erected monuments.

During the tour of a former "comfort house" in Shanghai's Pudong District, we met Mr. Qian Cang Zhan, an eighty-one-year-old former owner of the impressively large home that the Japanese soldiers took over as a comfort station in 1943. Before the Japanese invaded, his family lived in a few of the rooms while renting out the other rooms. When the Japanese soldiers invaded, they evicted the renters and let the owner and his family live in a place right outside of the house. A group of Chinese women were brought to the house as sex slaves. By 1943, the Japanese military were experiencing several defeats in battles. The military was in need of comfort stations to boost morale in order to encourage the soldiers to keep fighting. Officers, not just regular soldiers, were 'entertained' in this home. The soldiers could only visit during the day, while the officers had evening visiting privileges.

Zhan's firsthand account: "When the Japanese first disappeared, we didn't dare come into the house. Every day, while they were here, they raped Chinese women. They raped so many women. At the station, because of the rapes, the women were examined in a medical room in the house every week. Three people ran this comfort station. An outside wing in the house was where some soldiers lived. The officers lived in the main building. The comfort women also left a short time after the Japanese were gone. I want to let you people know because the Japanese committed crimes against Chinese women, and to this day they have not owned up to their war responsibility. I remember the German Prime Minister kneeling down to apologize at a concentration camp in Poland because of atrocities against Jewish people. Even now, the Japanese government refuses to apologize. I do still believe justice will ultimately win.

Not too long ago, a lawsuit was filed by forced laborers in order to sue the Japanese government, and they won in court. I was told many of you are history teachers. I hope you can tell the next generation the true facts of history."

In August of 1945, when the war ended, the Japanese soldiers and officers suddenly disappeared from this station. Then, a few years later in 1952, the Chinese government bought the house and converted it into a vocational school for the Port Transportation Industry. Professor Su is involved in lobbying to preserve this former comfort station and several others as historical sites.

Zhan pointed out that even the German Prime Minister showed unusual remorse on behalf of the Germans and apologized at a former concentration camp in Poland. The lack of contrition by the Japanese government and their visits to Yasukuni Shrine have caused a bitter rift between them and the people of China, Korea, and other nations invaded by the Japanese military during the Asia Pacific War. An official Canadian government apology for racially discriminatory laws and government-instituted injustices have brought healing to the Japanese, the Chinese, and the First Nations communities in Canada. Would a single apology bring healing to Wan and other survivors?

Chapter 6

"We have our part in building this nation's knowledge of itself, a task which seems to us as important for a whole people as for an individual." ~ Louis C. Jones

Discrimination Against Asian Victims

The rape and murder of these comfort women were not acknowledged as war crimes at the Tokyo Trials, or International Military Tribunal for the Far East despite the evidence and knowledge the Allies had of the comfort women and comfort stations from as early as 1942 and later from firsthand interviews by US military personnel.[63] As the Allied Forces moved through the Pacific and into

Asia they found Korean women as far away as Myanmar, Manchuria (northeastern China), Borneo, Papua New Guinea, the Rykuku Islands and the Philippines. These women were interrogated by government officials, and reports were filed with the Allied Command. In one report prepared by the US military intelligence (US Military Psychological Warfare Team based in Myanmar and India), a description of the experiences of twenty women in a report describes the women as being, for the most part, uneducated and naïve.[64]

Some Allied documents even categorized the women as camp followers,[65] suggesting that these women were willing participants, offering their bodies as prostitutes, even though the US military was aware of the Japanese military's use of deception and coercion to recruit the girls.[66] One Allied interviewer wrote a description of the so-called "camp-followers" after he interviewed twenty Korean comfort women in Myanmar in 1944: "The girls were young—eighteen to twenty-four was my guess. Their expressions varied. One or two appeared defiant, but most wore looks of fear and anxiety. Some had tears in their eyes or running down their cheeks, while some with their heads bowed low, appeared to be praying. None exhibited the coquetry usually attributed to camp-followers."[67]

There were no formal inquiries into why the Allied Forces did not bring the perpetrators and organizers of the comfort women system to trial as war criminals. The Allied Forces also engaged in rape and violence against women as an act of war against the "enemy," and to include sexual crimes as war crimes at the tribunal would force the Allies to harshly discipline and bring to trial its own soldiers. Furthermore, evidence for lenient attitudes towards prostitution and sexual violence against women is very clear in the Allied Forces usage of Japan's "emergency" comfort stations, provided urgently so that the local women would not be raped.[68] General MacArthur, the leader of the Allied Forces, was fully aware of these comfort stations during the occupation in Japan and did not demand they be immediately shut down.[69] In fact, the US also requested others be built on their behalf. After the war, the Japanese government was afraid that the United States and other Allied troops would commit atrocities in Japan in a similar manner as

Japanese troops did when invading China in 1937. In order to prevent rapes, on August 18, 1945, the Japanese government opened the comfort stations for use by Allied troops. According to Japanese documents and testimony from former comfort women, the women at these stations were forced to serve as sexual slaves to the American soldiers. The first comfort station opened solely for the use of United States troops in the Tokyo area on August 27, 1945, with reports that terrified Japanese comfort women began weeping and clung to posts in the building, refusing to move.[70] It is not clear whether these women served Japanese troops before the war ended.

In September of 1945, the chief of Tokyo's Public Health Section, Yosano Hikaru, met with the Surgeon General of the US Military to discuss the availability of women for the US Military. After this meeting, responsibility for the comfort stations was divided between Yosano and Colonel C.F. Sams, Chief of the US Public Health and Welfare Department.[71] These stations were only shut down because of the threat of sexually transmitted diseases and not because they realized it was a severe violation of these women and girls.[72] When a US chaplain, who was assigned to the occupation of Japan in 1946, protested to the base commander upon seeing officers setting up brothels on the base, he was reassigned stateside within weeks.[73]

Dutch Victims

The Allied interviews with the comfort women were for intelligence gathering purposes rather than documenting and gathering evidence to prosecute crimes of sexual violence against women at the Tokyo War Crimes Trial.[74] Some of the rapes committed during the Rape of Nanking formed part of the basis for convicting Japanese officials of war crimes.[75] The Allies at the tribunal, however, did not view the Imperial Japanese military's use of comfort women as a war crime requiring the prosecution of the Japanese, except for two cases: one involving Dutch women in Indonesia, but not the Indonesian women who were Dutch colonial subjects, and the other Guam female residents. The only Japanese military sex slavery cases that were brought to trial involved Dutch women at the end of the war. No further investigation was ever conducted.[76] The Imperial Japanese military had gone out of their way to cover their tracks in order to ensure the military comfort women system was buried before the war ended.

Professor Sarah Soh, a researcher on Imperial Japanese Military sex slavery wrote:

"Nonetheless, among the approximately fifty military tribunals convened at various Asian locales between 1945 and 1951, only one tribunal, conducted by the Dutch in Batavia (today's Jakarta), meted out stern punishments (including one execution) to Japanese officers who forced Dutch women into sexual servitude. The Batavia trial thus recognized the "forced prostitution" (to use the Dutch government's terminology) of thirty-five Dutch women as a war crime. However, it ignored similar suffering by a much greater number of native women in Indonesia, not to mention female victims in other Asian countries. What, then, is the meaning of the Batavia trial for the comfort women issue? Obviously, it was the action of a victorious nation-state protecting the human rights and personal security of its nationals in a colonial setting as a matter of national interest. It underscores the common deprivation of human rights of people under colonial rule."[77]

In 1942, the Japanese invaded Indonesia and soon began to force the Dutch civilians into prisoner-of-war camps. Many in these camps, when the Allied armies came to liberate them, were skeletal, lifeless, and barely had energy left to move.[78] There were several cases of women being forced into the military rape camps according to the Dutch government report.

More than fifty years after World War II ended, in 2000, a high-profile Western comfort woman survivor, Jan Ruff-O'Herne, testified at the second unofficial Tokyo War Crimes Tribunal called The Women's International War Crimes Tribunal for the Trial of Japan's Military Sexual Slavery. Jan said that when the Japanese military returned the Dutch comfort women to civilian internment camps near the end of the war, the soldiers separated and placed these women in different camps and threatened their lives and the lives of their families if they spoke of the crimes committed in the comfort stations.[79]

The Dutch held trials in Java, Borneo, and elsewhere in the Netherlands East Indies,[80] but the Batavia court was the only one to try and punish the Japanese for forcing thirty-five Dutch women into prostitution.[81] In the trials by the Dutch and the official government report by the Netherlands, the focus was on the experiences of women of European descent and did not adequately investigate the experiences of the Indonesian women who were former colonial subjects of the Netherlands. In the trials in Batavia, the Japanese were only tried for the use of Dutch women as sex slaves even though Indonesian women suffered just as much as they did. The racial inequality between Dutch and Asian or Indonesian victims in the court at Batavia is not surprising. Racism drove the moral panic over trafficking and prostitution in the late nineteenth and early twentieth centuries when there was outrage over the sexual enslavement of young, white impoverished English girls. It seems that due to the race and class relations in Indonesia, the same righteous indignation was not there for Indonesian or non-white women.[82]

The two trials in Batavia involved a hotelkeeper, as well as Japanese military officials, who were all charged with raping female interns in Ambarawa, Java. The hotelkeeper, Washio Awochi, was charged with the war crime of enforced prostitution and the indictment read: "In times of war and as a subject of a hostile power, war crimes by, in violation of the laws and customs of war, recruiting women and girls (as young as twelve and fourteen) to serve as prostitutes at his establishment. Under the direct or indirect threat of the Japanese military police, the Kempeitai, the women were held involuntarily and forced to serve Japanese civilians solicited by Awochi."[83]

Twelve women, who had been forced into prostitution, testified at the trial in Batavia and substantiated the charges. Awochi was found guilty of violating the laws and usages of war and he was sentenced to ten years imprisonment.[84] Another one of the accused was condemned to death and the others were sentenced from two to fifteen years for committing crimes against humanity, namely coercion to prostitution, abduction of girls as young as twelve years old and women for forced prostitution, and rape and inhumane treatment of prisoners.[85] The court martial also said the women were forced to work in brothels in Semarang and this was, "considered undesirable by Headquarters of the Prisoners of War and Civil Internment Camps as the conclusion might be drawn that this has been done under duress, this being in contravention of international law."

At the Tokyo War Crimes Tribunal, Japan's military was not prosecuted for crimes against Koreans during the Japanese occupation and against local people groups under the colonial rule of the Allied powers.[86] This kind of subjective decision-making in determining who or who would not be prosecuted and what constitutes a war crime is unconstitutional, arrogant, and racially discriminatory, reflecting imperialistic attitudes at best.

The definition of war crimes had included and continues to include atrocities such as rape, abduction of women and girls for forced prostitution, and coercion to prostitution. Japan's government is therefore responsible for the atrocities committed against not only the Dutch military sex slaves for the Imperial Japanese Military, comfort women, but women from other countries as well.

Holland's Redress Movement

Holland was occupied by the Nazi forces from 1940 to 1945. But the only traces of the war in Amsterdam that are visible are the Anne Frank Museum and the Corrie Ten Boom Museum, and both are haunting reminders of the Nazi occupation. The unusually flat landscape of Holland and the wide expanse of sky lend a sense of idyllic calm, as do the country's flatness and endless stretch of verdant fields.

In October of 2007, I flew into multicultural Amsterdam and took a train to The Hague to interview a Dutch survivor of Japanese military sex slavery, Ellen van der Ploeg. The Netherlands-based Japanese Honorary Debt Foundation[87] was hosting a conference on the 1907 Hague Convention[88] and its legal implications for survivors of Japanese war crimes. The 1907 Hague Convention prohibited the torture of prisoners-of-war and women. The members of the Japanese Honorary Debt Foundation numbered more than nine thousand dues-paying members. They state on their website that "around four hundred girls and women are known to have been forced into sexual slavery; many more have been abused, including young boys. Those who survived were left with permanent trauma (sic). Only a few of them are still alive." Their community had a tight bond formed from a common experience of intense suffering, and they had lobbied their government for years on the issue of obtaining redress from the Japanese government.

Ellen had been forced into military sex slavery in March of 1942, right after her high school graduation. There was the possibility that she would not want to talk. At eight-five years of age, she was getting tired of waiting for the Japanese government to apologize. Ellen's testimony was key, along with those of other survivors from Korea, and it influenced the passing of the motion in the European Union's parliament that called on the Japanese government to apologize. She had traveled to Japan, China, and Canada to testify and had met Kil Won-Ok *halmoni* from South Korea and other survivors from Asia at the Tokyo Tribunal in 2000 as well. I decided that I would only interview her if the chance came up naturally.

Those attending the conference met for drinks at the Kurhaus Hotel the first evening. The location of the conference was symbolic. This hotel was the very location where the Hague Convention was drafted more than one hundred years ago. Everyone was there to explore ways on how survivors could receive an apology from the Japanese government for war crimes committed against them in the World War II. The Japanese delegates squealed at the thought of Jan Ruff-O'Herne attending the conference. She ended up not making it, but it showed that even in these activist circles, there were superstars.

Devout Catholic and Australian citizen, Jan Ruff-O'Herne, has written her own book and is a strong voice for reconciliation with the Japanese. From the conversations I've had with the foundation members, I gathered that reconciliation would not be addressed unless the government of Japan offers a sincere apology and proper symbolic compensation.

I met some more people from the foundation and was soon seated next to Ellen. Her smiling eyes crinkled at the corners, and she shook my hand and laughed. Her silver-hair was pulled back in a hair band and a bun. Her dark eyes were round and misty. The other foundation members greeted her with warmth as she joked with the men. She had a wicked sense of humor. For a few days, she led me to believe she was sixty-five years old. She said it with such a straight face. Even though we had celebrated the sixtieth anniversary of the war not too long ago, in a suspension of disbelief, I thought, why would this lovely lady lie about her age? Her endearing, easy laughter rang out often, and her voice sometimes got hoarse because she was suffering from a cold.

During one of the morning sessions of the conference, I began by asking Ellen some very casual questions. When I asked her what she wanted from the Japanese government, she replied, "I've been waiting more than sixty years for the Japanese government to tell the truth and apologize. Why haven't they? It has been more than sixty years. In times of war, it is always the women who have to pay the bill!" She also mentioned Sudan and the women and girls who were raped there.

During the conference's documentary film session on prisoner of war camps in the Dutch East Indies, Ellen was moved by the film and sighed frequently. She also agreed to share her story:

"There were more than a hundred girls in the comfort stations that they called brothels. It is a lie that we were paid…You can't believe it…As I get older and older, I can't ever forget what happened when I was young. When you're young, you believe in life and believe in mankind." All of a sudden, Ellen, smiling ear-to-ear, burst into singing the theme song from the musical Annie. "Tomorrow… tomorrow…" We both laughed as I joined her in singing. Her inner strength was apparent.

"Are you ever discouraged that the Japanese has not apologized?" I asked.

"Yes, I'm still waiting after sixty years and nothing has happened. The Japanese government officials have no character."

"Are you optimistic now that an official apology will be given to you?"

"No, not at all," she said. "I have heard nothing that sounds like an apology I wanted to meet some Japanese officials here but I haven't seen one to tell them what happened to me."

Then she said in an animated way, "*Xie xie (Thank you). Zaijian, zaijian, zaijian (Goodbye, goodbye, goodbye).*" We laughed again. She had learned some Chinese from meeting with survivors and activists in China.

"What are you demanding from the Japanese government?" I asked.

"That they have the guts to behave like people with character. That they have the guts to tell the world we have been wronged in the comfort stations during the war. And that they apologize. We are not asking them for money," she said. "Apologize and say the war was cruel. Don't tell me they were always good and we're always bad. I said as long as the Japanese only tell their truth, I will tell my truth. I won't give up."

"You were very athletic when you were younger," I stated.

"Yes."

"Were you competitive?"

"Yes," she said laughing heartily.

"Is there something you'd want the world to know about you and remember about you?"

"I am just one person with all the good and the bad habits and so on. I try to be good because I am a lover of justice. Justice. Justice," she said with a lilt.

"What is your greatest weakness?"

"Oh, I don't know... I think that if you have experienced a war in Indonesia like me, it was today we're in the home and tomorrow we're in a prisoner-of-war camp with our mother, sister and little brother. Then you'll see the story of my mother when my ten-year-old brother was taken from her. It was so traumatic. I can't forget it," she said. "My little brother didn't cry. He thought he was going with other boys.

"I can't forget the changes in my own body after one month. You don't have your monthly period. It went away for three years. For three years. There was a lack of food. There was no food at the POW camp. I can't forgive them. Never," she said emphatically.

"What was the hardest thing about being in the comfort station?"

"Waiting for a visitor. It was always with fear in your heart. You don't know what's about to happen. And there was an old Japanese woman who had to give us lessons on how to keep our bodies clean. Remember--you are seventeen, and you don't know what happened with your body and there is a foreigner telling you how to keep your body clean. That is terrible."

"Were you ever beaten?"

"No, no, no."

"Did you have any health problems?"

"No. There was a doctor to examine us every three weeks. I didn't have any sicknesses. As soon as I was with my mother in Holland, I had to go to the doctor. Thank God I did not have any health problems."

She poured sugar and milk into her coffee and then exclaimed, "Beautiful color!" She laughed heartily. Ellen and a Korean military sex slave survivor had testified at the European Union before they passed the resolution that called on the Japanese government to officially apologize to the women. The lawyer informed us that later, in the fall, survivor Kil Won-Ok would testify in the Amnesty International Comfort Women Speaking Tour Campaign across four European capitals in November of 2007. In addition to Kil, Ellen and a seventy-eight-year-old

Filipina survivor, Menen Castillo, would testify in The Hague, Brussels, Berlin, and London.

Ellen quickly switched back onto our conversation. "Women and men are just the same. They are equal. It is wrong of the Japanese government to force women into sex slavery. You can't respect them. That's my point. You don't have to love or like them."

"Can you describe what it was like in the comfort station?"

"My Japanese name in the camps was Purugu. I still don't know the meaning of the name. They called me that because they couldn't pronounce my last name of Ploeg. I was born in – you'll never believe it because I have lived my whole life in Indonesia – The Hague. I'm now eighty-five. I was born on January 14, 1923. Many Dutch people working for companies had to go back and forth to Indonesia," she paused. "When I see your young faces, I feel old. I feel old."

"How old were you when you got recruited?"

"I was eighteen. School was not finished at that time. We were already kept in a prisoner-of-war camp—my mother, sister, little brother, and me. As soon as my little brother was ten, he was taken from his mother and put in another camp. That was the rule of the Japanese authorities. What was wrong was why the Japanese authorities didn't tell the truth. That is always my fight."

"What happened before you were taken to the camp?"

"It was 1942 when we had to leave our houses. My father was already forcibly taken by the Japanese. The Japanese authorities told us to pack our luggage… fifty kilos per bag. We had to go to the street and head to the POW camp," she said. "After that we were put in open trucks and went to the capital of east java, Surabaya. We were put on the train and taken to a real POW camp in Semarang. We stayed for a long, long time. Every morning it was the same ceremony, in the morning we had to bow down and line up. We had to learn in Japanese to respond. If we were wrong, we had to wait long and do it again.

"Food was just porridge… no meat. Potatoes, I hated it, hated soup. On a certain morning, there was a decree of the Japanese who told us that all young girls from twelve to twenty years of age had to parade for the Japanese officials. So we had to walk around and around.

All the officials looked at us. You could even have respect for an enemy because of their good behavior, but I can't have that for the Japanese because they have never apologized. On the second day, we had to go around and around... all girls, fifteen to seventeen years of age... third day we had to go around and around. There were several Japanese authorities in uniforms and big boots. They looked at us. At just one point, they put a finger to a girl and she was transferred out. Then one day, an official pointed at me. There were fifteen of us girls, and we were happy to leave the POW camp. We were promised beautiful fruit, food, and opportunities to study to be a secretary or nurse. It was heaven on earth, they said. We believed it and packed our luggage. But I lost my friends when they separated us and put us together with girls from other camps. That was their intention. No one knew what was going to happen to us. The mothers were told by the drivers who brought us to the comfort stations in Semarang, of what we had to do. As we were young, we did not know what was going on. We were soon asking what they wanted from us. An old Japanese woman came forward and told us we were for the pleasure of the militaries. For the first time we learned what pleasure was for men. We were young, fifteen or sixteen, so what did we know? They knew that.

"The drivers told our mothers there were four brothels and what the situation was for the young girls, and they couldn't do anything anymore. In the comfort station, there was a papa-san. He took the tickets from the Japanese military men. All the girls had a little room with a round table and two or three chairs, as well as a bed and closet and cupboard shelves to put clothes in. My favorite place was always the bathroom where, for hours, I could stay locked in by myself. I was there for three months and one day. You can't erase that experience from your young life at that moment. After three months, I came out of the camp, and we were brought back to our mothers again. There is a point where you can't confess everything because everything we experienced had made such a big impact on our characters.

"Jan O'Herne came out with a book called *50 Years of Silence* and married an Englishman. I heard about her book in Holland. I decided I would do the same in Holland for the girls. Jan has to be honored because she was the first one to come out with her story through her book," she said.

"How did you feel about coming forward?" I asked.

"I did not feel afraid. Not at all. You have to make the world know and make sure that it never happens again. It is always the girls who suffer the most. Look in Darfur at what happened. The girls were raped and murdered. It is always the women who pay the price in war."

"Do you feel like you've made a difference by testifying?"

"Yes of course, I don't know how, but the main point is even the Dutch people do not recognize these things," she said.

"There must always be the people who bring it forward. That's you," I told her.

"Yes I hope so."

"What was life like in the comfort station?"

"It was very boring. There was nothing to read, no music, no radio, no daily papers. I couldn't talk with my friends. The Japanese were watching us, and we wouldn't dare to speak freely. We had to be careful all the time," she said emphasizing the word 'careful.' We had to bow to people we don't even know and bow to the Japanese whom we hated."

"What was going through your mind when this was happening?"

"I had to be humble not because I was afraid, but because it would have been harder for me if I was not humble. Many women fought with the guards, but I didn't want to fight because I wanted to live to tell the world what they had done to me and other young girls."

"What happened to the girls who fought with the soldiers?"

"I always heard them screaming. I wanted to tell them they weren't accomplishing much with fighting because it was causing them physical pain not just emotional pain.

"What was the most painful thing you had to deal with after your time in the comfort station?"

"It was my own fault because I didn't want to tell my story right away and to tell my family what happened and how it happened. Many asked the same questions. All the girls from Indonesia to Europe had the same experience. They never told about their experience in the comfort station. For what reason do we have to tell that? I was furious about that question: How many men did you have to receive every night?

"Some people believe you and think you're innocent. Some said 'she looks innocent but she's not innocent' or 'she looks like a lady but she's really a whore,'" she said getting heated.

"After you told your story, how did that make you feel?"

"I felt great. For me, it was over. I told myself whoever asks me what my experience was as a young woman in the brothel, I shall always tell the truth from the beginning to the end. I have no secrets about that life. I can tell anybody and not feel ashamed because it was not my fault. But I was not strong enough to tell my mother and give her more sorrows than what she already has. I looked to nature to gain understanding that there is misery and pain in the world. There is much between here and above heaven that we don't know and understand," she said.

"Many people will find strength in your story," I told her.

Ellen's father was Dutch, and her mother was Indonesian. She returned to Holland with her mother, sister, and brother after the war ended. They lived in poverty, and both Ellen and her mother worked very hard to support the family. Her father had died in the war after he was taken into captivity by the Japanese military. "I have been married, but I didn't want to be a mother. That was the point the marriage broke down. After that period, I wanted to be alone to follow my own decisions and my own thoughts and didn't want anything to do with men. I like men, and I'd be sad if there were no men in the world. But they're not for me, and I know that now."

When asked to give a word of encouragement to Taiwanese survivors in a videotaped message, Ellen balked and said, "No way. They have to find their own way. I can't help them."

There was a surprising coldness in her comments. But it gave insight into how she has had to become tough for herself to protect her heart. This was her way of surviving. Despite Ellen's tough demeanor, she was especially tender with her friends. At times, at the end of the day or after a meal, she looked confused and called for her friends. "Where's Lieke? Where's Lieke?"

Ellen is waiting for an apology from the Japanese government and says she does not want rape to happen to women in war ever again. She has become a voice for suffering women experiencing sexual violence in war zones. And after all that she has endured from Japanese soldiers, she says she does not hate the Japanese people.

J.F. (Jan) van Wagtendonk, the president of the foundation, remarked that the Dutch government, unfortunately, does not take care of its veterans or survivors of war as well as the UK and American governments do. While these people should be honored as heroes in times of duress, instead they came home to Holland to accusations and little support. Jan recalls the Dutch from the East Indies were told to go back. If the Dutch government took care of its own, then the foundation would not have a reason to exist. Compared with other nations, the survivors of the Netherlands have been able to organize themselves politically and fight for their right to an official apology from the Japanese government. The members and leaders of the foundation are in their sixties and seventies. They are now asking how much longer they will have to keep up the fight. There are many more Dutch survivors who will never come forward with their stories. There are people in Holland who have stated that their aunts or someone in their family was forced into Imperial Japanese military sex slavery.

This may be the longest running international activist movement on behalf of victimized women. After the survivors pass away, this unprecedented international movement could lose momentum. However, the legacy of upholding human rights can go on if the movement hands over the reins of fighting for justice to the upcoming generations.

The North Korean Delegation

Besides the interview with Ellen van der Ploeg, some additional fascinating moments at the conference was with the North Korean delegation, made up of an older woman and man and a young woman in her twenties. The three delegates wore little pins with Kim Il-Sung and Kim Jong-Il's faces on them. I could barely understand some of the circ. 1950 Korean words they were using. As if frozen in time before the peninsula was divided, it seemed like they had literally walked out of a chapter of a history book.

Ms. Hong Son-Ok was the chairperson of the North Korean government's committee on Japanese military sex slavery. Hong had an old-fashioned beehive style on top and her side hair was pulled back. She wore eighties style glasses and her make-up was pasty white with bright red lipstick, just like in the typical, old North Korean pictures. She said the North Korean former military sex slaves were furious to hear the Japanese government calling them prostitutes who wanted to make money and denying that they forced the women. That's when forty-six of these women came forward in North Korea. In total, two hundred nineteen women have testified to the North Korean government of being enslaved in comfort stations, but only forty-six of these women were willing to speak out publicly.

Hong's assistant, Jong Un-A, was the translator for the interview with the North Korean delegates. The tall willowy Jong was extremely intelligent and spoke fluent French in addition to English. She was from North Korea's elite, and the government had sent her to foreign schools to mold her for future foreign service.

"What do these women want from the Japanese government?" I asked.

"They want an apology, recognition of past crimes, and compensation," Hong said.

"Do they hate the Japanese?"

"No, not hate. Hate is not the appropriate word. It is more than hate. They have said that they could not forget their sufferings even after their deaths."

Hong said the North Korean survivor with the most powerful story is Park Yong-Shim, the same woman that Japanese journalist Rumiko Nishino had interviewed. Nishino is a leading writer on Japanese war crimes such as military sex slavery and a founder of the Women's Active Museum on War and Peace in Tokyo that preserves historical documents and materials related to

Imperial Japanese military comfort women for future generations.

There is a famous American archive photo where Park is standing up looking uncomfortably pregnant. Park saw the photo and identified the woman as herself. "Before she died, her last words were 'I want my youth back!'"

Pak testified at the Tokyo Women's International War Crimes Tribunal for the Trial of Japan's Military Sexual Slavery (the non-legally binding tribunal) in 2000, and shared her story in the book *Downtrod Women's Cry* that documents the stories of forty North Korean women forced into sex slavery for the Imperial Japanese Military. Pak Yong-Sim tells her story in her words:

"I was born in Sogi-dong, Kangso District, Nampho City, on December 15, 1921. I lost my mother in childhood and grew up under a stepmother's care. When I was fourteen, I was sold as a maid to a tailor's shop in Hupho-dong, Nampho city. Around March of 1938, at seventeen, I was drafted by the Japanese. A Japanese policeman in a black uniform with the rank of lieutenant came to my place with a sword at his side, picked me and another girl of twenty-two and took us to Pyongyang by force.

"From Pyongyang Railway Station, we and fifteen other Korean girls were transported by train and truck to our destination, which was Nanjing, China. We were put in the Kumsuro Comfort House that was five hundred meters from the barracks. It was fenced in with barbed wire hung with empty cans. It was a three-storied brick building. Each room was 2.5 meters long and two meters wide and had a bed.

"I was called by the Japanese name *Udamaru*. I was allotted to room number nineteen on the second floor. On the door of each room hung a plate with the comfort girl's name and number. We didn't have any daily routine. When the sun rose, we ate a bowl of boiled rice and a few pieces of pickled radish and then were forced to "serve" the Japanese soldiers on their holidays, which came in turn once a week.

"Every day there were thirty soldiers on average. They were all vicious beasts. We had no rest, no holidays. If we disobeyed their demands, we were harshly punished.

"One day I begged mercy from an officer, as I was dead-tired from the continuous rapes and humiliation. He held his sword to my neck, threatening to kill me. Then he beat me viciously before gratifying his sexual lust.

"Those who were ill or undernourished were either thrown into the river or taken away somewhere. New girls were brought to take their places. I also saw two Japanese army privates stab a pregnant woman in the belly and murder her. For three years, we were forced to serve Japs at the Kumsuro Comfort House. Then, at the instructions of the Japanese military police, we were escorted by two Japanese soldiers to the Rashu Comfort House near Rangoon, Myanmar. We got there by way of Shanghai, boarding a five thousand ton military vessel and sailing for forty days. On the ship there were already forty Korean girls.

"In this comfort house I was renamed *Wakaharu* in Japanese and had to serve the Japanese ground and tank forces. During the day, I had to service about ten army privates and at night I had to serve the officers. The privates brought condoms. I had to service between thirty and forty army privates, so I was always in real pain. Two horrible years passed at the Rashu Comfort House before we were again moved, this time to Lameng, the border area between Myanmar and China. Since this was close to the fighting front, bombs sometimes fell and mortar shells flew back and forth.

"In this dangerous area we had to serve thirty to forty soldiers a day. There were twelve of us Korean girls in all. A private house was reconstructed into a comfort house, which was partitioned into twelve rooms with plywood. The Japs, who were usually drunk and hysterical after battle, whined about their sad lot and their lives "hanging by a hair" as they assaulted us. The terror and agony of pain we suffered in this place are really beyond description.

"Out of the twelve girls who were taken to Myanmar, eight died, due to the bombings or were beaten to death, or dead from disease. A girl of twenty-two from Kyongsang province was killed in an air raid. Ok Gyong from Nampho was murdered, stabbed to death by a mob of Japanese soldiers who had gone wild.

"When the war ended, we were taken as prisoners, along with the defeated Japanese troops, and sent to

Kunming POW Camp in China. It was an additional shock and humiliation for me to be detained in the POW camp for seven months in the company of men I loathed and whose victim I had been.

"Although ashamed of the disgrace of my past, I made up my mind to return home because I knew that my homeland was the place where I wished to be buried when I died. In February of 1946, I came to Incheon by ship and went on train and foot to Chongdan by way of Seoul and I finally arrived in Nampho nine years after I had been forced to leave.

"I have lived as a disabled person. I had to have my womb taken out because of the years of abuse. I suffer from heart disease, and I often lapse into disturbed mental states because of nervous exhaustion. My life has been without warmth of a family life and I have never known the joy of bearing a child. I adopted a child from an orphanage and am now living with his support.

"Whenever I look back on my bitter past there comes to my mind the images of thousands of Korean women, forced to leave home by the Japanese, many dying in an alien land while being subjected to the most horrifying suffering and torture. My ability as a speaker or writer is not strong enough to fully lay bare the crimes committed by the Japanese who occupied Korea. Whenever I think of those days, I feel I wouldn't be satisfied even if I were given the chance to tear all the Japanese to shreds.

"Even while pregnant, Pak was raped by the soldiers. She also had to supply food for the soldiers daily during the bombings in Lameng. Months later, Chinese soldiers found Pak and took her and three other women as prisoners. They were interrogated and photographed. At the prisoner-of-war camp, Pak required surgery when she began to bleed profusely. Her baby was born dead. Pak spent seven years as a military sex slave altogether.

"The book of testimonies that documented Pak Yong-Sim was published by the North Korean government to mark the fiftieth anniversary of "national liberation and the defeat of Japan" said Kim Il-Sung describing the comfort women as 'innumerable Korean women died in the prime of their youth because of inhuman oppression, exploitation, and unbearable personal insult at the hands of Japanese fascists.' The introduction by the 'Committee on the Measures for Compensation to the Former Korean

Comfort Women for the Japanese Army' further explains that 'even after the passage of half a century, the deep-rooted animosity of the Korean nation against the Japanese aggressors still remains, and why our people continue to call for revenge and for world denunciation of the Japanese aggressors.' Hong said the government preserved two comfort stations as museums in North Korea in Ranam[89] and Bangjin to preserve the memory of human rights violations committed by the Japanese army.

"Many of the North Korean women and teenagers who were forced into military sex slavery perished 'in sorrow and pain as stateless colonial slaves' and only a small number of survivors in their seventies and eighties were identified in 1995 when the book was published."

Back at the conference at The Hague, I asked Hong, the North Korean official, "How did this horrific experience affect these women in North Korea?"

"I cannot say exactly. Many had pain both physical and mentally and because they suffered so much, they couldn't marry, and they couldn't have children," said Hong.

"How did they support themselves?"

"Our government took necessary means to help them survive by giving them rice and building homes. The peoples' committee took care of them," she replied. "Also some young people wanted to support them and live with them. They were also taken care of in a hospital."

The forty-six grandma survivors became well known after their testimonies were published. Their neighbors visited them regularly after *Downtrod Women's Cry,* the book of their testimonies came out.

"They cannot get their youth back," she said. "These women called the soldiers *Japs* (derogatory name for Japanese)."

Hong shared that they are focused on teaching about Japanese military sex slavery to the younger generation. "Not only about comfort women but about past war crimes," she said.

"What does the North Korean government want?" I asked.

"We want the Japanese government to recognize past crimes and give an official apology. We will keep going until we get justice," she said with a militant tone of a general.

Near the end of the trip, the man from North Korea, leaned over to me while we were sitting on the bus and said, "The conference was a success."

Taiwan's Sex Slavery Survivors

In 1992, former Taiwanese sex slaves for the Imperial Japanese Military decided to come forward publicly for the first time in Taiwan. Liu Huang A-Tao was the first Taiwanese woman to testify that the Imperial Japanese military used deception and force in trafficking her and the other women she was with into sex slavery in 1942. She was promised a job as a nurse, but was forced to be a sex slave in Indonesia. Days after she arrived, she was injured in frontlines battle and her womb had to be removed. Liu Huang was inspired by the words of a Korean military sex slavery survivor, who said, "It is not us, but the Japanese government, that should feel ashamed."

Her courage in speaking out encouraged other women to do the same and catalyzed a redress movement. These surviving women surfaced after Hideko Itoh, a former member of the Japanese Diet, found three telegrams written in the 1940s that stated fifty Taiwanese women were conscripted as sex slaves for the Imperial Japanese military in Sarawak, Malaysia. In February 1992, Itoh made her discovery at Japan's Defence Agency research library two months after Korean survivor Kim Hak-Soon broke silence for the first time. The telegrams made requests for permits for fifty "comfort personnel" to travel by ship to Sarawak.

As a colony of Japan from 1895 until 1945, Taiwan was a source of girls and women as 'sex slaves' for Japan's Imperial military from 1938 as it tried to keep its ratio to one comfort woman for every one hundred soldiers[90].

After the exposing of Taiwanese comfort women, the Taipei Women's Rescue Foundation (TWRF), a non-governmental organization that dealt mostly with domestic violence and sexual violence cases at the time, decided to set up a hot line for survivors to come forward on February 20, 1992. The foundation said of the telegrams that it "proved beyond doubt that in World War

II, Taiwanese women were sent to Japan's frontline as sex slaves in the Japanese military."[91]

The TWRF confirmed about fifty-eight women were forced into Imperial Japanese military sex slavery and were still alive. They were between sixty-five and eighty years of age. They also conducted research in partnership with a Ministry of Foreign Affairs task force and learned that at least twelve hundred Taiwanese women, from all over Taiwan, were forced to be sex slaves between 1938 and 1945 and were not informed of what was ahead for them in the comfort stations. These women's ages ranged between fourteen to thirty years of age and were taken on warships to Hainan, China, Indonesia, the Philippines, Okinawa, Myanmar and Singapore. These women were raped by at least twenty to forty soldiers every day in the frontlines of battle where they faced disease, air raids and witnessed murder if they were not slaughtered themselves.

In July 1995, the government of Taiwan began to give monthly financial support to former military sex slaves, and by 1997, the monthly allowance was five hundred US dollars. The TWRF offered psychological counseling and medical support as well as funeral services for the elderly women survivors.

Ching-feng Wang, a lawyer and former Justice Minister, and the Director of TWRF at the time, conducted research trips to Korea and Japan and campaigned for governmental services for survivors and helped provide research for their lawsuits against the State of Japan. As a volunteer, Wang helped Liu Huang who led eight other Taiwanese survivors to file lawsuits against the Japanese government from 1999 to 2005 to demand a sincere apology and compensation.[92] Liu Huang said: "We're all cherished daughters in the eyes of our parents. Since the Japanese army robbed us of our virginity, it is not too much to demand an apology from such a government."[93]

All of the lawsuits failed to get justice for the women in Japan as the Japanese courts claimed with the expiration of the statute of limitations, the state of Japan is not legally bound to compensation the victims and that Japan had settled its war crimes compensation issues by signing the San Francisco Peace Treaty in 1951 and other country treaties.

On November 11, 2008, Taiwan's parliament unanimously passed a resolution that demanded the government of Japan to apologize for forcing women into military sex slavery before and during World War II and to compensate victims. Liu Huang A-Tao died at the age of ninety on September 1, 2011 before receiving the apology she fought for since 1992.

At the same Hague conference, where I met the survivor Ellen Van der Ploeg, I had an opportunity to speak with Graceia Lai, a social worker from the Taipei Women's Rescue Foundation, and she has linked historical Imperial Japanese Military sex slavery with the current problem of domestic violence in Taiwan. I learned that many of the women forced into military sex slavery came from poor aboriginal communities. The health of those who survived was damaged by their traumatic experiences in the comfort station and many suffered from uterine diseases, infertility, and neuralgia. Those who returned to Taiwan could only find work as waitresses, cleaners, and farmers.

Graceia told me that Taiwan is also the only country that was colonized by Japan where some citizens have expressed gratitude that their daughters could serve patriotically as volunteer sex slaves for the Imperial Japanese Military. She said these people were in the minority and felt this way because they were disappointed with the corruption of their own government and decided to identify with the Japanese colonialists.

In August 2009, I flew to Taipei and requested her help in arranging a meeting with an Ah ma. Graceia and Shu Hua Kang, the director of the Taipei Women's Rescue Foundation set up an interview for me with sixty-five-year-old Chen Lien-Hua.

Graceia told me then that Chen Lien-Hua does not want to give her real name (later she was willing to be identified even in the press). "This survivor has not shared her story with the public, nor does she plan on it," she explained. "Her family has not acknowledged it. She is ashamed to come out."

We walked up the stairs to a modest apartment building. Chen opened the door. Her plump face broke into a charming smile. She was a pleasant woman with a naturally happy demeanor. We sat on the couch, and she showed us photos of her activities and memberships in different community groups. She gazed and remarked that my diamond earrings were beautiful more than a few times, so I gave them to her.

Her daughter and grandson walked through the living room where we were sitting and walked past us into the kitchen. Chen told me, "My children don't speak about it. I don't want anyone to know."

She was taken away to Cebu, Philippines as a teenager. From a poor family, Chen was lured by a promise of a good job. It was June 1944. The Japanese name they gave her at the comfort station outside of the military compound was Namiko.

Here are her memories of her days at the military brothel:

"At not yet seven o'clock in the morning, people were already walking and talking outside. I struggled to get up, because my head felt like it was splitting, my stomach was swollen in pain, and my vagina was inflamed and in great pain. I had difficulty getting out of bed. Slowly, I got up, or the vicious old woman (the mama-san or female brothel manager) would have yelled outside my door. My mind went numb thinking about yesterday. From eight in the morning until ten at night, nearly thirty soldiers raped me until I had no strength left to cry.

"Every Monday, we had to have weekly physical check-ups at the military hospital. We were gathered at the front door and walked together to the hospital. It was a short distance away, but we all looked forward to this brief excursion once a week. Day and night, we were forced to be sex slaves, stripped of all human dignity. I wanted to die. Every time I thought about my parents back at home, my heart deeply ached like it was shedding tears.

"I climbed up on to the examination table. The doctor touched the inside of my thighs, and I screamed out of control. Nurses came to help. I squeezed my eyes shut, but the tears streamed down. Except a few days during my menstrual cycle, we had no rest from the soldiers. We were locked up in hell.

"Back at the comfort station, I saw a line of soldiers outside of my door. I walked by them, nauseated by the animal-like stench from their bodies. I wanted to vomit. It marked the beginning of yet another day of misery. I clenched my teeth, closed my eyes, and wept silently or sometimes, I sobbed continuously, until they left my body. I imagined myself as a piece of dead meat as I lay on the bed. This was how I coped. After he was relieved and washed himself, I carried the water basin to the bathroom and drew a fresh basin for the next soldier. I also cleaned my lower body with antiseptic. As antiseptic seeped into the wounds in my vagina, the pain was unbearable.

"At lunch, I sometimes had two bowls of rice and still felt hungry. Most of the time, though, I had no appetite. It felt like I was eating rice with an antiseptic odor. I felt nauseated. At first, I thought I was pregnant. Two weeks later, the antiseptic smell was everywhere. From the moment I opened my eyes in the morning, everything I touched— the bed, the clothes, the bowls and chopsticks, even my hair and skin—reeked of that smell.

"At ten o'clock at night, Mitue in my neighboring cubicle came to chat. I enjoyed listening to her Taiwanese tunes that seemed to soothe my homesickness. She was well read. Her writing was beautiful. She seemed to have come from a nice family, but how was she so unlucky to be tricked to be in this place? I reminded her that we had been here a month. As we talked, we held each other and cried. This one month felt like a year. I remembered our first day. We realized we were cheated. We were not to be nurses but sexual slaves. I would never forget how we in our twenties held each other and cried. I was nineteen with a wonderful prospect in life. And now, my youth, my virginity, and my dignity were all buried at this comfort station."

Chen Hua had experienced death many times over. Death to her dreams, death to the life she had before and death to innocence. The next day over coffee, I asked Graceia Lai, "Are the survivors willing to forgive their perpetrators? Or do they want an apology first?" She replied, "Some are willing to forgive. Chen does not want to. I have suggested to her that if you forgive, then you'll have a different life and perspective. I told her that forgiveness is good for you. Some say it is really hard to forgive. As for Chen Hua, she has changed her life, she's happy, but she says 'No way, she won't forgive.' Forgiveness should be from bottom of her heart...I respect their choice."

Lai used to speak regularly at high schools on Japanese military sex slavery to raise awareness. Her husband and teenage daughter actively support the survivors, even financially. For a few years, her daughter donated five hundred new Taiwan dollars to the women. "I love the *ah ma's (grandmother's)*," Graceia said. "I treat all the survivors like my own *ah ma (grandmother)*. I told them they can call me anytime and before they used to call me often. But now, they're getting old."

I asked her what kept her going in helping these women and persevering in the fight for justice on their behalf. "Their stories of resilience really touched me," she said. "They have gone through so much not only at the comfort station. After they came back to Taiwan, their family members, especially the men, despised them. One survivor we called Xiao Tao, which means small peach, had her suitcase thrown out the door by her uncle when she returned. He screamed, 'Our family does not have any dirty women!' She cried a lot. She is strong, has a strong mind, and is a survivor in society, too. I admire that they have gone through so much, yet they still keep going. It is not easy. For women, sixty years ago, it was a very conservative society."

I flew into Los Angeles from Beijing on October 4 to 7, 2007 to attend a global conference called 'The World Conference on Japanese Military Sexual Slavery' at the University of California at Los Angeles. A Los Angeles Times veteran journalist, Connie Kang, called this conference "historic" for bringing academics, lawyers, NGO leaders and activists from around the world together in the US to create a global coalition to put pressure on the Japanese government for legal reparations for military sex slavery survivors. Activists for these women had tried various avenues throughout the years and received recommendations from Amnesty International, the International Commission on Jurists, the UN Human Rights Committee and the ILO Expert Committee.

Motivated by the advanced age of the surviving women, this group wanted to build upon the awareness created by House Resolution 121,[94] also known as the Comfort Women Resolution, championed by California Congressman Mike Honda that was passed in July 2007.

Nelia Sancho, a human rights activist with the Asian Women Human Rights Council (AWHRC) was at this conference and she brought a survivor, Adela Reyes Barroquillo, with her to testify. Sancho was one of the founders of the Philippines-based NGO Lolas Kampanyera, a survivor group for victims of sexual violence and rape by the Imperial Japanese military. Sancho heard Kim Hak-Soon speak on her experiences as a former military sex slave for the Japanese miltiary in December of 1991 at an Asian Women Human Rights Council consultation on trafficking in women and said it was "shattering to one's soul"[95]. She has been involved in providing social services and legal support for the Filipina survivors.

Seventy-eight-year-old Adela Reyes Barroquillo, bore witness at the conference to what she suffered as a military sex slave for the Imperial Japanese Military. She was born into a poor family in Sigma, Capiz Province on

September 13, 1929. Her father was a farmer and her mother was a housewife. She was the youngest of seven children. She was twelve when the war broke out in December of 1941. Her family hid from the Japanese army in the mountains for two years. By 1943, she was fourteen and heard that it was safe to return to their family home in the village.

Here is Adela's story:

"The war was still going on in 1943. I went to the market and I saw my two friends Pestang and Nita, both around sixteen years of age. We had not seen each other for the past few years.

"We were very happy and we were laughing and talking. The Japanese foot soldiers came near us and told us to ride in their jeep. They were going to a party at another town. After the party, they told us to ride in their jeep. We weren't sent home. They took us to the army garrison. The soldiers told me to go into the garrison. I refused.

"He (Japanese soldier) was angry. I shouted for help. The other Japanese slapped me hard and kicked me. I felt pain all over my body and I was bleeding when I woke. I cried and cried. That's all I did. I was enslaved for (the Imperial Japanese Military) almost three months. Then some Filipino soldiers attacked the garrison. We girls escaped and crossed the river.

"I told my mother what happened to me but I did not tell my father and brother. My mother knows how ill I felt that day. I could hardly eat. I cannot sleep. I got nervous. I was afraid of these people, especially men in uniform. That was the time when every night I screamed because of what had happened to me. Seven years passed.

"The war was over. I told myself that I must go back to school so that I can forget my bad memories. I went to school. There I met my husband who was a friend during my high school days. We got married and had six children. He died. I did not tell him that I was once a victim of sex slavery. I feared he might not accept me. Several years ago, I heard about Lolas Kampanyera (survivors group for former Imperial Japanese Military sex slaves). I found somebody who told me that there is one organizer who can help me, but I must be interviewed about what happened.

"Now I would like to demand the Japanese government give me a sincere apology, justice, compensation. Now! The Japanese government must do the right thing for those who suffered. If something was done to you, whoever did it must recognize their actions and ask for forgiveness from you. And they must resolve not to do it again. The Japanese should make it right and we have the right to seek justice.

Adela has said that it is painful to hear the term "comfort women."

"We're not prostitutes," she said.

I asked Adela about her children and if they were supportive.

"That is my big problem. My children are very... sometimes they are ashamed of what I've experienced. One of my children heard that I joined the survivors group Lolas Kampanyera. She asked what it was for. I told her it was for sex slave victims of World War II. My children laughed and said, "Who are those people who were abused?" She kept her experiences from her children until they read of it in the newspapers. She denied it at first when they asked. But after time passed, she couldn't keep the truth to herself any longer. Her children became supportive and they have made peace with her past.

Sancho said of Adela, "She experienced much pain since then. She didn't tell her family, and she waited until her husband died to tell her story publicly. She was afraid he couldn't handle the truth. She immersed herself in getting an education. Adela is now a retired educator and government employee. She has dealt with her pain in this way."

Lola (grandma) Rosa Henson was the first Filipina survivor to publicly come forward in 1992 after hearing Kim Hak-Soon's testimony. After Rosa testified, other women felt inspired to step out of the shadows and share their stories with the Asian Women Human Rights Council and joined three different survivor groups that formed: the Lila Pilipina Lolas in 1994, the Malaya Lolas in 1997 and the Lolas Kampanyera in 2000. More than four hundred Filipina survivors of sexual slavery and war rape by the Imperial Japanese Military were documented. These organizations have launched a formidable nationwide movement in the Philippines and raised awareness through books, research, school exhibitions, lobbying at the Philippine government, and offering therapy and counseling for survivors. Nelia Sancho wrote in the book, *Justice With Healing* that "we have seen the survivors transformed from a victims to those who are empowered enough to articulate the call for a clear and unequivocal apology as well as legal compensation from the Japanese government."

Shim Dal-Yeon, another survivor, spoke at the conference. At the age of twelve, Shim Dal-Yeon said she was kidnapped by Japanese soldiers by her village in Chilgok County in North Gyeongsang Province in South Korea. The soldiers forced her onto a military truck and put her on a ship to a military base in Taiwan where she was raped by Japanese soldiers in a comfort station. She was so abused that she was unable to speak for years. In an Amnesty International report, she said, "I was battered and hit so harshly that sometimes I fainted, once a soldier cut my thigh with a knife. My mental state was so unstable, I was like a dead body, I just lay there; soldiers would still come in and rape me. I was so young, I was in complete shock."[96]

Here is her story as told at the conference in her words:

"The reason I was dragged (by the Japanese soldiers) was because I went out to collect greens. There was a truck and they asked us to get in the truck. We (my older sister and I) refused and held on to each other and the soldiers grabbed us by our hair and took us. I didn't know where they were taking us away. It looked like a warehouse and we were dragged there. Now I think it was a school. There were students there carrying backpacks and students were coming out of the school. They told the students to get on the truck and they did. We were taken away from there again. We were so scared, we were weeping. They told us to go into some kind of tent. There were women older than us. We were crying so much that a soldier stood guard over us. The soldier kicked us whenever we cried. So we were forced to remain there.

"I couldn't even sleep. They forced us into another car and we were dragged somewhere else again. Later on we were forced to get on a ship. We could not refuse to get on board. We were starved for a few days. They only gave us dry crackers to eat and some water. I don't know where it was exactly. They took my older sister and taller girls away first. They picked older girls first and took them away. And that was the last time I saw my sister. I couldn't find her after that. She told me, 'Please be a good girl, I'll come back to get you.' I waited and waited thinking about her last words. Other girls were taken away and never came back.

"Some guards were standing outside of the door and we were prohibited from speaking in Korean with each other. If we did they slapped, beat us and kicked us. I said I'm sorry, I'm sorry. We stayed quiet. We stayed for a day or two. Some people came and they took me away to a river and there was a small boat. They helped me board the boat and cross the river. We arrived at a bare mountain, no building, no shelter, nothing. I was thinking this is how I'm going to die. Oh my god. My sister said she'd come and get me. My parents didn't know where I was. I was so scared.

"I am not sure if they were soldiers. They dragged me. There was no tent or mattress or sleeping bed. I was dragged there. I was hurt very badly there. I was injured and they put bandages on my hand. I waited there and they tried to do something bad to me. The next morning I fainted and I bled so much. And I almost lost consciousness and the next morning someone asked me do you know what happened to you last night? You lost consciousness and you have just woken up. I tried to hide before the rapes. Every time I tried to hide they came after me and kicked me. I fainted every time the soldiers came. And they only gave us dry crackers. That was the only thing they gave us to eat.

"Every night the soldiers came and I was seeing some images, dark images, and I started shaking from then. I was scared every time by these images, the dark images. I couldn't think of anything and I fainted so easily. People told me afterwards that I fainted every time I saw the soldiers. So one of the girls told me I thought you died and I touched your heart and it was still warm so I knew you were still alive. They tried to revive me. I was constantly beaten and kicked… I thought I was going to die. I didn't really care if I would die or not. I was almost losing my mind at the time. I didn't care what was happening to me. I only wanted to know if my sister was coming to get me or not. That's how days and months passed. After a while they moved the camp around.

"One day we were moved to another location and it was so cold I couldn't stand the cold and my skin was peeling off and it was bleeding like a river. They gave me ointment but it was not helpful. My skin was peeling off; I was bleeding so hard. The blood was black. I don't clearly remember what happened. I don't know how much time has passed. I just survived because I didn't die. I don't know how I survived. I just said to them do whatever you want. I started laughing whenever they raped me, kicked me, bit me. I just started laughing. Whenever I was beaten I would lose consciousness and wake up later on.

"So I asked someone why I was treated so much worse than other people. This person told me it is because I don't listen to them. Others listen to the soldiers and do whatever they tell them to do. We were supposed to learn Japanese and speak in Japanese. But I couldn't learn Japanese and couldn't speak a word. They did not allow us to speak Korean.

"After a few years, I was discovered by a Korean couple with a son my age. The son told his parents about me. This Korean family took me back to Korea with them after the war. They tried to find my family but I couldn't remember my hometown and family name. They tried to feed me and give me medicine. Whenever they were out I did crazy things because I had lost my mind at the time. One night they asked us to go out so I followed them without thinking and he took me to one of the mountains – entrance of mountain. He told me to sit here and wait. I waited there and he left. After a while a man approached and asked me who are you? Why are you sitting here? I said my parents told me to sit here and so I'm waiting. This person said you cannot sit here or you'll die. Come with me. I think it was a Buddhist monk who was trying to collect food in the village and he was going back to the temple.

"It was a temple. I couldn't answer the monk's questions. He asked me to cook in kitchen and help with chores in kitchen. I didn't know how to do any of it but slowly I learned and they would give me some food too. That's how I got to stay at the temple. One day, my younger sister came to the temple and saw me. She started asking me questions. 'What's your name? Where are you from?' Then she said, 'You're my older sister and I'm going to take you with me' and she took me to her home.

"Later, I was told that my mother passed away lamenting until her death about why her two daughters were taken away. 'What did I do wrong?' she cried. My little sister finally found me. That's how I found my identity.

Shim began to cry. Someone in the audience asked Shim, "If you have one wish before you pass away, what would it be?" Shim said, "It is an apology from the Japanese government that I want. Every time I talk about this... I cry. Whenever I see children and people with babies. And I think of why I never had this chance. It makes me cry at home." Because of the physical trauma from her time as a sex slave, she had an operation to remove a tumor from her cervix and she suffers from an anxiety disorder. Shim has raised four of her younger sister's children after she passed away. "They treated me like a mother," she said.

A woman in the audience said, "I worked with the victims of the Holocaust and there were sex slaves in Germany, but they weren't able to talk openly to so many people like this. It is because they wanted to hide their secret and never want reveal it. I think it is amazing that these grandmas are so courageous to talk about their past."

I asked her, "What is one thing you'd want to say to the Japanese government?"

Shim responded, "I would like to receive an apology and redress from the Japanese government. The redress is not for me but I'd like to have a home, a place of my own. If I didn't go through that I would have had my own children and my life would have been vastly different."

Fellow survivor Lee Young-Soo is also from Daegu and she met Shim while she was trying to find other survivors in town. Lee said, in a confident manner, "Grandma Shim still does not have a clear memory of her past. She had no recollection whatsoever when we tried to help her. It is really sad and unfortunate. When I talked with her, I asked 'Are you Grandma Shim? Weren't you a victim of the Imperial Japanese Military comfort woman system? Don't you want to fight against them? Fight for an apology from the Japanese government?'

Shim became active in the redress movement. A picture book by Yoon-Duck Kwon called *Kkothalmeoni* (*Flower Grandma*) was published in 2010. It was based on Shim's life and experience as a twelve-year-old sex slave and was the effort of artists from Korea, Japan and China to promote peace between the nations. Shim passed away in December of 2010 before the book was published.

Chapter 7

"The essence of this tragedy is that it can never be fully communicated....
And yet, we are duty-bound to try. Not to do so would mean to forget. To forget
would mean to kill the victims a second time. We could not prevent their first
death; we must not allow them to vanish again. Memory is not only a victory
over time, it is also a triumph over injustice." ~ Elie Wiesel, Holocaust survivor
and Nobel Laureate.

Yasukuni

The outline of the Daiichi Torii, or the first shrine
gate, at twenty-five meters tall, looks even more imposing
against the azure sky and signals that one is entering a
sacred space. Trees line the meticulously groomed
grounds. Yasukuni Shrine sits in Chiyoda district, at the
very heart of central Tokyo. It is where the seat of
government rests in the Diet building and where the

location of the Supreme Court and Prime Minister's residence. The long concrete walkway to Yasukuni seems haunted in an otherwise serene atmosphere. I was with Judy, a Chinese-American documentary filmmaker, and Tim, a Tokyo-based Canadian journalist, to explore this place that was at the center of heated debates and controversy in Asia. This controversial shrine is regarded by many in Asia as a terrible symbol of Japan's past militarism. Whenever the prime minister and top officials visited Yasukuni, they paid homage to their military casualties, including Class A war criminals, those who committed war crimes in Asia such as genocide or the mistreatment of prisoners of war, violent riots erupted in Asia.

One can feel conflicted before walking into the Yasukuni Shrine, called the "Ground Zero" for ultranationalists because of the trifecta of the shrine, the smaller secular memorial, and the 'Families of the War Bereaved Society Office'[97]. I was eager to find and interview a former soldier. The shrine is dedicated to Japan's two million five hundred thousand war casualties which include women, children, soldiers, nurses, and young people from wars such as the Sino-Japanese and Russo-Japanese wars to the twentieth century wars. Since the main wars that are memorialized are those with China and other Allied nations, some see this shrine as symbolizing foreign invasions.

To many right-wing conservatives in Japan, Yasukuni is a symbol of nationalism, worship of the emperor as a deity, and love for their motherland. Every year, hundreds of thousands of people from all over Japan visit the shrine to honor those who died in war. In 1869, Emperor Meiji[98] ordered that a place be established to enshrine the souls of men who have sacrificed their lives for their country. The shrine's name is ironic and confusing. Yasukuni literally means 'peaceful country.' Its very existence, as a staunch nationalistic symbol, is jarring to see in the midst of Tokyo's skyscrapers and tech-savvy society. Everything about it points out that there was no change in Japanese society after the war ended in 1945. There should have been a regime change like there was in Germany. The Nazis were no longer in power, and today neo-Nazism is seen as a marginalized group.

The most controversial souls at Yasukuni are fourteen convicted, Class-A war criminals, including Prime Minister General Hideki Tojo and Iwane Matsui who were sentenced to death at the International Military Tribunal for the Far East (also known as the Tokyo War Crimes Tribunal) for their responsibility for the Nanking massacre in 1937. These war criminals, along with millions of others, are not merely honored, but they are worshipped as *kami (gods)*. War banners and military regalia surround the *kami* and wartime military relics are commemorated at the shrine.

This deep reverence and worship of the dead is part of the Shinto faith in which it is most honorable to treat the dead as if they were still living. Shintoism is a spiritualized form of nationalism. Deceased ancestors are considered as "guardian deities" who watch over living family members. Daily rituals of meal offerings and words to the dead are offered up twice a year, and the most important rituals take place which include offerings from the Emperor, and members of the Imperial family attend.

In 2001, Japan's then Prime Minister Koizumi's visit to Yasukuni Shrine strained Japan's relations with Seoul and Beijing. Both Korea and China had expressed concern over Koizumi's proposed visit on August 15th, the anniversary of Japan's surrender. One writer likened the Japanese shrine to a memorial of Adolf Hitler. Twenty South Korean men draped in Korean flags chopped off their pinky fingers to show their extreme displeasure, the news media reported dozens of emotional rallies that happened all over Asia, and lawsuits by the hundreds were filed against Koizumi—the plaintiffs calling his visit unconstitutional.[99] On December 26, 2013, Prime Minister Shinzo Abe visited Yasukuni as an anti-war gesture, infuriating China and Korea. On October 17, 2014, Abe sent a ritual (symbolic) offering to Yasukuni Shrine, instead of visiting. However, at least one hundred ten Diet members from across party lines visited Yasukuni, including Yasuhiro Ozato, a senior vice environment minister, and a parliamentary vice-minister in the education ministry[100]. And on February 18, 2015, Abe defended his visit in 2013 to Yasukuni by saying it was natural for Japan's leaders to honor their war dead.

At Yasukuni, there is a table of ultranationalists passing out literature in Japanese that spreads their belief that the surviving military sex slaves are liars and that other so-called atrocities committed by Japanese military were fabricated. It is known that these right-wingers are sometimes violent. Our raised eyebrows at their literature probably gave us away that we were on the other end of the spectrum. They quickly deduced that we were activists for victims of military human rights abuses. One young Japanese man began to circle us with a video camera. I shielded my face. Three more including a young woman began to descend closer on us. We managed to get away.

At every turn in the shrine, the monuments confirm the discriminatory attitudes towards other ethnic groups and affirm that the war was a good war. Statues of a bronze horse, a German Shepherd, and carrier pigeons, that were messengers, honor the roles these animals played in wartime. Taiwanese and Korean people died as Japanese. Therefore their nationalities are not recognized, as they are still considered colonial subjects in this shrine, even though the colonial period ended in 1945. A monument was added in 2005 to the memory of Dr. Radha Binod Pal of India, who was one of the judges at the International Military Tribunal for the Far East. The official Yasukuni website says, "Among all the judges of the tribunal, he was the only one who submitted judgment which insisted all defendants were not guilty."

To many Asians, the shrine represents a painful past inflicted by the Japanese military and colonial rule. How they feel would be akin to how Jewish people would feel if top Germans leaders were worshipping Nazi war criminals and those who orchestrated the concentration camps of the Holocaust. The matter of Yasukuni is a further humiliation and a slap in the face of the elderly sex slavery survivors and all former victims of Japanese wartime atrocities. It evokes the same horror as if hypothetically, the German president and parliament members still visited and worshipped at Hitler's grave and even marked it as a national memorial.

Compare the Japanese leaders to former German chancellor Willy Brandt. The black and white photo[101] of Brandt during an official visit in Poland as chancellor of West Germany in 1971 shows him kneeling in front of the monument that honored Jewish Poles who had been executed by the Nazis. The mesmerizing photo became an iconic image, symbolizing reconciliation between nations in the twentieth century, and won Brandt the admiration of the world. How uncharacteristic of a world leader to be showing that depth of humility and repentance. Would it be possible for the prime minister of Japan to kneel down at the site of a monument built to the memory of former military sex slaves and visibly show deep contrition for the military sex slavery and other wartime atrocities?

That day would bring healing.

My First Encounter with a Former Soldier

At Yasukuni, in the military and war museum, we ran into a slight man with a baseball cap on top of his speckled grey hair and silver rimmed glasses. He was a former soldier who appeared to be in his eighties. He first tapped me on the shoulder and proudly pointed to the

black and white photograph of the soldiers in Nanking--
soldiers with guns--and he said slowly with a firm tone
and deliberately, facing me with shoulders back and with
a glint in his eyes, that he was there.

When asked about *ianfu* (*comfort women*), his eyes
widened, as if he were jolted by a sudden rush of
electricity. He turned away and mumbled something
about how the nurses were well taken care of. I looked at
him trying to meet his eyes. But he kept turning away
while clutching his hat with both hands and stepped away
from me. I continued to engage him with the help of Tim,
our translator, who had warned not to mention *ianfu* to
any of the soldiers. I said *ianfu* again in case he did not
hear me. He kept walking and waved his hand as I said
ianfu yet again. Our friend and translator, Tim, a
Canadian journalist, looked sheepish. The soldier dashed
down the museum stairs at Yasukuni.

Later, Tim said the more effective way would have
been to draw him into a longer conversation and then ask
the questions. Of course that was the common sense thing
to do. It was horrible to pounce on him with that question.

He could have been struggling with his own demons over his actions during the war.

There was another World War II veteran at Yasukuni. This man told us the military comfort women wanted compensation money, alluding that they were prostitutes who were mad about being unpaid. Another Japanese man in his forties, a right-wing activist against building another war memorial outside of Yasukuni, told me that there was no evidence that women were forced to be military sex slaves. It was like meeting a Nazi veteran who said the Holocaust never happened.

Redress Movement in Japan

The Japanese government's evasion of war responsibility has galvanized a contingent of selfless lawyers and activists in Japan, including two high-profile attorneys and activists—Etsuro Totsuka and the late Koken Tsuchiya. Totsuka, a brilliant human rights lawyer, who was the first Japanese to speak on the Imperial

Japanese military sex slavery issue at the United Nations. This movement was significant and perhaps will be what turns the tide on obtaining justice for military sex slave survivors.

There are many more faceless activists, some of whom face harassment from right-wingers. The late Saburo Ienaga[102] fought against the dangers of government control over education, and in his books, he has shown how primary school textbooks from the twenties and thirties glorify the war and teach that the emperor is god. Ienaga, himself, was taught that all Japanese people were descendants of the sun goddess Amaterasu, and that the emperor was a living god. The historian, professor, and activist against government censorship of school textbooks, spent more than fifty years of his life challenging the Japanese Ministry of Education that textbooks should tell the truth of what happened in history including military war crimes. His campaign was motivated by his own guilt, that as a high school teacher during the war, he taught from textbooks that spread war propaganda to students who were soon sent to the frontlines of war.[103] At the time, he was too afraid of the government to speak out against the war. Ienaga is a hero and was nominated for the Nobel Peace Prize in 1999 and 2001. His courageous campaign against revisionist textbooks and for the right to free speech, even while suffering from Parkinson's disease, has won him admirers from all over the world.

The late Yayori Matsui[104], a journalist and one of the leading activists for military comfort women, supported school textbook reform and women's rights in Asia and helped launch the movement in Japan for raising awareness about military sex slavery. She was known as a woman of action. In 1998, she founded the Violence-Against-Women-in-War Network, Japan (VAWW-NET), and the office houses a museum on Japanese military sex slavery. The work at VAWW-NET has been linking historical Japanese military sex slavery with the fight to eradicate violence against women around the world. The organization played an instrumental role in pulling together a major international conference called the Women's International War Crimes Trial, held in Tokyo in 2000. The symbolic trial convicted Emperor Hirohito and found him as the one responsible for the policy that allowed the Imperial Japanese military to force Asian women into sexual slavery before and during World War II.

During the landmark proceedings, the judges of the women's tribunal heard hours of testimony from seventy-five survivors and reviewed affidavits and video interviews by countless experts. The Tribunal's Judgment found Emperor Hirohito and other Japanese officials guilty of crimes against humanity and held that Japan bore state responsibility and should pay reparations to the victims. The Japanese government continues to remain ambiguous about military sex slavery because simply-- truth and justice have been perverted. This was allowed to happen due to how Japan was dealt with at the end of the war. If Hirohito and the other high ranked officials responsible for crimes against humanity were tried and executed at the end of the war, just like the Nazis were, there wouldn't be a historical memory problem in East Asia.

Historians believe there were tens of thousands of Japanese women who were forced into military sex slavery. Some of them were working as prostitutes in

Japan before their enslavement in rape camps. They took these secrets to their graves. In Japan, the only well-known military sex slave of Japanese descent to come forward is a survivor who wrote a memoir *In Praise of Mary* under a pen name Suzuko Shirota.[105] A radio interview with Shirota in 1986 brought the military sex slavery issue to the public, more than the books that were written on it, and led to a widespread awareness.

When Shirota was fourteen, her mother died, and her father began gambling. He sold her to a brothel to pay off his debt. At eighteen, she was raped by a client and contracted syphilis. Soon after, she was forced into the military rape camps in Taiwan. On the way there, she remembers other Korean and Japanese women on the boat with her. Shirota ended up in a rape camp that was privately run, but the military and government kept close watch and made sure the women would not escape.

In her 1971 memoir she wrote, "I became, in name and reality, a slave. On Saturdays and Sundays, there would be a line and men would compete to get in. It was a meat market with no feeling or emotion. Each woman would have to take ten or fifteen men."

She returned to Japan after the war but continued to work in prostitution because she had no alternatives. She eventually worked at a brothel frequented by US troops in the city of Fukuoka. She ended up living with an American soldier, but he abandoned her. Then, she found a Christian group that had a shelter in Tateyama for women-at-risk, and she lived there until her death in 1993.

There is also another activist, Yoshifumi Tawara, who is well-known for his fight against revisionist history textbooks. He is the Secretary General of Children and Textbooks Japan Network 21.[106] He has worked closely with Saburo Ienaga from the beginning of Ienaga's decades-long battle with the Ministry of Education in Japanese courts over whitewashed textbooks. Tawara was an instrumental member of Saburo Ienaga's inner circle while Ienaga was campaigning for the truth of the war to be told in Japanese school textbooks. Tawara has given up his life and career to this cause, quitting his stable job at the publishing company a few years before retiring, which is unheard of in Japan where many work until retirement.

At his office, Tawara explained that Emperor Hirohito was the biggest war criminal and most responsible for Imperial Japanese military sex slavery and other crimes against humanity not brought to trial but given immunity by the United States and Allied forces. United Nations investigators and the international judges for the Women's International War Crimes Tribunal for the Trial of Japan's Military Sexual Slavery in 2000 urged the Japanese government to identify and punish surviving perpetrators involved in the recruitment and institutionalization of comfort stations during the Second World War.[107] One Japanese military officer who should have been brought to trial for his involvement in the military comfort women system, instead went on to become the leader of the nation years later. Furthermore, former Prime Minister Yasuhiro Nakasone, established comfort stations and wrote about it in his memoirs.

"The major difference between Germany and Japan was that war criminals were not all brought to trial by Japan. Some convicted Class-A war criminals were released from prison and allowed to be active in political circles. Nobusuke Kishi, a war criminal, became prime minister in the 1950s," Tawara said. He explained that the blurring of lines between past and present is what's preventing the government and the public from taking responsibility for war crimes.

"If you really want to put an end to the past; squarely face the war issues. There has to be distinctive line between August 15, 1945 and after. It has to be totally different. No clear difference before and after, status quo continued. Japan lost its chance," he said during our interview at his office that had stacks of books and papers lined up virtually on every available tabletop space. "I believe the Japanese public is responsible to hold our government accountable to make an official apology and issue compensation to victims like the military comfort women even though they didn't commit the crimes. We need to make Asia into a peaceful community. During the late nineteenth century, until 1945, Japan has always been waging war every decade. I think the Japanese public should reflect on that fact."

As one of the pioneers of the redress movement in Japan, Tawara, has seen all the ebbs and flows of the right-wing attempts to control history. The late Ienaga

Saburo filed his highly publicized lawsuits against the State of Japan between 1965 and 1997. Tawara supported these legal battles from the beginning and was the executive of the civic group that fought alongside of Ienaga.

"The lawsuit end was marked by a ruling given by the Supreme Court at the end of August 1997. They ruled that deleting or modifying phrases regarding the Nanking massacre or Unit 731 or atrocities including rapes in the Nanking massacre is illegal and unconstitutional," said Tawara.

That marked a great victory for Ienaga and his fellow activists. The group reflected on the last thirty-two years of fighting against revisionist texts and formed a new organization in June of 1998 of which Tawara became secretary general.

Activists like him face continuous threats from the right-wing and he has received letters saying: "What you are saying is a major crime against the emperor. You're not qualified to be a Japanese citizen. You're a spy for China and North Korea. Get out of Japan."

He remains unfazed by the abusive messages and has sacrificed his career and much of his time to the fight for truth in textbooks, even giving up his pension by quitting his job at the publishing company a few years before retirement. In the 1990s, he became involved in the redress movement when lawsuits were filed against the Japanese government on behalf of military comfort women and Chinese victims of war crimes. He supported their cause as the two issues of redress and textbooks are closely intertwined since both involve the fight for truth and facts during the war.

"Many cabinet ministers are saying Japan did not commit wartime atrocities and say that the victims are all making false accusations. If they believe that then they don't believe an apology or compensation needs to be made," he says. "If the Japanese government offers an official apology and official compensation, wartime atrocities are reality then and that's not something they want to admit."

He agreed that there is a bitterness and a lack of honesty motivated by racism towards other Asians, and that this has led to a profound lack of trust for Japan. "As a premise for making such a peaceful community in East Asia, it is necessary to establish proper historical notion of what has really happened," he said adding that he is involved in a project to promote reconciliation with scholars from China, Korea and Japan.

A committee of fifty-four scholars from China, Korea, and Japan has written and published a middle-school textbook based on common history, including war invasions from the late nineteenth century until the post-war modern era, from a cross-border point of view. This is the first work of its kind.

What he said next helps explain why the Japanese public seems apathetic to unresolved Imperial Japanese military human rights abuses like the sex slaves: "Most Japanese people do not know anything about these issues because they haven't been given a chance to learn. As a result, they're indifferent. Why they became like that is that for a long time after the war, Japanese textbooks failed to mention what really happened in war and human rights abuses. That's why the public became like that. It took forty years after the war to add the mention of the Nanking massacre in junior high textbooks. The Japanese public failed to learn about this chapter of history during the war."

The experiences of these women are not as known in the west as the Holocaust. One contributing factor is the silence of the United States government. Why has the US failed to do more to bring justice for these former sex slaves? There were several reports compiled by the US Military that mentions the Imperial Japanese Military was directly involved in establishing and operating the sex slavery system.[108] You could say not only was the United States guilty, but every Allied nation that ignored these sex slaves was complicit in covering up this issue, relegating it to the wastebasket of buried history.

How should the world have responded? Subsequent crimes against humanity against women could have been lessened or possibly averted. Think of the Balkan wars of the 1990s, the Rwandan massacre in 1994, the ongoing War in Darfur that began in 2003, or the Second Sudanese Civil War from 1983 to 2005 and the present South Sudanese Civil War where women and girls were attacked by men who used rape as a weapon of war to terrorize and destroy families and communities. Rape, sexual slavery, and forced marriages were common in the Sierra Leone civil war; systematic rape as a weapon was used in the armed conflict in the Democratic Republic of Congo and in Liberia's civil war and in Uganda.

Would these women and girls have been spared these horrific ordeals? What would have happened if the Tokyo War Crimes Tribunal championed the rights of women and made a "never again" commitment to end sexual violence, sexual slavery, and rape, as a weapon of war, in armed conflict? Several human rights activists have said that it would have impacted significantly in the arena of war and sexual violence against women.

It wasn't until a later trip to Tokyo that I realized how much opposition these Japanese activists and intellectuals face from their own people. I had scheduled meetings with leading redress activists to get some answers on the Japanese government's stonewalling and refusal to take legal and moral responsibility for military comfort women. The existence of Yasukuni and the continual visits by government leaders makes one ponder. Was Yasukuni at the heart of this issue of how the Japanese government has avoided taking on full legal and moral responsibility for forcing hundreds of thousands of women into systemic rapes and for trivializing other war crimes by the Japanese military? Yasukuni, a place dedicated to the cult of the imperial ruler[109], means the heart of imperialism and nationalism is still alive, and the worship of Hirohito has not ended.

Mishiko Nakahara, the vice-chair of VAWW-NET, remembers learning in her textbooks that military comfort women were voluntary prostitutes. "Almost all Japanese soldiers knew about comfort women because there were books on comfort women that were published. They wrote and called them prostitutes. I didn't know what their actual circumstances were. At that time, I didn't have knowledge of feminism," she said. In 1991, after Kim Hak-Soon testified of being forced into a nightmare of military sex slavery, Nakahara remembers that was the first time she saw them as women just like her.

"Of course they're older than us. But from this one woman, from Kim Hak-Soon, I learned what the Japanese did to them. When I found this out, it made me so angry at Japanese men, the military, and government. There are so many cases in Japan that the Japanese government refuses to admit," she said, with passion that seemed uncharacteristic of her serene appearance. "1991 was a very important year for Japanese activists. And for comfort women. I realized that year what the Japanese military did to women, not necessarily only Korean but including Japanese, Chinese, and women from every country in the pacific and southeast Asia."

Nakahara had just retired from her post as professor emeritus of Southeast Asian history at the time I met her. The seventy-year-old became part of the redress movement after meeting former military sex slaves in Malaysia while she was researching the Japanese occupation of the region. She was also a close friend of the late Yayori Matsui. At VAWW-NET, Nakahara said they had discussed barring the use of the term comfort women. "We call them Japanese military sex slaves. Last year, at a conference in Korea, Professor Yun Chung-Ok told us that the women do not like to be called comfort women," she said.

Nakahara's interest in war came from her childhood experiences. As a little girl, she witnessed air raids and her own house burning down. She had experienced the American occupation of Japan, and later in college, she explored war and why people fight and murder one another. It was at Waseda University in the 1960's where she caught on to the growing feminist movement. She was one of the few female students and was not very comfortable in the chauvinistic culture of the classroom and campus life. As a feminist, she became disturbed by why there were so many government documents about military sex slavery written by men but no documents written on agony or pain by these women.

She had an open personality and was very forthright, which was not very common among women her age in Asia who are culturally accustomed to more subtle communication.

"Why is the government refusing to issue an official apology and compensation to former military sex slaves and war victims?" I asked.

"I think from the beginning of post-war years the Japanese government has refused to recognize any of their war responsibility. Emperor Hirohito is guilty. I want him to be put on trial. No one discussed his responsibility in the war," she said. "People should have the right to try perpetrators of Japanese military sex slavery in Japanese courts. But the concept of gender justice is new and one cannot expect the government to protect women's rights."

One of the most significant gatherings for activists and survivors of military sex slavery as well as survivors of sexual violence in modern day armed conflict was the Tokyo Women's International War Crimes Tribunal on Japanese Military Sexual Slavery in 2000. At this symbolic trial, the issue of comfort women was raised in Japan and internationally, and a judgment was made against perpetrators, who have already passed away, including Emperor Hirohito and the whole issue of large-scale rape that was planned by the Japanese government that occurred before and during World War II. At this landmark event, Emperor Hirohito was indeed tried and found guilty.

A year later, the judgment was reissued at the Hague International Criminal Court. The aim of this tribunal was to show that the state of Japan, through its officials and government personnel, had broken international laws and breached several treaties[110] and therefore were criminally responsible for acts of rape and sexual slavery as crimes against humanity. The Tokyo Women's International War Crimes Tribunal emphasized that the issue of Japanese military sex slavery is very relevant to the sexual violence that occurs in wars today.

"Crimes against women, especially sexual crimes in war, have never been punished. That's why it has continued," Nakahara said. "The Tokyo Tribunal was a very exciting event and gave rise to a new concept of gender-based justice. Every day we were surrounded by right-wingers (ultranationalists). Actually, right-wingers came and rushed into the place the one time I was not there. One right-winger threw a can at a woman and was arrested. The brave woman brought the case to court. The right-wingers threatened the local government to forbid us to use the venue. Sometimes, we had to cancel meetings."

Next, I met with Ken Arimitsu, a full-time activist for redress on issues like military sex slavery. He is another sacrificial activist. His friends and family support him financially every month. His office has a clear view of

Yasukuni Shrine. He is a skinny middle-aged man with glasses and seems very self-disciplined and very intense in his manner and his walk. Before our interview, he served us tea in paper cups. Later I discovered that it is quite a feminist statement for a Japanese man to pour tea, a so-called woman's job, for two women. This uncharacteristic gesture reflected his unbiased values and how he could have empathy and compassion for the military sex slaves. His main concern is redress for survivors; not a memorial for military sexual slavery victims, which is something VAWW-NET is trying to work towards. "I feel a sense of urgency because the survivors are aged and dying one by one," he said.

"My friends say I am crazy to be working so close to Yasukuni," he said with a laugh. He spoke of his meeting with Rosa Henson, the first Filipina military sex slave survivor, and how it was a watershed moment for him. He was the first Japanese person to meet her. He stated that most of the redress work is now focused on changing legislation in Japan. It is difficult work to lobby for change in policies especially when the Japanese do not understand why this redress movement is so important.

Arimitsu has also worked with the Japan Fellowship of Reconciliation (JFOR), a Christian non-governmental organization in Japan that has been around since 1926 and was the first organization to bring the Japanese military comfort women issue to the United Nations.[111] Their work in Japan and abroad focuses on anti-war efforts, human rights, restoration of justice, and promoting reconciliation based on the teachings of Jesus Christ.

Since 2000, Arimitsu has tried to lobby for a bill called *Promotion of Resolution for Issues concerning Victims of Wartime Sexual Coercion Act* to be passed. Senator Shoji Motooka from the Socialist Party introduced it first, and then in 2002, Democratic Party Senator Tomiko Okazaki did. It was introduced in the house again in 2008, but it did not get passed. In 1990, Motooka was a Diet member and during a Diet budget committee, he called for a government inquiry into whether military comfort women were forced into sex slavery[112]. Okazaki has met with survivors and their activist supporters and promised to lobby for compensation and an apology from the government. The bill calls on the nation of Japan to "singularly express an apology for the violation of the honor and dignity of the victims of wartime sexual coercion and implement necessary measures to restore their honor as soon as possible." Importantly, it also emphasizes reconciliation with other nations, saying that as Japan takes responsibility to restore the honor of the women, "the objectives of this Act lie in providing the necessary fundamental grounds for the resolution of the issues concerning the victims of wartime sexual coercion and, by doing so, in improving the trustworthy relationship between the peoples of the concerned nations and our people and in making it possible for our country to occupy an honored place in international society."

If this bill passes, this could be the beginning of healing for survivors and healing between nations.

JFOR with Japanese Diet members re-introduced a bill in 2003 called, *Promotion of Resolution for Issues concerning Victims of Wartime Sexual Coercion Act* that was supported in an unprecedented way by nearly all of the NGOs and supporters of military comfort women in other Asian nations and the government of the Republic of Korea. In a report to the United Nations Commission on Human rights, JFOR stated that this bill, if passed would be "the first ever significant landmark, however, which could make a symbolical opportunity for a major reconciliation over the fifteen years war that was waged in 1931 by Japan."[113]

"In Japan, what can effect justice and change for military sex slave victims?" I asked Arimitsu.

"Our society needs to be changed. We need to change the minds of ordinary Japanese citizens. Half of all Japanese citizens are still conservative, influenced, moved, and swayed by the right-wingers. We need to start a dialogue with them. We must understand their method of thinking. We should change the way they think so they can accept Japanese military sex slavery happened. To accept the stories of former military sex slaves is very difficult. Without such a process of changing one's mindset, it is difficult to achieve redress for war victims. Thus, the textbook issue is the focus," he replied.

After we said our goodbyes to Arimitsu, I prepared for another interview with Rumiko Nishino, a journalist and author of several books on Japanese military sex slavery and war crimes. She has been one of the chairwomen of VAWW-NET since her friend Yayori Matsui's death, and as an anti-war activist, she was involved in war redress issues from the time she began interviewing former Japanese soldiers and before Kim Hak-Soon went public with her story. She gained more insight into the issue as several of these soldiers mentioned military sex slaves; and also after reading Kako Senda's book *Military Comfort Women* in the early 1970s. But in 1991, Kim Hak-Soon's testimony deeply impacted her. She signed up for the movement and has not looked back since.

She was the one who broke the news that Unit 731 that conducted gruesome medical experiments on prisoners-of-war had tested sexually transmitted diseases on women in their laboratory. Nishino was a gifted researcher and interviewer. She was the kind that did not suffer fools, a no-nonsense kind of person.

"Out of all the military sex slaves, is there a particular person who has moved you the most?" I asked her.

"Of course all the women's stories have left an impact on me, but the one who has left the biggest impact is a North Korean survivor, Pak Yong-Shim (the one who was photographed beside a grinning Japanese soldier looking miserable while pregnant from rape, with other military sex slaves in Yunnan province, China). There's not a day that goes by that I don't think about her," she said.

"Why is that?"

"She struggles with post-traumatic stress syndrome. I've also spent the most time with her and have seen more aspects of this woman. I saw how she suffers emotionally and psychologically. Sometimes she goes into a slump and looks out the window; she feels like she's been shamed and is a stained woman, and that's why she does not want to live any longer. She's tried to commit suicide several times."

Nishino first met Pak in Tokyo at the Women's International War Crimes Tribunal for the Trial of Japan's Military Sexual Slavery in 2000. Pak's testimony was offered as evidence to the trial. She was taken from North Korea and transported by the Japanese military into comfort stations in Nanjing, China, then to Lashio, Myanmar, and Yunnan, China. Nishino arranged to visit Pyongyang and met two former military sex slaves including Pak and spent extended time with her. Nishino has written a book on this woman and has included a former Japanese soldier's point of view, who happened to be stationed in the same area as Pak.

"How do the soldiers view military sex slaves?" I asked.

"I feel there are two types of soldiers. One type who feels the war was a war of aggression and invasion. They have a strong sense of guilt. They want to talk about it. They feel it is important for Japan to address these wartime issues for the future of Japan and for peace with other Asian countries," Nishino said. "The second type is the ones who deny this was a war of aggression and say it was a war of liberation. They feel it is unreasonable to teach the younger generation to condemn the older for what they did. They feel they had tried to protect their country, and they accuse the former military sex slaves for giving false testimonies. These soldiers say the women were willing and volunteer prostitutes."

"What motivates you to keep researching this issue?"

"It is a question I get asked a lot. Even recently, I've met people I haven't seen in ten years. They ask me, 'Are you still involved?' Implying why are you still? The military sex slavery issue has not been solved; that's why I'm still involved. I'm reminded of my meeting with Kim Hak-Soon and she said 'There's nothing wrong with us, there's nothing to be ashamed of. The Japanese government should be ashamed for denying their responsibility.' The state of Japan has not done enough to offer redress and justice and it has not made a sincere effort to apologize. I want Japan to be a better country, and through the resolution of this military sex slavery issue, I believe it can be."

Nishino believes a lack of empathy for other Asians who suffered during the war is to blame for the unsettled closure. "Recently Prime Minister Koizumi visited the Yasukuni Shrine. The basic understanding, for the Japanese government and people to understand why these wartime atrocities and redress issues are important to resolve, is not there. The Japanese people do not know why it bothers the Chinese and Koreans to see the prime minister visit Yasukuni," she said. "The Japanese government must resolve this issue. They cannot leave it. They must apologize, make redress and offer reparations. The Japanese society must realize what happened was a crime and it should not be repeated," she said. "But the government has left it ambiguous."

Nishino has seen, firsthand, in survivors like Pak, that time does not heal sexual violence. She believes that sexual violence against women and children still occurs in wars today because there has never been proper redress in the past in international courts and in the nation itself over the Imperial Japanese military sex slavery system.

"When there is a war, violence against women is always committed. But I want violence and rape to be recognized as war crimes, and I want to see perpetrators punished. If this does not happen, it'll be repeated in every war, and it is happening in the Iraq war," she said. "Through an Iraqi women's association, I know of four hundred women who have been sold as sex slaves--mere goods. In fifty years, today's Iraqi women will bear the scars from the war."

Why these Japanese military sex slaves were ignored and forgotten for more than fifty years is a complex mystery. Why were those aware of the sex slavery system silent? Why were the Allies silent when they knew about the sex slavery? Germans are well aware that they were responsible for the Holocaust, and "German guilt" is one phenomena springing out of that. The people in Japan, unlike the Germans, do not have a common knowledge of the atrocities the military committed in other countries.

An activist considered a heavyweight on the topic of military sex slavery in Japan and internationally is Professor Yoshimi Yoshiaki. He is battling the goliath problem in getting the government to speak the truth, and he does so in his own humble, self-effacing way. He wrote a landmark book *Comfort Women,* and it has become one of the main resources for activists and researchers. He was an academic warrior and a hero for his steady lobbying work and research on behalf of the military sex slaves at international forums and in Japan. His work in raising the banner of truth in Japan about its war past is honorable. He recognizes that in order for their country to go forward and be at peace with its neighbors, former wartime enemies, and colonies, they must deal with military sex slavery and other war atrocities, like Germany has, and look it square in the face.

When I was in town, he happened to be lobbying the Japanese Diet again, and I had a chance to hear him speak. The path for him was carved out when he heard Kim Hak-Soon's story for the first time, when she spoke of her suffering as a Japanese military sex slave in an NHK (the Japan Broadcasting Corporation) interview in December of 1991, several months after she first bore witness as a military sex slave survivor to international media. Unknowingly at that moment, a Japanese professor witnessed part of his activist and academic destiny on TV. In that interview, Kim was asked why she was filing a lawsuit in the Tokyo District Court to seek an apology and compensation from the Japanese government. She responded, "I wanted to sue for the fact that I was trampled upon by the Japanese military and have spent my life in misery. I want the young people of South Korea and Japan to know what Japan did in the past."[114]

Her words awakened in Dr. Yoshimi Yoshiaki, a sense of outrage at the Japanese government's denials of direct involvement in military sex slavery. A few years before he heard Kim's testimony, Yoshimi was searching the archives for his research on poison gas the Japanese had used in China when he stumbled across some of the most important archival documents for the growing women's rights movement in Asia at the Japanese Self-Defense Agency. The only thing is, he did not know it at the time. And no survivors of sex slavery had come forward, so he did not feel there was a need to publish them. After hearing Kim, he realized he had made copies of government papers in his research files that would expose the Japanese government's direct involvement. He went back to check those official documents in the Self-Defense Agency's National Institute for Defense Studies Library[115] and confirmed six documents from the 1930s that proved the Imperial Japanese military planned, implemented, and managed comfort stations in northern China. These papers also had the personal seals of high-ranking Imperial Japanese Military officers. He published them in a daily newspaper, the Asahi Shimbun, and he became a target of political right-wingers who threaten his life and call his home every night.

"Despite the testimonies of former military sex slaves, the Japanese government kept denying responsibility. The government kept denying while I had this paper. I thought if I researched more, I may find more information, and I felt I needed to get the facts straight for the Japanese government. I had no idea the avalanche effect my findings would have. At the time, I didn't think about what the government would say in response to these documents or how they would react," he said. "What struck me most was I felt this needed to be resolved in order to make the Japanese and Chinese relationship better. I thought it was important."

Part of the problem is the public's inability to empathize with the war. They are stuck in a historical amnesia, according to Yoshimi. "The Japanese public does not think brothels or comfort stations were human rights violations. When it comes to World War II, the bombing of Hiroshima and Nagasaki is what Japanese remember. They feel like they are victims and do not think about other aspects of the war or war casualties," he said. "It was inevitable that they became self-centered. In the same way, Americans do not know much about the

Vietnam War and the pain inflicted on the local people there during the war."

Yoshimi's find in the Defense Agency had an immediate and forceful effect on the government's stance on military sex slavery. The Japanese government stopped claiming that only private businessmen managed the comfort stations or the recruitment of the women and girls. They backpedaled and issued an ambiguous statement about its part in organizing a mass mobilization of young women to be sex slaves in the frontlines of war.

At this time, Yoshimi began to research the military comfort women issue in earnest. And what he found has been groundbreaking. It has been used as evidence for the lawsuits and United Nations and other international forums on Japanese military sex slavery. Yoshimi says the critical difference between the Japanese system of sex slavery and other armies' usage of wartime brothels is that the Japanese military was the "main actor" and created and expanded the system of rape stations and regulated daily human rights violations. The military elite saw the military sex slavery system as a vital part of the war effort.[116]

It is no surprise that the Japanese government has either destroyed or held back archival documents. According to the government documents that have been found by Yoshimi, the first confirmed military sex slavery station was indeed established in Shanghai. The Japanese military waged war in northeastern China on September 18, 1931 in what is known to the Japanese as the "Manchurian Incident." The Chinese military offered little resistance, and soon after, the Japanese military began to set up the puppet state of Manchukuo[117], in northeast China and Inner Mongolia in March of 1932.

That same year, in 1932, the Japanese military attacked Shanghai, in what is referred to as the First Shanghai Incident. The news of soldiers raping local women reached Yasuji Okamura, the Vice Chief of Staff of the Shanghai Expeditionary Military. He then contacted the Governor of the Nagasaki Prefecture[118] to provide a group of women, called "military comfort women corps,"[119] who would offer sex to soldiers in the field. He believed this would prevent the rapes of Chinese women.

The Japanese military was directly involved in running these stations. Okamura ordered his senior staff officer, Okabe Naosaburo, to build "comfort facilities" in March of 1932. That was how the first rape station came to be. Okamura wrote: "To my shame, I am a founder of the comfort women system. In 1932, when the China Incident occurred, a few rapes were reported. Then I, as Vice-Chief of Staff of the Shanghai Expeditionary Military[120], followed the practice of the navy and requested of the governor of Nagasaki Prefecture to send a group of comfort women. I was pleased that no rapes were committed afterward."[121]

In Staff Officer Okabe's diary, he wrote that "soldiers have been prowling around everywhere looking for women" and he "often heard obscene stories" regarding their lewd behavior with local women. He believed that having "options for resolving the troops' sexual problems" would reduce the incidences of rape. Okabe ordered Lieutenant Colonel Nagami Toshinori to set up the comfort station and base it on the Japanese navy's model.

Yoshimi calls the Japanese military sex slavery or comfort women issue a "hidden problem" between Japan and Korea and other nations such as China. He started off by saying, "Internationally these issues are being debated, but the Japanese government is trying to hide their responsibility. A government official said the military sex slavery was run as a private business by civilian business people. We're here today to examine the truth of what happened."

Everyone was extremely polite at his seminar. Senator Kumiko Aihara (Democratic Party of Japan) was also in attendance. In a subdued and polite manner, Yoshimi was calling on the government to open up the archives because he believed there was enough hard evidence to force the government to accept both moral and legal responsibility for forcing women into military sex slavery. It was very civil, almost too civil compared to the press conferences and lobbying efforts in North America.

When asked why there was a block to opening the archives, he said, "I think it is more of a political power struggle. There are people opposing it and resulting in its bureaucracy and opposition from some Japanese lawmakers. They want to keep the compensation as low as possible." He says these politicians do not want to pay even higher amounts of compensation to survivors of military sex slavery and their families. These lawmakers are from conservative or right-wing backgrounds that believe the government has already resolved the issue of comfort women and sufficiently apologized to the victims and offered compensation through the Asian Women's Fund. Yoshimi also believes that it is part of the government's strategy to say there were no government documents on the military sex slavery in an effort to control its war history.[122]

When asked why the Japanese government was giving an unclear apology to survivors of military sex slavery, Yoshimi answered, "The first reason is compensation. Up until now the Japanese government has not paid compensation to individuals. There was an unusual exception with the Dutch and English prisoners of war. They were paid a small amount of money. There is a fear that they'll have to pay a lot of compensation."

The compensation comment was surprising because the Japanese government had just committed five billion US dollars for civilian, non-military aid in Afghanistan.[123] Why five billion for Afghans, and according to Yoshimi, not one yen of government compensation was paid to former military sex slaves?

"It is ironic that they're giving Afghanistan money when the world is watching – to make themselves look good – but no compensation to survivors. That is shocking," I said to Yoshimi as he nodded his head in agreement. What was really the root of this? Was it about making the past honorable? Was it an issue of racism where they felt the other "inferior" Asian groups did not deserve a sincere apology?

Yoshimi says the controversial Asian Women's Fund[124] (AWF) was ambiguous, and that the government needs to think about what moral and legal responsibility actually mean so that they can offer a direct apology. Because of this fund, many in Japan feel the government has already taken responsibility for military comfort women and they believe that the issue has been resolved.

In the rest of the seminar, Yoshimi made a case for the military being involved in every aspect of the sex slavery system, including managing the comfort station managers on top of ordering them to be built. In Manchuria alone, there were four hundred comfort stations. "Private businesses were involved but the military built comfort stations, gathered women, and maintained them. Some officials still strongly believe it was private," he said, adding that it was puzzling to him that the officials were so convinced of their position when even they had no way to prove certain aspects of the system. "I wonder why right-wing government officials are so strong in their opinions because all of the military sex slavery operations were carried out in secret. Somehow they manipulated everything to make it appear as if it were the private organizations, but ultimately, the military ran things." The military hid their role, and in order to recruit women from Japan, Korea and Taiwan, the government made requests to the Interior Ministry of Japan and the colonial government leaders in Korea and Taiwan to gather the women.

Yoshimi presented the official documents that he found which proved the wartime comfort stations were built by order of the military. "We have documents that prove women were abducted and kidnapped. Courts are even admitting it," he said. "But the Japanese government is not taking responsibility." Yoshimi emphasized that the acts of abduction, deceiving women, and trafficking were illegal at the time from a legal standpoint and vastly different from state-regulated legal prostitution. The law that prohibits human trafficking was established and put into effect in 2005 in Japan.[125] "The state regulated system was human trafficking and violation of freedom, therefore it is slavery. The comfort women were enslaved; there was no freedom on housing or freedom of going out. It was impossible to refuse being raped. The women were put in cruel environments while being placed in war zone or occupied territory and had to accompany soldiers all day long."

He ended his talk by calling on the Japanese government to pass the bill that calls on the government to give an apology that restores honor to military comfort women and "take responsibility of legal issues."

As the audience got up from their seats, I ran over to Kumiko Aihara, a member of the Japanese Diet House of Councillors, to ask for her thoughts. "I've been working for eight years to pass a resolution for an apology to survivors. Many members will not accept this. There is a lot of proof that this system happened. The most important thing is to resolve this issue before the survivors die and to let the younger generation know about historical facts," Aihara said.

"How do we communicate that military sex slavery is a human rights issue and not a Japan bashing issue?" I asked.

"This problem is a war-related problem. There will be other issues arising out of this as well. For example, forced labor victims—the Japanese government is afraid of paying reparations."

"Do you believe if the 'Promotion of Resolution for Issues concerning Victims of Wartime Sexual Coercion Act Bill' is passed, it'll heal relations with China and Korea?"

"That's what I hope," she responded.

"Why do you desire racial reconciliation?"

"I used to live in mainland China as a little girl. My parents educated me that war casualties existed on both sides and that Japan was not the only nation that was devastated."

Aihara was taught that Japan was not the only victim in World War II, otherwise her stance on this issue might be different today. She believes education is critical in teaching the upcoming generations about the truth in war and the truth about military sex slaves.

Next was the interview with Yoshimi. In his quiet manner, he had made some very bold pronouncements that effectively called out the Japanese government on lying and covering up their involvement. It was very radical, and yet because I heard his talk through a translator and the sheer civility of the time, it did not initially strike me as a revolutionary thing.

"I think you're the Martin Luther King, Jr. of Japan because you're fighting for justice and anti-discrimination like he did. You're a voice for the oppressed military comfort women."

Ken Arimitsu, who was also present in the room, laughed and said, "Yes, it is true. He is."

Yoshimi seemed genuinely embarrassed and laughed heartily. While he is an academic and not as expressive as MLK Jr., who was a world-class orator and pastor, the interesting thing is that Yoshimi is himself Japanese just as the oppressors he fights against, and King was a voice that rose up from his own people who were the oppressed.

Many have pointed out that the fundamental difference between Germany and Japan and the way they dealt with wartime atrocities could be Germany's "guilt-based" Protestant foundations versus Japan's shame-based culture. When asked why the story of young women trafficked into rape camps in Asia was forgotten and if it was part of the Asian shame-based culture, Yoshimi had a theory of his own. "It was the great social pressure that wouldn't let the survivors go public. In Korea, the first empowered movement was the women's movement. During the cold war, the power of the government was very strong. After the war, people had more freedom to speak out for themselves. I suspect that in China, there were a lot of victims but they couldn't speak out. They were forgotten. Very few survivors were willing to admit what they had endured. The opposing forces were bigger. More than just shame culture, it was about protecting their honor."

It was true. Speaking out would put their reputations at stake. Therefore, it gave prominence to the barriers the handful of outspoken survivors had to overcome. Yoshimi shared of a Japanese woman he had met.

"I spoke with a Japanese comfort woman survivor, and she was afraid she wouldn't be able to work if she had testified," he said. "She owned a dress shop. She was afraid that customers would find out and as a result, she'd lose customers because they would accuse her of being a prostitute during the war."

"She feared her testifying would affect her siblings and children and that her children would be unable to get married. Yes, I think it could have happened just like she said," he said. "The Japanese public in general has to change the notion that comfort women were voluntary prostitutes."

The communal aspect of Japanese and Asian culture where the family as a unit is emphasized over individuality was also a heavy consideration for this survivor. He spoke of how poor women at the time and even now had to go into prostitution to support families. It was perplexing to think about why the Japanese people still viewed the military sex slaves as prostitutes, even though they had testified to the media that they were forced into slavery. The influence of the media has a lot to do with the public's perceptions.

"There's a division of opinions. Specifically, Yomiuri Shimbun Newspaper[126], which has the widest circulation, has never said these women were victims. The Asahi Shimbun[127], a left-leaning national newspaper, has said that these women were forced. The reason behind Yomiuri is that the owner, Watanabe Tsuneo, is close friends with right-wing, former Prime Minister Nakasone," he said. "And newspapers have not reported that Nakasone has built comfort stations, even though he has. They're afraid of retribution and being blackballed. The big media companies are still saying these women are lying and that the comfort women were not forced."

He also added that the politicians who call the women prostitutes are nationalistic and part of that includes vilifying the so-called enemy of your national identity. "Some people still think the comfort women did it out of their own volition, their own choice. There are two contradictory ideas on this: the first was that the women were forced into systematic sex slavery and the second was that the comfort women did it of their own free will."

Yoshimi pointed out these women were forced, even if no violence or persecution were used, and trafficked through kidnapping, abduction, and deception. The point is they were taken against their will and trafficked into slavery even though the Japanese government denies this and says the sex slavery system was run by private businesses. It was the military, he reiterates, that supervised and controlled the comfort women and the brothel managers– even the rules for how the comfort stations were run were decided by the military, which conducted tests for sexually transmitted diseases.

He has found in his research that the Japanese troops would choose the location of a new, wartime comfort station, and that it was either directly managed by the military, or they would offer support by supplying food and construction of the buildings. One Japanese military unit, in Indonesia, even offered free clothing, daily living supplies, and cosmetics.

The next day, my translator Anny and I went to Yoshimi's office. The tiny elongated office was filled wall-to-wall with books in a maze of shelves. He poured tea for us, just as Arimitsu had. This very humble act demonstrated that he is a feminist. How was Yoshimi able to have compassion for the military sex slaves while other Japanese, such as former Prime Minister Shinzo Abe view military comfort women as mere prostitutes? Although it seemed like there were not many people like Yoshimi in Japan who used their academic platform to be a voice for the voiceless to the government, he humbly said that there are many Japanese like him, and that he is merely doing his own research work.

"Whatever you do there's always a price. It is not special sacrifice. Yes, it has been worth it," he said. "There's a lot of social impact internationally, and my goal is to impact internationally."

Yoshimi also explained that in his early twenties, he had seen tragic romantic plays and TV dramas and had read novels that portrayed the plight of impoverished women. They helped him empathize. It was the kabuki theater plays that opened his mindset.

"The Kabuki is a typical theater from the Edo period in Japan. There are many stories of *yujyo* (*prostitutes*), about the women who are put in the brothels, and about how the women who were there were suffering greatly because they were sold to those places," he said. "Many women sought true love and would fall in love with their male customers, but the story would usually end up in a double suicide."

"Do you have a spirituality that influences you to do your work? Or was it more of an academic meets justice type of work?" I asked.

He cleared his throat and seemed surprised by this religious question. "I think that I just inherited common Japanese beliefs and mindset rather than those from Buddhism. I was born and raised in a farm village in Yamaguchi prefecture," he said. "When I was a young boy, my grandmother would take me to the temples, and I would listen to the preaching of the monks. I don't practice it, but I have some faith in it."

When asked how he had, as a Japanese man, handled his interviews with the survivors of military sex slavery who had suffered at the hands of Japanese soldiers, he stated that it helped that he had a female interviewer to assist him in asking the questions of the elderly survivors. "It was difficult (to do the interviews). Most women survivors I've met are my mother's age, and it is really heartbreaking to think about them," said Yoshimi. "When I think on it, it is hard on me. Personally, I think it is not good for a man to ask these questions. I hesitate because I am Japanese and these women were victimized by Japanese men, so there seems more of a reason to keep a distance."

One of the most detrimental impacts of the Japanese government's denial of the truth is damaged relations with nations like China and Korea. "But in order for reconciliation to happen, it is critical for the Japanese government to take action, and for the truth to come out about comfort women, the rape of Nanking massacre, Unit 731, chemical warfare, and forced slave labor,"

Yoshimi said. "The government does not realize the gravity of the problem. They weren't educated about this when they were in school. Their textbooks did not talk about war responsibility."

"The people in Japan who are denying that the Japanese government was directly involved in military sex slavery are similar to Holocaust deniers," I said.

"Yes, I think it is similar," Yoshimi agreed.

"In Japan, it is as if the Nazis still continued in the government in Germany. It is evil. If they can deny this, who knows what else can happen in the future."

"In Germany, anti-Nazi political measures were implemented, and people's individual responsibilities were questioned--but not in Japan--and those people are still linked to the government," he said. "The Chinese cite Yasukuni Shrine and denial of comfort women as reason to hate Japan." Yoshimi also added that he feels hopeful that relations between the two nations will improve. In the meantime, he says there are two laws that have to be passed: the first law is for the archives to be opened to researchers; the second law to be passed is regarding apology and compensation to former military comfort women.

While he is not optimistic about the second bill being passed, he said it is important for people to think about the essence of the military comfort women issue. "They have to understand it is a positive thing for this problem to be solved, and they have to get that. By solving the military comfort women issue, it will help resolve other problems of sex trafficking and sexual violence against women and I'd say even gender discrimination."

It was enjoyable to spend time with this humane, compassionate, humble man. Like a giddy fan of a movie star, I asked him to autograph my book. It was thrilling to meet someone who lived by his convictions no matter what the cost. From Yoshimi, one can learn what true sacrifice is and what it is like to give your life to a meaningful cause you believe in wholeheartedly. His commitment to these elderly women is moving because he is a Japanese man living in a generation away way past the time period of these inhuman crimes.

All of these activists have given a large part of their lives and careers to see the elderly women survivors obtain justice. Several survivors have given the remaining years of their lives to fight for justice. What will it take to move the state of Japan to stop denying and own up to the past? It is a stand against all the historical forces that caused them to invade and colonize other nations and force women and children into sexual slavery for the military war machine.

Chapter 8

"The Japanese military itself newly built this system, took the initiative to create this system, maintained it and expanded it." ~Yoshiaki Yoshimi

Former Japanese Soldiers

Some of the most inspiring moments I've experienced while researching Japanese military sex slavery were during my meetings with the three former Japanese soldiers in and near Tokyo: Waichi Okumura, Tetsuro Takahashi, and Yasuji Kaneko. Following their repatriation to Japan from internment as war criminals in China, these three joined the Association of Returnees from China (Chūgoku Kikansha Renraku Kai), or often referred to as Chukiren, an organization that launched in

1957. One of the aims of this association was to promote Japan-China friendship and lobby for formal diplomatic relations between the two countries, which happened in 1972.

For more than five decades, these men and other members of Chukiren spoke of their involvement in war crimes, even when the association dissolved in 2002. They were seeking closure, or perhaps forgiveness, before they died. They were looking for young people to carry on their legacy in the peace movement in Japan. Each of these ex-soldiers had experienced a watershed moment, a turning point that caused them to break Japanese cultural traditions and tendency to glorify the war. These brave men are significant in bridging differing opinions in Japan on the war, as they were eyewitnesses and perpetrators themselves. They have become some of the most loyal supporters of survivors of Japanese wartime atrocities.

These men were transferred to China after having lived in horrible conditions in a Soviet Gulag[128] camp. The Soviet Union army captured Japanese soldiers in Manchuria (northeast China) and imprisoned them in prisoner-of-war camps in the Soviet Union. Tens of thousands of Japanese soldiers are thought to have died in the Gulags and thousands were in captivity until December 1956, more than a decade after the end of WWII, before they were able to return to Japan. The Soviet Union used the Japanese as part of the labour force and kept them longer than the other Allies.

In what is known as the Miracle of Fushun [129], the Chinese at the Fushun War Criminals Management Centre, a prisoner-of-war camp, had given amnesty to two of these soldiers I met. This caused the soldiers' turning point. During their time in Fushun, a Chinese prisoner-of-war camp, Takahashi and Kaneko scoured their souls to examine their own loyal worship of the emperor and the impact the war crimes by Japanese soldiers had on the victims and their families. They were able to empathize in such a profound way that that they were able to endure accusations of being brainwashed by the Chinese Communists from Japanese nationalists.

Fellow Truth Seeker: Waichi Okumura

Okumura is one of the few who are critical of previous prime ministers' visits to Yasukuni Shrine. He refuses to see the deceased soldiers as gods. The former soldier was born on July 13, 1924 and had been conscripted into the military in November of 1944. He was a high-profile anti-war activist, a man on a mission to find the truth of why he was forced to stay behind in China for three years after the war ended in 1945. He was also an active supporter of survivors of Imperial Japanese military sex slavery and arguably their most effective advocate as a former soldier and living witness.

I was feeling eager to meet Okumura, but at the same time I was apprehensive that I might find out something about the Korean soldiers in the Japanese army that might confirm that my great-great uncle was involved in some aspect of the comfort women system. Okumura chose a small restaurant with chic sixties style furnishing and a cozy smokers' atmosphere. Dressed in a turtleneck and black jacket, Okumura shook my hand as I did an East-

West awkward mix of bowing my head and shaking his hands with both of mine at the same time. The first thing I had noticed was that he could not look me in the eye. His eyes darted everywhere else and never met my gaze.

He had been in Shanxi, China after the war ended and fought in the civil war with the Kuomintang (KMT) military[130] against the communist forces led by Mao Zedong[131], the leader of the Communist Party in China (CPC). He had never met a Korean Canadian woman before but told me he had seen many Korean military comfort women in China. He had been given the opportunity to hear these elderly women bear witness many times.

He was compelled to see atrocities by the Japanese military recorded truthfully and to investigate why a large group of Japanese soldiers were left behind in China after Japan surrendered. This impulse took him to China three times after the war. He's been featured in a documentary called *The Ants* which portrayed his efforts to expose the secret Japanese military orders that stole eleven years of his life that was spent in China after the war and stripped him of his military pension upon his return to Japan because of his involvement with the Chinese army. On official record, Okumura and the other soldiers were considered "volunteers" in the Chinese nationalist military. They battled this claim in the courts to prove that the Japanese military had forced them to stay in China against their will.

The eighty-four-year-old said he had never experienced killing or using sex slaves, yet he stood guard while other soldiers raped local women. He had met comfort women in China and had spoken with others who had raped them on a regular basis. He and two thousand six hundred other Japanese soldiers were fighting against the Mao Zedong-led Communists until he was captured by them in 1949. Then he spent the next seven years as a prisoner-of-war.

"I was twenty years old in 1945 when the war ended. The Korean people—both comfort women and soldiers— were sent back after the war ended. The Kuomintang leader, Chiang Kai-Shek,[132] separated Koreans and Japanese. There were two thousand six hundred of us left in China, and we didn't know why we couldn't return home. We had to fight for Chiang Kai-Shek as volunteers.

In March of 1946, our names were eliminated from an official list of soldiers in Japan.

"I went back to China several times because I wanted to know what had happened. I found out ten years later in 1956, when I finally arrived home in Japan, the government didn't want to admit they left their soldiers in China. Because of the Potsdam Declaration[133], Japan had to leave China and Korea. So two thousand six hundred of us lived together in China. From 1946 to 1949, we fought for the KMT against the Communists until they put us in detention in an area south of Taiyuan, Shanxi Province.

"Were there any military comfort women during the three years after the war ended?" I inquired.

"Yes there were comfort women during the three years," he said.

"You mean after the war ended?" I said incredulously.

"When the (Japanese) troops gathered in a place, the first thing they did was built a comfort station. It was inevitable for the soldiers to get comfort women to encourage them to fight," he explained.

"Why was it inevitable?"

"Some Chinese girls were sold by their parents because they were very poor. Not all daughters were sold like that. Some were forced. In Japan, the same thing happened as it did in China where when the farmers didn't have much money but had a lot of children, they resorted to selling their daughters who were considered of less value and esteem than sons. It was considered normal to sell young girls into sex work. There was a military headquarters in Shanxi and an official comfort station where some of the women were sold by their parents," he said. "The Japanese soldiers captured girls from neighboring villages whenever they went out on the field to fight. The number of girls captured was usually much larger than the girls at the comfort station headquarters.

"There was a hierarchy with the comfort women based on racial discrimination. On holidays, senior soldiers visited comfort stations. The generals and the captains of the military would use Japanese prostitutes who went to China to earn more money as it was deemed an honor to be able to serve the nation by "serving" the soldiers. The next level below were officer types, and they could only use Korean comfort women. The lowest foot soldiers were given Chinese comfort women. I remember seeing Korean ladies and were told they were dancers and entertainers. They thought they were going to China to dance for the military, but to their shock, they were raped."

"After the war ended, did you see the KMT use military comfort women?" I asked.

"I don't know," he responded. "I, personally, have not seen Japanese soldiers rape the local Chinese women. Some Korean women married Japanese soldiers and formed families, however after the war, the Communist government couldn't accept that they were married and forced them to leave, thus separating husband and wife. The Communist military did not use comfort women." Perhaps the Communists were in 'survival mode' after fighting the Japanese forces and then the KMT.

"How did the Japanese soldiers perceive the military comfort women?" I asked.

"In those days, there were brothels and prostitutes everywhere in Japan. It was perceived as normal for men, so soldiers did not think it was evil or immoral since it was accepted in our Japanese culture," he said. "Two condoms were also distributed by the state health department to each and every soldier so they would not contract venereal diseases. The soldiers who used comfort stations knew nothing about those girls' poor backgrounds. They assumed these girls came for the money and were paid by the government, so they did not feel any guilt."

"What else do you know of the military comfort women in your area?"

He paused and looked mournful. "The soldiers were paid three yen a month. When they went to use a comfort woman, they had to pay one-and-a-half yen each time. They paid half their monthly salary for fifteen minutes with a comfort woman. Many soldiers grumbled after coming back from the comfort stations. Each woman had to deal with four men per hour. There were lines, lines, lines for this girl, that girl. There were highly favored girls, and officers fought against each other to monopolize their favorite. I felt bad to hear of this. I also saw officers fighting and saying, 'I want to take that girl.' The troops who were far from the headquarters could only go to the comfort stations on holidays or special occasions, so they had to find and capture the women themselves. Those units of troops usually ambushed and kidnapped the local women. They raped them so they would not have to pay. The soldiers then brought them back to the makeshift camp where they built huts and used the girls until they were no longer able to have sex. I don't know about the number of girls. They just went to villages nearby and even raped old ladies."

"Why do you think they raped these women?" I asked with an aching heart.

"Lust drives them. Soldiers went to neighboring villages to steal and loot, and then they sold the goods to finance their visits to the comfort station. When the communist party became stronger, the soldiers couldn't go to villages to pillage anymore, or else they'd risk getting killed.

"At the end of the war in August of 1945, we knew the war was officially over. Chiang Kai-Shek ordered us to stop all comfort station operations. But we were forced to stay behind and form a new army division. A comfort station was built, as usual, and more were established as the raping of locals continued. I've read many published diaries of Japanese soldiers. The first thing the Japanese military did when they arrived at a new location was open up a bar to offer liquor, and the comfort women or bargirls would be in the back. There were bars for the soldiers everywhere."

"How do you feel about the comfort women now?" I asked gently.

"We need forgiveness," he simply said and closed his mouth. "My words are not enough. There's a big difference between the way the Chinese and the Japanese view the war. In China, people can specifically say that 'the war affected my family like this' or 'the war affected my family like that.' It is very specific. But in Japan, people say 'Hiroshima and Nagasaki were bombed' or 'Tokyo was bombed.' The Japanese people do not talk of how the war affected their families directly. In China, they know how their ancestors suffered. It is important to talk about family matters. Then we can talk about war and therefore take a closer look at World War II and wars in general." Even through translation, his depth and the breadth of his passion for justice is apparent in his eloquence.

In 2002, a male librarian in Japan introduced Okumura to survivor, Liu Mian Huan of Shanxi Province. The librarian wanted Okumura to financially support some of the former sex slaves. "Liu suggested that I share publicly of my experiences after I told her my story," Okumura said.

A tender and highly unlikely friendship formed between this former soldier and the survivor. They were both survivors on opposite sides of the war in China. He met her again in 2005 and also met mainland China survivor and vocal activist Wan Ai Hua in 2002.

"Wan Ai Hua was supposed to be doing farm work in the field, but it was too hot for her. She fainted when the Japanese soldiers put her in prison and raped her. It was so painful for her to remember the past, and when we went to the place where she was tortured, it was emotionally difficult for her. I had known of their existence because senior soldiers used these Chinese women as sex slaves, but it was when I met them in person, when I started to feel sorry towards them even though I did not abuse them.

"Wan Ai Hua was the sub chief of her village. She was very talented and had power. She was also part of the underground communist party during the war with Japan. Now she is a very earnest Buddhist, and you know that communism and Buddhism are totally at odds in beliefs and ideology. Marx does not believe in God. But she totally changed," he said.

"Why are the Japanese public and government ignoring Japanese military comfort women survivors and your case?" I inquired.

"It is because if the government admits all these facts, it means the government and the emperor are guilty of unsound acts. I do not believe the Japanese government will admit they ordered us to stay or that they forced women into sex slavery. If the government admits to wrongdoings, then it will collapse. Even after the war, the Japanese government insisted on using the same nationalistic anthem that praises the emperor, and they continued to use the very flag that flew over all their military operations as they invaded other nations. I think these things should be replaced by a new anthem and a new flag. All teachers and students are supposed to stand up when we sing the national anthem, however some teachers are against nationalism and do not stand up. Oftentimes, teachers who don't stand up to honor the flag are reported on. It is the worst in Tokyo."

"So you believe the survivors will never hear an apology?" I asked.

"The government must apologize to comfort women survivors. This is an issue of human rights. If our mother was misused or disgraced, can we be silent? If our mothers were raped, we'd feel terrible. Almost every woman was raped in all of the villages, wherever the Japanese soldiers went. I wanted to have my own spontaneous truth and reconciliation commission, and I have come forward to testify on my own." A truth and reconciliation commission aims to learn about and deliberate over past crimes by a government or individuals to resolve related conflict in the present. Amnesty is extended to some perpetrators of crimes as well as reparations to victims.

"Have you forgiven yourself?" I asked.

"I've done things where I cannot forgive myself," he confessed. "But I did not rape anyone. I guarded those who did. Everyone works together in a military unit, and each has a role. I feel collective guilt. It is not only the military but Japan itself. I am a member of this community. I'm an offender and also a victim. Chinese people whom we fought against were also victims and offenders because they killed the Japanese, too. That's what war is."

He feels guilt, a concept other Japanese activists in Japan use in relation to their responsibility for crimes against humanity. He could not forget the memory of his first murder, so he made peace with his past during one particular trip in China. He returned to the killing field, where in February of 1945, he was ordered by his officer to stab and kill an innocent Chinese with a bayonet. He remembers clearly that was when he realized he became a murderer, and a Japanese "devil," a term the Chinese used for the Japanese military. What troubles him is that war could happen again.

"It is really dangerous. The spirit of militarism is rising. I want all the military bases to be out of Japan. I want the younger generation to know how miserable and evil it is in war. In war, it is justified to kill people. I want to bear witness and tell people how horrible war is. Japan should be totally independent. All the things we left in China are under the command of the American government. We're still under the influence of the US, and I believe the Americans and Allies must apologize to the Japanese."

In an interesting parallel, like the former sex slaves for the military, he too was haunted. He was compelled to find the answer as to why he wasted eleven years in China. He kept asking himself why he had to stay behind. He filed a lawsuit in 2001 to sue the Japanese government with twelve other soldiers who were left behind, but he lost the case even though they had evidence that they were forced to stay by a military order. The Supreme Court rejected the soldiers' final appeal.

"The order to stay in China is said to have come from the headquarters of troops, but I believe it came from Tokyo, and the government was in charge. I'd like to find the evidence. So far I have paid 1.6 million Yen for archival government documents. I haven't found anything yet. We want compensation for those lost years," he said. "But money is not the issue. I just want the Japanese government to acknowledge that they were the ones to order us to stay. However, the government is indifferent to us."

Due to years of smoking and drinking, he has had two different kinds of cancers in his throat and chemotherapy will not help. He laughs at the irony. "I never had fear of death during the war and now I do after the doctor told me I have cancer."

"My body hurts. I got shot, and I also shot others," he said.

He humbly bowed.

"Okumura-san, I pray that you'll be released from your guilt and shame," I said to him and held his hand. His eyes were still dark pools. I continued on, "I hope you'll find true freedom." He bowed again humbly. Then, there was a visible impact on him, as if something had literally lifted from his mind and shoulders. He finally looked me in the eyes, and there seemed to be peace.

What an enlightening time I had with a man, a renegade in his own culture, who has faced his past and his demons and has transcended the prevailing attitudes of almost all former soldiers to glorify the war and even society that wants to forget the "bad" parts of the war.

Okumura passed away on May 25, 2011 in Nakano, Tokyo.

Miracle at Fushun: Tetsuro Takahashi's Atonement

An activist sent me an email of the two former soldiers I was to meet on Saturday. The first interview in the morning was with Tetsuro Takahashi. "He lives in Tokyo. He does not have experience killing Chinese, but has experience as Japanese soldier," the activist said.

It is infuriating to think that if a Korean had grown up in Japan, he/she would be deemed a second class citizen and looked upon with disdain for no reason other than he/she was born ethnically Korean. It is the same for Japanese people that face discrimination in China and subtle racism in countries that were invaded or colonized by Japan. The very same kind of open racial contempt is perpetuated by the Chinese and Koreans who say racist things of Japanese, based primarily on historical resentment and unresolved war issues. How astonishing it is that racism is prevalent in these nations and there is a resignation about it that nothing can change.

Before the translator, Yumiko, and I arrived at his apartment, she told me that the three taboo topics in Japan are: military comfort women, the Nanking Massacre, and the Emperor.

When Takahashi answered the door, he was dressed in a grey sweater and slacks. He radiated intelligence and civility. He asked his wife to get us some tea and snacks; he spoke kindly and was attentive to my translator and me.

As soon as I pulled my recorder out, he said, "I have no direct experience with Chinese and Korean comfort women. While in Jinan, I went to a restaurant called *Sakura* and it was a comfort station. In another rural area, there were about ten Korean women in a comfort station."

"Japan has such discrimination towards Koreans and Chinese, however it is not always overt. I was raised to have discriminatory attitudes towards Koreans and Chinese. Basically, Japanese children are educated to discriminate against them, and this still remains as an undercurrent in society. The military sex slavery issue is very much a result of this racial discrimination. In the Greater East Asia Co-Prosperity Sphere[134], the Japanese were superior among the Asians. As part of the basic policy, the Japanese government established a shrine in every colony and forced everyone to bow and worship the emperor.

"I was born on February 15, 1921 in Miyazaki prefecture in Kyushu. I had a typical childhood. After World War I ended in 1918, until the 1930s, we had an economic depression. I studied history at school and everything at that time revolved around the emperor. He was god. It was the emperor religion. When a child was born, every family had the emperor's photo to pray to. It is the same with Kim Jong-Il in North Korea, but in Japan, it was more intense than North Korea because there was no other information about anything else at that time. My parents prayed to the emperor every morning, and we did the same at elementary school. For history lessons, we studied the emperor's family tree and all the names of the emperors in history class. Everyone believed the emperor was the most important person. No one in the entire society doubted that.

"In 1941, I graduated from the Osaka Foreign Language University at twenty years of age. All Japanese men were conscripted into the military. I worked briefly for a trading company in China, but in February of 1944, I was drafted into the military and assigned to the 59th Division that was stationed in Shandong. That's where I stayed until 1959.

"I had a girlfriend. At that time, women were discriminated against. They did not have voting rights. Personally, I did not discriminate. The prostitution system was widespread, and it was not illegal to use a prostitute. During university, I visited prostitutes with my friends. It was part of the culture. These prostitutes mainly came from the northern areas where many poor parents sold their daughters to brothel owners. The Japanese soldiers did not believe they were being aggressive with the women in the comfort stations or villages. They justified their actions. I personally did not know about rape at that time. The frontline soldiers frequently raped, and that was different from the comfort stations in their mind. It was legal for them to use military comfort women."

Takahashi did not seem to think it was morally wrong to use prostitutes. That mindset has not changed much from his day. Many men in Asia still use prostitutes as evidenced by the flourishing and widespread sex trade, and therefore these men do not believe it brings damage to the women.

"What was your role in the military?" I asked.

"For six months, I was trained. In October of 1944, after the training, I joined the communications and propaganda department. I created musical theaters to promote the Japanese military to the Chinese as a way to counter the Chinese resistance movement.

"Right now, there's a right-wing movement in Japan, and they say that Japan was not the aggressor. However we need to learn of the truth of our past history. Without that, there is no peace for Japan's future. This right-wing movement is very dangerous."

It was surprising to hear a former soldier express eloquently the need for historical truth. "How is the right-wing ideology dangerous for the future?" I asked.

"The fact that people deny and blame the comfort women as voluntary prostitutes is the most shameful point of this comfort women issue. The right-wingers want to conceal that this happened. To prevent repeating such aggression, we must learn the history of military aggression against China and Korea. I can understand what the Chinese and Korean survivors of Japanese wartime atrocities feel and the reasons why they cannot forgive the Japanese military. History should not be distorted. It should be corrected."

"Wow. What led you to have these convictions?"

He paused and then explained, "After the war, I was detained for six years and taken to Siberia for five years to do forced labor work until 1950. I worked in a coal mine in Siberia. There were more than two thousand concentration camps and six hundred thousand Japanese soldiers. It was a terrible experience working in such dangerous conditions. At least sixty thousand soldiers died in the camp. We were treated very cruelly."

"How do you feel about the Soviets?"

"I hate them. My time in Siberia was like hell. I have hatred for Soviets," he responded calmly. "It was awful.

We had to work in construction on a railway and a road. There were German and Polish soldiers in the camp, too. Our prime minister will negotiate with Russia on Japanese prisoners-of-war in Siberia. I'm not demanding compensation on the Siberia issue, but there is such a movement in Japan.

"In 1950, the USSR sent one thousand one hundred of us Japanese soldiers to a concentration camp in Fushun, Liaoning Province in China. That's where I had stayed until 1956. We were treated well, and the Chinese people treated us humanely. By 1950, there were almost six hundred thousand soldiers repatriated to Japan from Siberia.

"We reviewed what we did in China and learned that Japan was the aggressor and realized how brutally we treated the Koreans and the Chinese. We reviewed the atrocities that were committed. We learned these things in China when we were treated well. In Siberia, it was too cold at -20 degrees, and there was no time to think because of the forced labor work."

The "Miracle of Fushun" was where Japanese soldiers were surprised to be treated with dignity and were given

Japanese meals and medical treatment. They were "re-educated" by confessing their "sinful acts" and reflecting on them. In 1956, military tribunals were held in China, and only forty-five were indicted. All of the former soldiers, including those convicted, were allowed to return to Japan by 1964.[135] Takahashi himself had charges against him dropped.

They were able to do some soul searching and realized they had brought so much pain on people like themselves through the war crimes committed. For Takahashi, this time in China was revolutionary and caused him to abandon his loyalty to the Emperor, even though he had grown up worshipping him and fighting the war for him. He began to see that he was in "bondage" to the "Imperial cult." Further change in worldview came after reading the writings of Mao Zedong.

"This concentration camp period is a very important part of my life. I have spoken out against war and want to prevent war from happening again at all costs. Let war never happen again. We were placed into two camps in China: in Taiyuan there were one hundred soldiers and in

Fushun, there were nine hundred sixty of us. A total of forty-seven people died in both camps, and one thousand sixty-two former soldiers were able to return to Japan. I did not file a lawsuit in court, but I have helped Taiyuan soldier returnees for forty years. They have re-opened Fushun as a museum.

"In the area of Fushun, more than three thousand women and children were massacred by the Japanese. It is a tragedy. They were mostly gunned down by machine guns. There were some survivors who were ten years old at the time and are about seventy years old now. I was impressed by these survivors. In February of 1956, we had a chance to tour China, and we listened to the stories of massacre survivors. The survivors shared of how they lost their parents, brothers, sisters, and children. We were totally shocked."

In 1957, after he and the other former soldiers who were imprisoned in China were repatriated back to Japan, they formed an activist peace group called Chukiren, which means a network of former Japanese war criminals repatriated from prison camps in China. He was the former secretary general of Chukiren, and the men in this group, unlike other former soldiers, did not glorify the war past but regularly testified to the "acts of aggression" and human rights violations.

In Kawagoe in Saitama Prefecture, confessions by three hundred Japanese veterans in documents to crimes such as rape and the murder of civilians, are exhibited at the Chukiren Peace Memorial Museum. The museum raises awareness of Japan's human rights violations in China and other nations, a side of the war that is rarely in the spotlight in Japanese society. The Chinese Embassy in Japan provided more than five thousand pages of handwritten testimonies by the former soldiers in concentration camps in China. Chukiren was dissolved in 2002 because many of the members were dying off. But its activities were taken over by a new group associated with the museum with several members in their twenties and thirties.

"I support the military comfort women and their fight for an apology. It is important because already more than sixty-four years have passed. In Japan, the comfort women issue is not resolved as a war crime. It is critical to recognize war crimes and the need for compensation to victims in China and Korea but this unresolved. The activists and survivors are trying to find resolution in court for individual claims.

"I think it is very natural for victims. It was a nation's crime. Japan committed war crimes therefore the government needs to apologize. This is very important and means reconciliation. The reality is compensation is urgently needed for victims. We must consider their feelings and needs. I want to demand that Japan as a nation must apologize and provide compensation to all victims including military comfort women. But the Japanese government and right-wingers want to see the war as meaningful and don't want to think that it was useless or that it was a bad war. I've noticed discrimination from the Chinese," he said matter-of-factly.

In spite of the discrimination he senses from the Chinese, the work of Takahashi and his Chukiren members have persevered, and they have been courageous in bearing witness and standing for peace. They have been important early bridges of healing and reconciliation with the Chinese, and their acts of confession and repentance are indeed reconciliatory.

The spirit of forgiveness, reconciliation, and bridge-building evidenced in Chukiren group's early work with the Chinese is nothing short of miraculous. These Japanese war criminals were offered amnesty – it was one of the earliest Truth and Reconciliation commissions – where they confessed their crimes and then the judge set them free. No one was executed. This new freedom dramatically transformed Takahashi and Kaneko.

A core group of members persevered through the tensions within the organization due to the decades of turbulence in China during the Cultural Revolution[136] after the war. Building friendship between Japan and China was a major tenet of Chukiren. In the 1950s and 1960s, the former Japanese soldiers drove the movement to return the remains of the Chinese victims of forced labor and for improving political ties between Japan and China at a time when there were no diplomatic relations between them.

There was strong resistance to the establishing of the People's Republic of China in 1949, so it was a time of great struggle. To complicate matters, the Cultural Revolution began in 1966. "The staff at the camps who treated me and the other Japanese soldiers humanely now were blamed for their kind treatment of us Japanese, and were severely persecuted," he said.

Takahashi strongly supported the Japan-China friendship movement even when he experienced persecution for it, and he continued to testify around Japan about his time in China and his regret over the atrocities inflicted on the Chinese and supported lawsuits filed by Chinese war victims in Japanese courts. He published the organization's publication called "Chukiren" which fought against revisionist historians who called the periodical "a source of masochistic historical perspective[137]."

China granted amnesty and forgiveness, and that forever impacted the souls of these men.

These men have done more for the victims and for healing relations than those who were not shown forgiveness. This story is not so well-known, but the principles of peace and forgiveness exercised here has fostered understanding between former enemies and it must be taught to the younger generations.

Takahashi demands that Japan, as a nation, apologizes to victims of all Japanese wartime human rights violations and that the feelings and needs of victims be brought into consideration. I feel this must include an apology to the families of the deceased for the ones who have passed away before hearing the long awaited apology. There is no time limit on issuing apologies to victims of egregious war crimes. This acknowledgment means the protection of human rights for women everywhere and particularly the ones degraded in modern day sex slavery.

At the end of our interview, I expressed my wish for reconciliation as a Korean woman with Takahashi. I told him that even though I did not have any relatives who had experienced military sex slavery, I am a Korean woman and therefore I wanted to say that I hoped he finds healing from the past. I used to, while researching Japanese wartime atrocities, despise these Japanese soldiers. I told him that God forgives him, and I explained that I am a committed Christian and that because God forgives us of all of our sins, we must forgive and love one another. His eyes and entire face lit up. He looked like a different man from when we first sat down on the couch. His shoulders relaxed and a sense of peace came upon us. He thanked me several times.

Yasuji Kaneko's Redemption

Yumiko, my translator, and I walked to the subway to go to our next interview. I had plenty of advance notice that the next interviewee had raped women when the comfort women became too expensive and frequently went to the rape stations. Yasuji Kaneko's hands had trembled when he was first ordered to kill. Gradually, it became a mindless chore for him. The issue of military sex slavery is a sensitive one for Kaneko's wife because he had often visited the comfort stations.

His wife smiled sweetly at us and welcomed us in when we arrived at their home. We sat down on the tatami mat floor of Kaneko's sitting room.

"You're a hero for speaking out about your war crimes," I said to him.

He smiled shyly and did not respond. He was short in stature and had white shaggy hair and glasses. His legs hurt so he could not walk for long periods of time. He pushed himself on a chair and began to tell his story.

"I was released as a war criminal in 1956 in Fushun, China. I had experienced the same experience as Takahashi. The Fushun prisoner of war experience changed me. With other soldiers, I had taken part in a cruel war and brutally killed, bayoneted, and beheaded people. I raped and abused women.

"In 1956, three hundred ten of us prisoners of war gathered in front of a judge. I thought we were about to be executed because we did so many terrible things during the war. But the judge called each of us by name. We waited for our death sentence or more prison time. Finally, the judge said we were all released from indictment. We were all so astonished. I was so overjoyed. About fifty of us cried to hear that we had been set free. But we still had some doubt and couldn't understand what the Chinese were thinking of us. The staff of the concentration camp of Fushun organized a farewell ceremony, and the manager of the camp presided.

"I said to the Chinese staff, 'We committed so many cruel crimes. Why do you forgive us?' They responded, 'We don't want war anymore. Please go back to Japan and have a good family. Let's become friends.' I still doubted and thought these Chinese would ask for compensation money from Japanese soldiers, but our former Prime Minister Kakuei Tanaka met Chinese Premier Zhou Enlai. And we learned that China has never demanded compensation from Japan. This is the very reason why I'm working in this group Chukiren to bring real peace and friendship with the Chinese people."

His honest confession was surprising. He was basically a reconciliation ambassador. His family had become part of his bridge building with China.

"I told my wife what I did, and she also came with me to China. She learned the story of Fushun and how they set us free. She was touched by the story. Later on, my wife and I donated one million yen to the Fushun camp facility so that they could set it up as a museum where visitors could go and learn from it.

"We invited the manager of Fushun, Mr. "K", and his wife to visit Japan with his two sons. I still communicate with them regularly."

"Have you forgiven your captors from the Soviet Union?" I asked after remembering Takahashi's comments about hating the Soviets.

"No, I cannot forgive them. I did not have enough food to eat. They beat me. I had a really horrible experience in the Siberian concentration camp. I had to dig tunnels there, and it was extremely cold. We were treated very inhumanely. The toilet was outside in the freezing weather, which shows that they did not treat us as human beings. It was terrifying to use the washroom at midnight in the minus twenty degree Celsius frigid weather.

"We were constantly looking around for something to eat. I picked up what seemed to be a potato, but it turned out to be frozen horse dung. I was so hungry that it looked like a potato to me. Once, I went to the warehouse to pick up cleaning tools. I saw piles and piles of dead naked bodies of Japanese soldiers. It was too cold to dig graves for them. It was a cruel and sad sight. I thought of their mothers or family members seeing their bodies and how unbearable that would be. There was a shortage of food constantly, and we ate insects we found while cutting trees. We ate stray dogs in the camp."

I interrupted Kaneko and asked, "Did you have to resort to cannibalism?"

"No, we did not eat humans in Siberia, only small breeds of animals. I appreciated China and how we were treated warmly and humanely. They helped us return to Japan. I worked so hard to make a good family just like the judge ordered us.

"I did not know about the plight of the comfort women at that time. Every time I went to the comfort station, there were about five to six Korean women there. Each time, it cost 1.5 yen. We got paid 8.80 yen a month. I was conscripted on November 2, 1940, and was sent to the Qingdao port to train for three months before going into China."

"How many comfort stations have you seen? I asked.

"I've been to at least three comfort stations, and there were ten young women at times. Almost all of them were Korean, and one or two were Japanese. The soldiers waited in line, and we had no time to talk with them. Altogether I've seen thirty women at one location. There were also teenagers and Chinese women," he said while he pointed and tapped his genitals to make a point. Kaneko also suggested that the manager of the rape station could not profit very much from the fees he took from the soldiers.

"Many of these women used opium. The manager of one of the comfort station who ran it as a private business profited from drug dealing, and he allowed the sex slaves to use drugs. Even ten comfort women could not make him much money since they brought in 1.50 yen each," he said. "The military comfort women were used to transport opium sometimes. They carried opium in a condom and hid it in their vagina. The drugs were cultivated in Manchuria."

"Did you use opium?" I asked.

"No, I tasted it, but I did not use opium," he said.

"Why did the men use comfort stations, and why did they rape?" I asked.

He paused before giving a raw and honest answer. "The comfort stations are expensive. It costs 1.50 yen out of our monthly salary of 8.80 yen. Rape is cheap– it is free. At the time, the men did not think it was wrong to use comfort stations because we paid for it. We only had 3.80 yen after five yen was deducted for other things. We had to scare and terrorize the locals, so that's another reason why rapes were committed," he said.

"What if the military comfort women were Japanese?" I asked.

"If we had Japanese military comfort women, it might have demoralized our soldiers because it would be as if their sister or mother were in the comfort station, and that would be so discouraging. To prevent being raped, the Chinese women made their faces really ugly and kept their bodies dirty. The soldiers raped secretly. They knew it was wrong to rape, and they were afraid they'd get in trouble."

"What do you think now of rape and using the comfort stations?"

"Of course I feel sorry for that. It was during the war, and it was a special circumstance in the battlefield. I did not know when I would die. Every day I faced death, and therefore I wanted to have sex with a military comfort women before I died."

"Why do some men and former soldiers refuse or are unable to see these sex slaves as deserving an apology from the Japanese government?"

"At that time rape was cheaper than paying for the tickets at the comfort station. The soldiers did not feel bad or guilty because the comfort stations were managed by the military, and we paid for it."

"Why do they not see the former sex slaves' fight for an apology as a human rights issue?"

"There are two reasons. The military established the comfort stations and managed them. And secondly, they paid money to use the comfort stations, and therefore they don't have feelings of guilt or see their actions as human rights violations. But I agree with the former military comfort women and support their fight for an apology and compensation."

"What do you want people to remember about your story?"

"Never again should we have war. We need peace. Only one thing I want to say is that I can't forgive the high ranking officials in the Imperial Japanese Military."

"What about your captors from the Soviet Union? Can you ever consider forgiving them in the future?" I asked again to see if I'd get a different response.

He was silent for a moment, and then he quietly said, "It is so painful that I cannot think about forgiving the Russians. Frontline soldiers like me became prisoners-of-war, however many high-ranking officials and officers did not get jailed. They were not forced to take responsibility. I feel angry about that because they caused the war, so they must take responsibility for causing the cruel war. I'm a victim in this. The ones responsible evaded responsibility and were set free. I was a scapegoat. Also, the most painful thing about Siberia was the food shortage. Many soldiers died during that time. I was shocked to see the piles of dead bodies. Is there any person who is happy that their son died in war and is honored in Yasukuni Shrine?"

Kaneko's eyes filled with tears, and he began to cry. His chest heaved as he managed to talk. "My mom waited for my return. This is a sad memory for me. My mom waited for me for more than ten years. She touched my face and soon after passed away," he said softly. "I returned in July of 1956, and she died in October that year. There should be no more wars. That's all I want."

Even in his old age, the memory of his mother still moved him to tears. Both Kaneko and Takahashi vehemently hated the Russians because of the abuse and ill treatment by the Russian guards, the constant hunger, and the outdoor toilet in the unbearably cold weather.

Now, he was a liberated man. He was free to admit his guilt in committing cruel war crimes and even raping women. For a Japanese man, that is considered counter-cultural and extremely shocking. He seems to possess this freedom because he received forgiveness from the Chinese and that profoundly impacted his life. After coming so close to death during the war and in Siberia, he was given a second chance in life when he returned to Japan. But ironically, he could not forgive the "Soviets" as he and Takahashi called them. He hated the Russians with a vengeance to the point that he could not even bear thinking of the act of offering them wholesale forgiveness, the same kind of which he was a beneficiary of from China. But he chooses to focus on his life-changing time in China.

What an extraordinary example that China has set as the very first government to implement this type of reconciliation act and amnesty. Sadly, the architects of this amnesty were persecuted for it during the Cultural Revolution. Let it be the benchmark: to show extraordinary mercy to our enemies. The radical power of forgiveness transformed these former soldiers into the most powerful, grateful witnesses for truth, justice, and reconciliation between the nations.

I wanted to say something to Kaneko about reconciliation and healing. He was the one who needed to hear it most out of the three soldiers I had met on this trip, but instead I conveyed that I admired him for speaking out and that he should not feel defined by his past. These soldiers build hope that reconciliation is possible.

Chapter 9

"Through truth and justice comes reconciliation and healing, and where there is healing for the past, there is hope for the future."
~ Former United Nations special rapporteur Gay McDougall, the lead investigator on a special report on comfort women and violence against women in war.

Jan Ruff-O'Herne's Extraordinary Example

One of the most powerful stories to emerge in this activist movement for an apology for survivors of sex slavery is Jan Ruff-O'Herne's. She has forgiven her attackers--the Japanese men--in the rape camp she was forced into for three months. She is arguably one of the most powerful and persuasive voices for several reasons. For one, the poised Australian Dutch woman can clearly articulate her experiences and demands for an apology, unlike the other survivors who do not speak English. She also widens this issue beyond Asia. Ruff-O'Herne, a survivor of both sex slavery and three and a half years in a Japanese prisoner-of-war camp, remembers "starvation, torture, punishments, illnesses, and seeing somebody dying every day."[138]

She has exercised divine forgiveness for her perpetrators and found freedom through it. She has spoken this message of forgiveness to several audiences in Japan and has an indisputable moral authority that has won her the right to be heard particularly by the Japanese and the government. How could they ignore her appeals for an apology and for acknowledgment? She has clearly not spoken out of vengeance or hatred. Most of the survivors have said that they could not forgive the Japanese soldiers or the government. Ruff-O'Herne is an exception.

Indeed it is rare to find someone initiating the release of forgiveness without hearing the one who performed the injury extending a heartfelt apology. She had only shared her story with one person—her husband—until the day she watched Kim Hak-Soon bear witness of her years as a sex slave on television. At that moment, Ruff-O'Herne knew it was her time to speak out and campaign for justice as well.

It is only through the power of prayer and her abiding faith in God that enabled her and the seven other Dutch women in the same house to survive their terrible experiences in sex slavery,[139] during which she was "raped day and night" by Japanese soldiers for three months.[140] "Without my faith I couldn't have even survived the time that I was in the comfort stations. My faith has always been the backbone of my whole life," she says.[141]

Through their darkest moments, Ruff-O'Herne and the girls supported one another. "We really needed each other. And they sort of looked to me to give them strength through my faith and through prayer. I used to pray with the girls. There was one Catholic girl, too, and we used to say the rosary. God knows how many rosaries we prayed together," she said. "When I met Lys again in Holland after fifty years, the first thing we asked each other was:

'How many rosaries did we pray together?' This is what helped us get through this period."[142]

During her childhood, Ruff-O'Herne, her parents, and five siblings lived on a prosperous sugar plantation near Semarang, in what is now called Indonesia. She was planning to become a nun and was studying at a Franciscan college when the Japanese invaded and forced her family into one of the Ambarawa prison camps in 1942. "My experience as a woman in war is one of utter degradation, humiliation, and unbearable suffering. During World War II, I was a so-called 'comfort woman' for the Japanese Military, a euphemism for military sex slave. I was born in Semarang (Java) and had a most wonderful childhood, until my life was torn apart by the war. I was nineteen years old in 1942 when Japanese troops invaded the former Netherlands East Indies (Indonesia). Together, with thousands of other women and children, I was interned in a Japanese prisoner-of-war camp for three and a half years.

"Many stories have been told about the horrors, insults, brutalities, suffering, and starvation of the Dutch women in Japanese prison camps. But one story was never told--the most shameful story of the worst human rights abuse committed by the Japanese during World War II—the story of the comfort women and how these women were forcibly seized against their will.

"Why did it take so long for these women's ruined lives to become a human rights issue? Perhaps the answer is that these violations were carried out against women. Women are always the victims in war. We have all heard it said: They are only women; this is what happens to women during war. Rape is part of war, as if war makes it right. Rape in war is a power game. It is used as a reward for the soldiers. In some countries like Bosnia, Rwanda and Kosovo, rape is also used as a weapon, and a means to genocide.

"It was February of 1944. I had been interned in Ambarawa prison camp together with my mother and two young sisters for two years. I was returning to my barrack from one of my heavy camp duties. Suddenly there was a great commotion. A number of Japanese soldiers arrived in military trucks. We were expecting to be called for roll call, however this time the order was given: All single girls from seventeen years and up were to line up in the compound. We did not like this command and immediately became suspicious.

"There was an air of fear throughout the camp, and some girls tried to hide. We were assembled in a long line, and we trembled with fear as a number of high-ranking Japanese military walked towards us. We did not like the look of these Japanese. It was the way they looked us up and down, and the way they laughed among each other and pointed at us. The young girls stood there frightened, heads down, not daring to look up. The Japanese paced up and down the line. At times our chins would be lifted so they could see our face.

"Up and down they marched, sneering, pointing, touching. After some discussions among themselves, half the girls were sent away. I was left standing with still a long line-up of girls. My whole body was trembling with fear. The selection process continued until ten girls were ordered to step forward. The others could go back to their anxious waiting mothers. I was one of the ten. I could hear crying and shouting of the women, as they tried to pull us back, fighting bravely with the Japanese. "Through our interpreter, we were told to pack a small bag of belongings and report immediately to the front gate, where the trucks were waiting to take us away. We were not told any details. The girls and their mothers, and indeed the whole camp, protested with all their might. The entire camp was in uproar, screaming, crying, and fighting.

"It was all in vain. Oppressed and bullied by the enemy, broken and enslaved helplessly by a brutal force, we were sheep for the slaughter. The guards stood over us as we packed a few things. I packed my Bible, prayer book, crucifix, and rosary beads. At that moment, they seemed to me the most important things--like weapons, and they would keep me safe and strong.

"Flanked by the guards we were taken to the front gate, and we had to say goodbye to our mothers and loved ones. My mother and I could not find words to speak. We looked into one another's eyes and threw ourselves around each other. There, in that moment, it seemed as if we both died in each other's arms.

"By this time all the girls were crying, as we were forced into the trucks. We huddled together like frightened animals. We had no idea where we would be taken. We soon realized that we were travelling on the main road to Semarang. As we came closer to the city, we drove through the hillside suburb of Semarang. The truck stopped in front of a large house. Seven girls were told to get out. I was one of them. We were soon to find out what sort of a house we were forced to live in. Nervously, we kept together as we were ushered into the house by the Japanese officer who seemed to be in charge. Each girl was shown her own bedroom. I could not sleep that night and neither could the other girls. We ended up altogether in the one big bed, huddled together in fear, and finding strength in prayer.

"The next day some more Japanese came to our house, and we were all called to the living room. We were made to understand that we were here for the sexual pleasure of the Japanese. In other words, we found ourselves in a brothel. We were to obey at all times; we were not allowed to leave the house. In fact, the house was guarded and trying to escape was useless. We were in this house for only one purpose--for the Japanese to have sex with us. We were turned into military sex slaves. My whole body trembled with fear, my whole life was destroyed and collapsing from under my feet.

"We protested loudly that we would never allow this to happen to us, that it was against all human rights, that we would rather die than allow this to happen to us. The Japanese stood there laughing, saying that they were our captors so they could do with us as they liked, and if we did not obey, we would suffer. They produced papers for us to sign, written in Japanese, which we could not understand. We refused to sign. We were beaten, but still did not sign.

"The following day, we saw the front room of the house being turned into a reception area. We were ordered to have our photographs taken. We all looked at the camera angrily or with sad expressions on our face. The photos were then placed on a pin-up board in the reception area. We were given Japanese names, and flowers were put in our bedrooms.

"A Japanese woman arrived at the house. At last, a woman, I thought. A woman would understand and help us, surely. But the woman showed no pity either. In the meantime, the whole house was being geared up to function as a brothel.

"Opening night arrived. We were all terrified, and we huddled together in the dining room. We were all virgins, and none of us knew anything about sex. We were all so innocent, and we tried to find out from each other what to expect and what was going to happen to us. As we sat there waiting, fear completely overpowered our bodies. Even to this day, I shall never forget that fear, and in a way, it has been with me all my life. I knew that the only thing that could help us was prayer. I opened my prayer book and led the girls in prayer.

"As we were praying, we could hear the arrival of more and more military to the house, the crude laughter and boots treading the floor, the excitement among the officers. We were each ordered to go to our own rooms, but we refused to go. We stayed closely together, clinging to each other for safety. My whole body was burning up with fear. It is a fear I can't possibly describe, a feeling I shall never forget and never lose. Even more than fifty years later, I still experience this feeling of total fear going through my body and through all my limbs, burning me up. It comes to me at the oddest moments. I wake up with it in nightmares and feel it just lying in bed at night. But worst of all, I have felt this fear every time my husband was making love to me. I have never been able to enjoy intercourse as a consequence of what the Japanese did to me.

"The house was filling up with the Japanese. We sat waiting in fear, huddled together until the time had come, and the worst was to happen. One by one, the girls were dragged into their bedrooms crying and protesting. They pleaded, screamed, kicked, and fought with all their might. This continued until all the girls were forcefully taken to their rooms.

"After a while, I hid under the dining-room table. I could hear the crying coming from the bedrooms. I could feel my heart pounding with fear. I held tight to the wooden crucifix that I had tucked into my belt around my waist. I had been wearing the crucifix like this continually. I thought that wearing it might convey some message, and it would keep me strong.

"Eventually, I was found and dragged out from under the table. A large Japanese officer stood in front of me, looking down at me, grinning at me. I kicked him on the shins. He just stood there laughing. My fighting, kicking, crying, and protesting made no difference. I screamed, 'Don't! Don't!' and then in Indonesian, *'Djangan, djangan.'* He pulled me up and dragged me into my bedroom. He closed the door, and I ran into a corner of the room. I pleaded with him in a mixture of English and Indonesian and tried to make him understand that I was here against my will and that he had no right to do this to me.

"I curled myself up in the corner like a hunted animal that could not escape. 'O God, help me.' I prayed, 'Please God, don't let this happen to me.' The Japanese officer was in total control of the situation. He had paid a lot of money for opening night, and he was obviously annoyed, so consequently he became very angry. He took his sword out of its scabbard and pointed it at me, threatening me with it. I told him that he could kill me, that I was not afraid to die, and that I would not give myself to him. I repeated again and again, 'Djangan, djangan, (don't, don't).' But he kept pointing the sword at me, touching my body with it, threatening to kill me. I pleaded with him to allow me to say some prayers before he would kill me. While I was thus praying, he started to undress himself, and I realized that he had no intention of killing me. I would have been no good to him dead. He was getting impatient by then, and he threw me on the bed. He tore at my clothes and ripped them off. He threw himself on top of me, pinning me down under his heavy body.

"I tried to fight him off. I kicked him. I scratched him. But he was too strong. The tears were streaming down my face as he raped me. It seemed as if it would never stop. I can not find any words to describe this most inhuman and brutal rape. To me, it was worse than dying. My whole body was shaking when he eventually left the room. I gathered what was left of my clothing and ran off to the bathroom. I wanted to wash all the dirt, shame, and hurt off my body.

"In the bathroom, I found some of the other girls. We were all in shock and crying, not knowing what to do, trying to help each other. We washed ourselves as if we could wash away all that had happened to us. I dared not go back to the dining room and decided to hide myself. I hid in a room on the back verandah. My whole body kept shaking with fear. 'Not again, I can't go through this again,' I thought.

"But after a while, the angry voices and footsteps came closer, and I was dragged out of my hiding place. The night was not over, and there were more Japanese waiting. The terror started all over again. I never realized suffering could be as intense as this. And this was only the beginning. At the end of that first horrific night, in the early hours of the morning, seven frightened, exhausted girls huddled together to cry over lost virginity and to give each other comfort and strength. How many times was each one raped that night? What could we do? We were so utterly helpless. How could this have happened to us?

"In the daytime we were supposed to be safe, however the house was always full of Japanese coming and going, socializing, and eyeing us up and down. Consequently, we were often raped in the daytime as well. As soon as it started to get dark, the house would be 'opened,' and a terrible fear would burn up my body. Every evening, I tried to hide in a different place, but I was always found and dragged into my room after severe beatings. One morning, I decided to cut off all my hair to make myself look as unattractive as possible. I cut my hair until I was quite bald. 'No one would want me like this,' I thought. But of course, it did not help me one bit. The rumor spread that one of the girls had cut off all her hair, and it turned me into an object of curiosity.

"As the months passed, all of us girls lost weight. We hardly touched our food. We shared our fears, pain, and humiliations. We were exhausted, and our nerves were stretched to the limit. Continually, we put in a protest to any high ranking officer that visited the brothel, but it always fell on deaf ears.

"Always and every time a soldier raped me, I tried to fight them off. Never once did any Japanese rape me without a violent struggle or fight. They threatened to kill me often, and they severely beat me frequently. During the fights, I hit out strongly and delivered mighty blows and kicks and scratches, and injured the Japanese. Because of this and because of my persistent fights, I was told that if I did not stop, they would move me to a brothel down town for soldiers—a brothel with native girls where conditions were worse.

"One day, a Japanese doctor arrived at our house. I immediately thought that he would be able to help us. Surely, as a doctor, he would have compassion for us. I requested to speak to him, but he showed no interest and no signs of compassion or apology. Instead, the doctor ended up raping me on the first day of his visit.

"In the days leading up to the doctor's visit, gynecological type of equipment had been installed in one of the rooms on the back verandah. From then on, we were to be examined for any possible diseases. Each time the doctor visited us, he raped me during the day. The door of the doctor's examination room was always left open, and to humiliate us even more, any other Japanese were allowed to look in while we were being examined. They would come into the room or stand at the open door to look at us while we were being examined. This humiliation was unbearable, and as horrific as being raped.

"More anxiety came when I realized that I was pregnant. I was absolutely terrified. How could I give birth to and love a child conceived in such horror. Like pillars of strength, the girls gave me their support, and they advised me to tell our female Japanese guard that I was pregnant. I approached the woman, and as a solution to the problem, she produced a bottle full of tablets. I could not kill a fetus, not even this one. I continued to refuse the tablets. Eventually they were forced down my throat. I started my period shortly after.

"During the time in the brothel, the Japanese had abused me and humiliated me. I was left with a body that was torn and fragmented everywhere. There is not an inch of my body that did not hurt. The Japanese had ruined my young life. They had stripped me of everything. They had taken everything away from me: my youth, my self-esteem, my dignity, my freedom, my possessions, and my family.

"But there was one thing that they could never take away from me. It was my faith and my love for God. This was mine, and it was my most precious possession, and nobody could take that away from me. It was my deep faith in God that helped me survive all that I suffered at the brutal, savage hands of the Japanese.

"I have forgiven the Japanese for what they did to me, but I can never forget. When the war was over, the atrocities done to me would haunt me for the rest of my life. I could not talk about it to anyone as the shame was too great. I had no counseling, and I had to get on with my life as if nothing had happened. After seeing the Korean comfort women on TV, I decided to back them up in their plight for an apology, and for justice and compensation. In December of 1992, I broke my fifty years of silence at the international public hearing on Japanese war crimes held in Tokyo, and I revealed one of the worst human rights abuses to come out of World War II. It is by telling my story that I hope these atrocities against women in war will never be forgotten and will never happen again."

After keeping her secret for fifty years, Jan Ruff-O'Herne was the first European survivor of Imperial Japanese military sex slavery to come forward with her story. One journalist described Ruff-O'Herne as having "a captivating lightness of spirit." Even her own children had no hint of her wartime experiences.

Jan Ruff-O'Herne has largely withdrawn from public life. In Holland, the Dutch activists spoke of her fondly but did not mention her message of forgiveness. "How can we forgive the Japanese for all they've done?" cried one older man in his sixties whose family members were killed by the Japanese soldiers.

But Jan Ruff-O'Herne did forgive. Through her faith in God, she overcame hate, bitterness, and revenge. She was able to meet with a Japanese soldier and extend forgiveness in person. Her act of forgiveness does not mean the denial of her perpetrators' guilt nor does it change the facts of what happened, but it transcends them.

Her act of forgiveness is divine and brings to mind Nelson Mandela who forgave the ones who had imprisoned him for years. Both Ruff-O'Herne and Mandela have discovered the key to unlocking the prison door of bitterness and revenge. "You can't imagine the shame that we have lived with...After you've experienced those atrocities, you feel dirty, you feel ashamed, you feel soiled, and we carry that shame all our life," she said.[143]

But they have chosen a higher road, and in doing so, they have modeled true justice and righteousness to their oppressors. For more than fifteen years, Ruff-O'Herne has fought for justice for herself and other comfort women, and she has always emphasized that "an apology will give us back our dignity."[144] Ruff-O'Herne said a formal apology would help the healing process to begin for her and the other survivors. "After sixty years, a lot of us are already dead," she said. "I'm eighty-four, and it is about time that Japan acknowledges wartime atrocities."[145]

With two other Korean survivors from Seoul, Lee Young-Soo and Kim Kun-Ja, Ruff-O'Herne gave a moving testimony in February 15, 2007 before a subcommittee of the US House of Representatives.[146] She testified to win support for House Resolution 121 that called on the Japanese government to take historical responsibility and issue a formal apology. "This is really the pinnacle of all the campaigning that I have done over the past fifteen years for justice for the comfort women," Ruff-O'Herne said.[147]

Since 2007, in a series of milestones in the international activist movement in support of Japanese military comfort women, the governments of Canada, the Netherlands, South Korea, Taiwan, and the European Parliament have all passed resolutions that demand justice from the Japanese government for these military sex slave survivors.[148] This resolution movement continued into 2009, in Japan, as the city councils of Takarazuka, Kiyose, Sapporo, Fukuoka, Mino-o, Kyo-Tanabe, Koganei, Mitaka, and Ikoma have also called on their government to bring resolution and an official apology to these women.[149] In the last several years, the United Nations bodies, including the Human Rights Committee, the Committee against Torture, and the Committee for the Elimination of All Forms of Discrimination against Women, have continued to make similar calls to the Japanese government on justice for the survivors.[150]Amnesty International said that the continued denial of justice prolongs the humiliation and suffering of these women, which is another on-going human rights violation.[151] While survivors with support from international lawyers and activists have been fighting for an apology and compensation, there has not been much traction on this issue with the Japanese government.

There are a multitude of reasons for why justice is being delayed, including but not limited to, the very denials from the Japanese government itself. It is human nature to desire to honor their history. And in their denials is a clear preservation of chauvinist history. Also, the survivors' own governments failed to fight for their human rights in an era where women's rights were not considered important and in the international arena. Discrimination against Asians prevented these sex slave survivors and other victims from being ignored. Other factors are cultural pressures to stay silent on sexual abuse and rape and the stigma they came up against from those who suspected they were enslaved sexually.

The Allies reinforced the injustice the survivors of sex slavery endured and allowed the perpetrators of the system and other war criminals to continue in their political careers, which would had been wholly unacceptable in Europe. For instance, in 1957, Nobusuke Kishi became Prime Minister for three years. This is shocking, in light of his being indicted as a Class-A war criminal, which was a charge against those in the highest decision-making bodies in the military. He served as a minister in Prime Minister Hideki Tojo's cabinet, an office that oversaw all of the manufacturing and every detail related to arms and weapons for the military during the war. The Nazi German equivalent of Kishi would be Albert Speer[152] who spent twenty years in prison for his war crimes from 1946 to 1966.[153] If Speer had become the leader of Germany, there would have been condemnation from the world. But Kishi's term was met with only silence from Japan's allies and regional neighbors.

Germany has paid reparations beyond what was required by treaty or law to victims under the Nazi regime and Holocaust including forced labor victims. The German government and companies involved in the use of wartime slave labor have also financed a fund to compensate survivors of Nazi slave labor in August 2000. Worth 5.1 billion Euros, the German Foundation Act established this fund. By 2005, they had accepted more than seventy thousand claims for compensation.[154]

Among the Japanese activists was a huge, disproportionate sense of responsibility towards the survivors. They went against the grain in society. But all the calls for an apology by foreign governments and activists have been met by resistance or blatant justification in the form of continual visits to Yasukuni

Shrine or approval of school textbooks that glorify the war. What if a Japanese Prime Minister fell on his knees in a former comfort station or in Nanking to ask for forgiveness just like former German Chancellor Willy Brandt was on his knees before a monument that honored the Jewish victims of the former Warsaw ghetto uprising of 1943. His visible act of deep repentance on December 7, 1970 moved many in Poland and Germany and brought healing to survivors' families.[155] In contrast, the apologies given so far by the Japanese government officials have only inflamed the anger and bitterness of survivors and their supporters towards the Japanese state.

A repentant Japanese prime minister would catalyze a reconciliation process for peace in the region. The role of government in this case is one critical way to bring reconciliation by acknowledging the truth and issuing an official apology. It is very difficult to forgive if there is no open acknowledgement of the injustices that wounded you or your people.[156] A genuine remorseful apology issued by the Japanese government would lift the shadows off of Japan and her neighbors and restore deep trust and friendship. Japan is mostly alienated in East

Asia. We could then see the beginnings of an unshakable alliance between Japan, China, and Korea.

Denials by former Prime Minister Shinzo Abe and his controversial visits to the Yasukuni Shrine with other lawmakers such as Deputy Prime Minister Taro Aso, whose family-owned company has used both Allied prisoner-of-war and Korean slave labor[157], have tarnished Japan's image in the international arena and aggravated diplomatic relations– drawing criticism from the US government even as late as December 2013– indeed, Japan's wartime atrocities is an extremely painful and sensitive sore spot. However, it must be a blind spot for the Japanese government that is largely unaware of the extremely negative impact and tarnishing of Japan's international image that its denials of wartime atrocities have on other nations. Could Abe, who has publicly cried over Japanese kidnapped by North Korea, have the same compassion on the former Imperial Japanese military sex slaves?

Racism has contributed to the war wounds, and racial healing is still needed. The wound inflicted from Japanese military invasions and colonialism still remains.

Minority Koreans and Chinese face apartheid-like conditions and underlying persecution in Japan while the nation presents a gross contradiction by being a huge supporter of the United Nations while angling for a seat on the Security Council. They dismiss lawsuits from victims that demand compensation while they have given $50 million to a humanitarian project in Afghanistan. The Japanese government also had an opportunity to apologize on the world stage after the United States House of Representatives and House Foreign Relations Committee, as well as government bodies in other nations, passed similar resolutions as House Resolution 121, but they have done nothing.

Do the Japanese government and Japanese people regard the survivors of Imperial Japanese military sex slavery differently in light of the lessons from a terrible injustice that had happened to the Japanese in the West? The Japanese were treated as second class citizens and basically jailed on the basis of racial discrimination during World War II in Canada and the United States. After the Japanese military attacked Pearl Harbor in the US on December 7, 1941, Japanese Canadians were moved out of the West Coast due to "military necessity."[158] Some senior members of Canada's military and police force opposed this order to relocate Japanese Canadians believing that they posed no security threat to Canada. However, this injustice of exclusion from the West Coast continued until 1949, four years after the war. It was part of a racist movement to eliminate Asians entirely from the West Coast.[159]

When World War II was nearly over, Japanese Canadians were told to prove their "loyalty to Canada" by "moving east of the Rockies" immediately, or sign papers to agree to be "repatriated" to Japan when the war ended. Many moved to other parts of the country, and never recovered the loss of their property and possessions. Out of about four thousand Japanese who were living in Canada, half were born in Canada and had absolutely no connection with Japan, but were exiled to Japan in 1946.[160]

My junior high French teacher was interned as a child. In his fifties, still scarred from the experience of incarceration, he often spoke of his family's time in the horse stall where they had to use the horse drinking trough as a toilet. I've been told that not many in Japan know about the Japanese internment experience in North America. These Japanese Canadians and Americans suffered greatly during the war for no other reason than for their Japanese ethnicity at a time when their nations were at war with Japan.

But after years of struggle and fight for an apology, the Japanese Canadians finally achieved victory more than three decades later. In September 1988, the Government of Canada formally apologized in the House of Commons and offered compensation for wrongful incarceration, seizure of property, and the disenfranchisement of Japanese Canadians during World War II. Prime Minister Brian Mulroney's said to the House of Commons on September 22, 1988:

"I know that I speak for Members on all sides of the House today in offering to Japanese Canadians the formal and sincere apology of this Parliament for those past injustices against them, against their families, and against their heritage, and our solemn commitment and undertaking to Canadians of every origin that such violations will never again in this country be countenanced or repeated."

The historic redress settlement for the Japanese Canadians included:

A Payment of twenty-one thousand dollars to all surviving evacuees;

A clearing of all criminal records related to violations of the War Measures Act.;

A re-instatement of citizenship to the "repatriated" Japanese;

A twelve-million-dollar community fund;

A twenty-four million-dollar contribution to the establishment of a Canadian Race Relations Foundation.

Through the official government apology, the Japanese across Canada received collective healing. It is possible for a government to admit it was gravely wrong in implementing racist policies that were not only morally wrong but a terrible violation of basic human rights. Japan could learn from Canada where once racist laws segregated Chinese and Japanese from their fellow citizens of European descent. Canada's racist past includes: the Japanese internment experience in Canada, discrimination against the Chinese through unfair immigration laws that kept their wives and families from immigrating and painfully separated families, the violent riots against the Chinese in Chinatown in the first half of the twentieth century, and the Komagata Maru incident[161] in 1914 where three hundred seventy six immigrants from India were refused entry. Canada was a white man's country.

Today, Canada espouses a multicultural policy that embraces diverse cultures and encourages racial harmony while discouraging discrimination of any kind.[162] Canada, unlike Japan, has issued an official apology to people groups it had discriminated and committed terrible acts of injustice against. In his historic official government apology to members of the aboriginal community, the prime minister stated in his speech, "The government recognizes that the absence of an apology has been an impediment to healing and reconciliation."[163]

In 1998, former Prime Minister Jean Chrétien offered a statement of reconciliation on behalf of the government, but it was rejected by members of the aboriginal community and perceived as insincere. After a century of inflicting abuse and cultural loss to members of the

Aboriginal community, the Canadian Prime Minister Stephen Harper formally apologized in the House of Commons for the physical and sexual abuse that occurred in an old network of federally financed, church-run residential schools that are no longer in operation. The government oversaw these schools that forced Aboriginal children to learn English and adopt Christianity and Canadian customs as part of a government policy called "aggressive assimilation" in about one hundred thirty such schools in Canada from the nineteenth century to 1996.[164] About one hundred fifty thousand First Nations Inuit and Métis children were removed from their families and forced to attend these schools based on the belief that Aboriginal culture and ways of life were racially inferior. Harper's apology was the first formal apology from a Canadian prime minister. Before Harper had given the apology, many had been expressing the desire for a sincere, heartfelt apology. A small group of Aboriginal leaders and former students were gathered. Some of them wept as Harper spoke:[165]

"I stand before you today to offer an apology to former students of Indian residential schools... The treatment of children in Indian residential schools is a sad chapter in our history. Today, we recognize that this policy of assimilation was wrong, has caused great harm, and has no place in our country. The government now recognizes that the consequences of the Indian residential schools policy were profoundly negative and that this policy has had a lasting and damaging impact on aboriginal culture, heritage and language. While some former students have spoken positively about their experiences at residential schools, these stories are far overshadowed by tragic accounts of the emotional, physical and sexual abuse and neglect of helpless children, and their separation from powerless families and communities.

The legacy of Indian Residential Schools has contributed to social problems that continue to exist in many communities today. "It has taken extraordinary courage for the thousands of survivors that have come forward to speak publicly about the abuse they suffered. It is a testament to their resilience as individuals and to the strength of their cultures. Regrettably, many former students are not with us today and died never having received a full apology from the Government of Canada.

The government recognizes that the absence of an apology has been an impediment to healing and reconciliation. Therefore, on behalf of the Government of Canada and all Canadians, I stand before you, in this Chamber which is central to our life as a country, to apologize to Aboriginal peoples for Canada's role in the Indian Residential Schools system.

"To the approximately eighty thousand living, former students, and all family members and communities, the Government of Canada now recognizes that it was wrong to forcibly remove children from their homes and we apologize for having done this. We now recognize that it was wrong to separate children from rich and vibrant cultures and traditions that it created a void in many lives and communities, and we apologize for having done this. We now recognize that, in separating children from their families, we undermined the ability of many to adequately parent their own children and sowed the seeds for generations to follow, and we apologize for having done this. We now recognize that, far too often, these institutions gave rise to abuse or neglect and were inadequately controlled, and we apologize for failing to protect you. Not only did you suffer these abuses as children, but as you became parents, you were powerless to protect your own children from suffering the same experience, and for this we are sorry.

The burden of this experience has been on your shoulders for far too long. The burden is properly ours as a Government, and as a country. There is no place in Canada for the attitudes that inspired the Indian Residential Schools system to ever prevail again.

"You have been working on recovering from this experience for a long time and in a very real sense, we are now joining you on this journey. The Government of Canada sincerely apologizes and asks the forgiveness of the Aboriginal peoples of this country for failing them so profoundly. We are sorry." It was a remarkable statement by Harper and covered issues of compensation and a commitment towards healing and reconciliation to begin a new future based on mutual respect. It was particularly helpful in the healing process to have Harper address the generational pain and impact of the residential schools.

The First Nations people in the House of Commons room began to tear when the Prime Minister mentioned the ongoing, generational impacts and pain from residential schools.

The apology was received by the Aboriginal leaders and the Assembly of First Nations National Chief Phil Fontaine, a victim of residential school abuse himself, responded to Harper's apology. "Brave survivors, through the telling of their painful stories, have stripped white supremacy of its authority and legitimacy. The memories of residential schools sometimes cut like merciless knives at our souls. This day will help us to put that pain behind us.

"This day testifies nothing less than the accomplishment of the impossible. For the generation that will follow us, we bear witness today. Never again will this House consider us the Indian problem just for being who we are. We heard the government of Canada take full responsibility for this dreadful chapter in our shared history. We heard the prime minister declare that this will never happen again. Finally, we heard Canada say it is sorry."

To demonstrate the importance of the apology, the government canceled all work on that day. In the morning, one hundred people gathered in a sunrise ceremony behind the government building to say prayers for former victims who had died before hearing the historic apology. The government finalized a CAD $1.9 billion compensation plan for victims. The government also established a Truth and Reconciliation Commission to investigate the impact of the residential schools. The Commission will contribute to educating all Canadians on the Indian Residential Schools System.

On June 22, 2006, Prime Minister Harper gave an official apology to the Chinese Canadians for the discriminatory Head Tax. The Chinese Head Tax was a fee charged to each Chinese person entering Canada to discourage Chinese immigration. Harper expressed his "deepest sorrow" for the subsequent exclusion of Chinese immigrants from 1923 until 1947. He said, "For over six decades, these malicious measures, aimed solely at the Chinese, were implemented with deliberation by the Canadian state. This was a grave injustice and one we are morally obligated to acknowledge."

The Prime Minister said the Government of Canada will give symbolic ex-gratia payments to those who paid the Head Tax and to the spouses of deceased Head Tax payers and offer a fund for community projects that heal the impact of past immigration restrictions.

Historic justice through government apology and acknowledgment is possible. An official government apology has brought a degree of healing to Japanese Canadians, the Canadian aboriginal community and the Chinese Canadians. The day a Japanese prime minister says a heartfelt "I am sorry," with an offer to provide compensation and a Truth and Reconciliation Commission to examine the legacy of wartime atrocities such as military sex slavery, and to remember the victims who died before an official apology was given, will be a breakthrough victory against historical hatred and racism, Japan's role in this reconciliation movement is paramount.

Although an apology has been given to survivors of Imperial Japanese military sex slavery by several high level Japanese politicians and some prime ministers, there has never been an official government apology, nor has it expressed deep and humble contrition to touch the hearts of victims and their families. The shallow apologies issued so far have not satisfied. Victims were not healed. The Japanese government continues to save face. For activists, and this is true of the overseas Asian community, what drives their fight for an apology is the cover up by and the moral ambiguity of the Japanese government. It is a war against perception since those who are not familiar with the issue believe that the Japanese government has already apologized numerous times.

The younger generations in Japan, unlike the youth of Germany, do not know of Japan's war responsibility and military actions during the Asia Pacific War and the military's institutionalization of rape including the widespread use of rape camps. The government has approved high school history textbooks that whitewash the military's involvement in using comfort women and has even tried to cover up a report from a United Nations human rights investigation.

What does the future hold if the younger generations do not know of military comfort women and Japan's crimes against humanity? If their texts do not educate about the war, children will grow up with skewed perspectives, and when they do read of the atrocities, acceptance will be nearly impossible. It would be the inverse of my story. When I was sixteen, I had no idea that girls my age were forced into sex slavery by the Japanese government and military until I had heard it from a Korean news source. There was no information about this in the Eurocentric history textbooks at the time. It was shocking to find that there was hardly any information on it at the library.

Chapter 10

"After working with lawyers and civil rights teams for many years and with the survivors, he now believes the elderly women need healing and eternal salvation more than compensation."
~ Zhang Shuangbing, an activist and supporter of Chinese survivors of Imperial Japanese Military sex slavery

War Wounds

It was nearly a seventy-five-year-old secret, a secret the elderly women in Shanxi, China themselves could not forget. These women had survived an ordeal that almost killed them in the rape camps organized by the Japanese military that had enslaved them during the war.

Over coffee in Vancouver, Chui Mai Kan and I immediately slipped into a deep conversation about these women in January of 2011. We were incredulous that the stories of these women in Shanxi were unknown until this time. Many of these women had never shared with anyone, not even their own families.

How my meeting came about with Chui Mai seemed like it was a divine intervention. She had been taking groups from Japan to China to apologize to the comfort women survivors and was only visiting Vancouver for a week.

"What got you started on this journey for these sex slave survivors?" I asked.

Chui Mai explained how she was struck by these women and their experiences while watching a documentary on Japanese military sex slavery during a visit to Singapore in 2005. Intense anger and sadness welled up within her at the shame and injustice they suffered. A deep desire to hear their stories in person compelled her to track these women down in the proverbial needle-in-a-haystack search in March of 2006. She lived in the southern part of China and only had the name of the town and province these women lived in. "It was the plight of the women that got to me. They were neglected and abandoned by everyone, even by the Chinese government. They were victims of the Japanese military, but they were not given priority or the help they needed," she said. Chui Mai was on the same quest I was on: To find these women, to tell their stories, to look for answers as to why these women were overlooked, and to make sure they were not forgotten.

The atrocities and sex slavery system were issues that Chui Mai had heard about in her childhood during the 1960s in Singapore. "We all knew there were comfort women where the Japanese military was stationed in Singapore," she said.

Her mother had also lived through the war in Malaysia. She had to run for her life and hide in the jungles as a girl, while her younger brother contracted malaria and died. Food was scarce and daily rice was mixed with gravel with a little bit of sweet potato added in. Chui Mai says her mom could not eat another sweet potato after the war ended. Chui Mai was never told to hate the Japanese, but there was something unspoken, even though she was not bound by hatred and an unforgiving heart as so many of the Chinese in mainland China. When Chui Mai's Japanese friend, female pastor Naoko Okamura, apologized on behalf of the Japanese for attacking Singapore, Chui Mai's mother responded with a quick wave of her hand and said, "It's okay. It is all in the past."

But the Chinese in mainland China keep remembering the past in ways that negatively portray the Japanese and stir hatred towards them. Since moving to China in 2001, Chui Mai has been exposed to a lot of media coverage on the Japanese invasion. "It is so shocking how much negative sentiment there and hatred there is in the media," she says. There was one incident that Chui Mai credits as a turning point and made her realize the Chinese hatred for the Japanese was a deeply spiritual problem.

During her class in spring of 2004, she showed a Japanese film that was based on a three-generation love story. The first love story was beautiful, and at one point, there was a ten-minute footage of male characters leaving to fight in the war in northeastern China and the Philippines. That's when havoc broke out in the classroom. Her usually shy and quiet students began speaking loudly in Chinese and lost control. There was a lot of rage. "Why did you show us this movie? Why are you hurting our feelings?" Someone wrote on the black board in red chalk, "Do not forget our national shame," which is an integral part of the national education curriculum and ideology. Every Chinese student knows this phrase by heart. The students went on to angrily lecture Chui Mai and said, "Don't you know they're Japanese devils? They speared babies and raped women. They disemboweled pregnant women!"

That night, Chui Mai couldn't sleep. "The reaction of the students was too shocking for me. Through it, I learned this is not just a historical or political issue, it is really spiritual," she said.

With this revelation, she began to think of how to bring Japanese Christians to apologize to these elderly survivors of Japanese military sex slavery. "They have not only been denied financial and material aid, but they haven't received deep inner healing from the past. I wanted to bring Japanese Christians to apologize to them because I knew that it could bring eternal healing and that we could share the gospel," she said, "That's the only hope they can have."

A battle for truth

After living in China for more than six years and asking everyone how they felt about the Japanese, almost everyone has cited the atrocities the Japanese military committed during the invasion of China as the reason for hating the Japanese. This hatred is strong, like a prison. One Chinese survivor in southern China had given birth after being raped by a Japanese soldier. Her half-Japanese son suffered extreme persecution all of his life and could not find a regular job or get married. He works in the fields with his aged mother. The two of them cling to one another as they were both ostracized for something they had no control over.

"This wound wasn't healed at all after the war and was caused by bitterness and hatred for the Japanese. I saw this wound was on the churches in China who are not aware of the depth of this hurt and are trying to ignore it," Chui Mai said. "We need to know the truth and the truth will set us free. I've heard from both sides, Japanese and Chinese that the truth has not been shared with the right perspective, especially in Japan. The Japanese have distorted truth and tried to wipe away what the atrocities committed by the government and military. They haven't admitted what they did was wrong. The Chinese are opposite. They always remember. All these roots are spiritual because truth is either denied or distorted."

The education system in China from elementary school to higher levels drill into the students to "never forget their national shame," to never forget the pillaging of villages, the rapes, the bayoneting of pregnant women and murder of civilians by the Imperial Japanese Military. "Both nations are not rooted in Judeo-Christian values and foundation. One is atheistic, and Japan's main religion involves worship of all kinds of gods. Our God is a God of peace. God sent his only Son to die for peace and that we'd be reconciled with one another. He wants us to be peacemakers with others, even our enemies. Or else people will continue to hate one another, never forgive, and be enslaved to denial," she said.

"So this is how your support for former military sex slaves began?"

"My mission is for reconciling the Chinese and for Japanese too. But It is really more so for the church to be healed and reconciled with the Japanese. This wound must be healed, or else China cannot truly move forward and prosper."

The principles for Chui Mai's ministry Healing River-Rainbow Bridge germinated at this time and soon her vision was solidified to engage in reconciliation work for the healing river to continue to flow to the survivors of military sex slavery and their children, grandchildren, and all future generations. In a short time, she joined a team comprised of Chinese, Koreans, Japanese, Americans, and Canadians. Because of her experiences with the Chinese students and their angry reactions to the Japanese, she felt the cornerstone of the reconciliation work was for the Japanese team members to apologize to the survivors so that healing, restoration, and blessings will flow to them as well as their future generations. In the last four years, their remarkable reconciliation work has taken them to Beijing, Shanghai, Nanking, Dalian, Shenyang, Harbin, Shanxi, Zhengzhou, Luoyang, Xi'an, Hainan, and Hong Kong.

In many house churches, Chui Mai shared the message of reconciling with China's historical enemy, the Japanese. But she felt that these Christians were either ignoring or not aware of the problem. One dynamic female pastor shared with Chui Mai after her team of Japanese friends shared and repented to the Chinese congregation.

"The pastor said the reconciliation work in China is important because it is cutting chains of bondage. Every time these Japanese Christians apologize and the Chinese respond by recognizing their bitterness and forgiving the Japanese, it is breaking chains." Then she shared her own testimony about how her heart was very cold and indifferent during the time the Japanese team came. She simply thought that since the Japanese government had not admitted their wrongdoings, it was only right that the Japanese people apologize to them. It is only when the Japanese members rose up from their knees after repenting and were about to go back to their seats that she heard God whisper to me, 'All have sinned and have fallen short of the glory of God. All have sinned, even you, a spiritual leader.' This pierced her heart. She led people to pray and bless Japan, something that she had not planned to do. She called one of her co-workers, an ethnic Korean Chinese pastor. The Chinese, Japanese, Korean pastors prayed in their mother tongue and blessed each of the people. It was a powerful time."

There were two other pastors who shared with Chui Mai about how their churches had visions for Japan. What was remarkable about his story was that as a young man, he had intense hatred for the Japanese and wanted to physically weaken the Japanese he would occasionally see on the streets. He was angry at Japan, even after becoming a Christian, and the bitterness did not go away--not until God spoke clearly to him to forgive the Japanese, a huge miracle in itself, and gave him a vision to reach Japan with the gospel. Another large Korean Chinese church has started a bible study in Japanese in order to prepare for evangelism work in Japan.

Many reconciliation ministries have been established in places like Israel and Rwanda, but so far, there are no organized efforts to reconcile the Chinese and the Japanese.

In March of 2006, Chui Mai met a couple in Taiyuan, Shanxi. But her search for the survivors of military sex slavery was fruitless. She says the tide turned after her friends prayed for her. Later in June, the couple she met called her and said they had a lead. Chui Mai and a Chinese friend went to Yuxian, Shanxi to meet a government official. He introduced her to a teacher named Mr. Zhang Shuangbing, who wrote a letter requesting financial support for a survivor with breast cancer and for the other survivors.

Zhang was a champion for these forgotten women. He stumbled across one survivor in his village more than twenty years ago. This woman had married twice after the war--one husband died and the other abandoned her. She was lonely, desolate, and sick. Zhang's heart was touched by her constant tears, and he began to get to know other women who had survived being forced into sex slavery by the Japanese military. He began to help them. Getting compensation for these survivors consumed his life, and he began to support a Japanese legal team that filed lawsuits in Japan on behalf of these elderly women. Zhang was the right connection and was the key to unlock this new calling for Chui Mai.

Zhang took Chui Mai and her Chinese friend, Li Mei, to see Sanni Xing, or Grandma Xing as he called her. As Chui Mai tells the story, her eyes well up with tears, and It is obvious by the pained look on her face that she has wept over this woman and what she has had to endure.

They found grandma Xing sleeping on a traditional bed in Northern China called *kang* in a dark smelly cave or grotto. Her home was on the edge of a huge rock formation and in this region, it is common to have caves transformed into homes. She had only one adopted son and he lived in a new house in front of her cave while he put his eighty-one-year-old mother in the old decrepit house that reeked of disease and human waste. She had battled breast cancer for two years and now it was in the advanced stages. Her son had no money to send his mother to a hospital for treatment. Grandma Xing was in deep pain and agony, and no one was around to help her relieve herself, so she had to crawl to do so. Her son and daughter-in-law worked in the fields all day and left her with only one *mantou* (bread).

Chui Mai and her friend wept when they lifted her blanket to see how she was treating her cancer.

"Our hearts were crushed by what we saw. She was naked and her right breast as well as the right side of her body was just rotting flesh that was oozing with pus and blood. She was gasping for air and groaning because of the pain," Chui Mai said. "Grandma Xing said, 'After my mother died when I was fourteen or fifteen years old, nobody really loved me. I had never felt loved. Not even when I got married. My mother used to feed me millet porridge. I was captured by the Japanese soldiers when I was thirteen years old, and dragged from village to village and from mountain to mountain by them. I lost my small toe on one of my bound feet. After the war, I was married but had no children.'"

Grandma Xing had nothing else to add. That's how simple and pure her heart was. "How can you treat your mother like this? You have to take care of her," Chui Mai and her friend, Li Mei, said to Xing's son and daughter-in-law. Zhang had written a letter to the local government office asking for medical aid of twenty thousand Chinese yuan (three thousand US dollars) for her but the local government office could only give a maximum of three thousand Chinese yuan (four hundred fifty-eight US dollars). He also sent out an appeal on the internet and shared of Xing's medical needs at a gathering of officials and business people, but no one cared.

They went back again the next day. Grandma Xing said she felt peace for the first time and slept like a baby. Chui Mai and her friend left some money with Zhang and asked him to hire a maid to take care of grandma Xing's daily needs and to pay for regular medical check-ups. After this visit, a maid starting taking care of her. A doctor and nurse began visiting her once or twice a week. The last day before she passed away, she ate her favorite foods--watermelon and eggs. Grandma Xing passed away about a month after finding peace in God for the first time in her life.

Chui Mai's turning point was in meeting Grandma Xing. "These women were victims but they were not given the help they needed. They haven't received not only financial and material aid, but they haven't received deep inner healing from the past. I wanted to bring Japanese Christians to apologize to them because I knew that could bring deep healing," she said. "That's when I wanted to bring Japanese friends especially Christians to meet them."

Later that year, Chui Mai brought two other Japanese women on a second trip to visit the elderly women. Xing's son and daughter-in-law took them to their mother's gravesite and there, Chui Mai and her friends mourned over the loss of this woman's youth and the suffering that followed her after she survived her time as a Imperial Japanese military sex slave. Their goodbyes to Grandma Xing at her grave was a profound time of reflection and resolve that the elderly women needed healing and closure before their deaths.

Since 2006, Chui Mai and her international team met twenty-five more elderly survivors and the Japanese Christians led by Tomoko Hasegawa repented on behalf of the military and apologized to these women. Tomoko and the Japanese team members wanted to see God's healing impact these women. Most of the survivors were bitter at both the Japanese and Chinese governments. Ten of them have since passed away in the last five years, and one family did not even want them to visit their mother again. They explained that their mother did not want them to return because she felt shameful. She didn't want to rouse attention from other neighbors and villagers. Sexual enslavement is seen as a shame and humiliation from the past."

In July 2006, Chui Mai and her friend Li Mei visited a woman in eastern Shanxi. Chen grandma was full of hatred for Japanese government. Her husband was a fighter in the communist army and received a military medal. But during the Cultural Revolution, he was stripped of that medal and wasn't given recognition and compensation he deserved as a war hero. Her family suffered during this time. She hated the Chinese government for their woes at that time and for not taking care of her. Chen told Chui Mai she wanted to take revenge against the Japanese, and she wanted her children and grandchildren to carry on the work of revenge after she died. When she said these words, her face seemed to be contorted by anger and bitterness.

Chui Mai brought two Japanese women to visit Chen several months later. "The Japanese women asked Chen to tell her story and experiences as a military comfort woman. After taking a number of medications due to her multiple health problems, and after taking a few deep breaths, Chen started telling us her painful and tortuous experiences with a lot of tears," said Chui Mai. "When the Japanese sisters cried and knelt down to apologize to her, Chen also cried and embraced them. I could see the anger and bitterness disappearing from her wrinkled face and demeanor, and I hope from her heart, too. Her bitter demeanor changed, almost totally. Chen said, 'I have forgiven you. All I experienced is in the past.' The apology seemed to unlock the door to the deep recesses of her soul and spirit that have been locked and trapped by such unspeakable pain, sense of injustice, anger and hatred. When that door opened, the healing grace of forgiveness and unconditional love was able to flow into her heart. I was very privileged to see that happened in that woman. She's very joyful now. Her life has totally changed."

Forgiveness unlocked the bitterness and broke chains of hatred that hindered healing from happening in Grandma Chen.

"There was another woman (a survivor) who did not say or express much of her anger and bitterness against the Japanese military and government. However, when the two Japanese knelt down to apologize to her she appeared to be very uncomfortable in her facial expression and body language. She refused to say that she had accepted their apologies even though the Japanese women asked for her forgiveness a few times. She was trying very hard to suppress her feelings and pain inside of her, and she could not even cry. We gave up trying to get a response from her as we knew we could not force that from her. Although we were very sad at her negative response, we had peace as our Japanese friends had done their part and responsibility in apologizing," Chui Mai said.

River of Hope

Since the Imperial Japanese Military left the area in 1945, Chui Mai's Japanese team members were the first foreigners and the first Japanese to visit twenty-five survivors from military sex slavery in Qingxian County and Wuxiang County in southern Shanxi. Both the Imperial Japanese Military and the Communist military had their headquarters in Shanxi. This region had some of the most protracted and intense battles and bloodshed between the two armies. It is still one of the poorest regions in the province. Unlike the women in Yuxian in eastern Shanxi who have received a lot of media attention and financial support, these survivors in southern Shanxi have not visited Tokyo or participated in lawsuits in Japan. These women in southern Shanxi have been forgotten for nearly seventy years.

After Chui Mai and her friend's first visit in September of 2006, a few foreign and local teams have since visited the women bringing mainly financial gifts.

Mr. Zhang, the teacher and Chui Mai's local guide in Shanxi, said, "There are other teams that have visited the women but they only bring in financial aid. Only your team and work have brought real healing to the women." Even government officials were visibly moved by the apology from the Japanese Christians.

In Shanghai, there were two former rape stations, referred to as comfort stations by the Japanese military. They had a gloomy aura and even one of the current inhabitants said the sad history kind of clings to the walls.

"What is a common theme in the women's stories?" I asked Chui Mai.

"Some of them in the east still have nightmares of being attacked by the Japanese soldiers, a form of post-traumatic stress disorder. The women in the south were not affected by nightmares. The sex slave survivors in the east, whenever they'd see Japanese soldiers on TV, they cringed in fear and had flashbacks of their time in the rape camps. Many of these women are depressed and it has to do with the legal issues. Most of the women and families had pinned a lot of hopes on getting an official apology and compensation from the Japanese government. They worked closely with Japanese lawyers. It was bold of them to come out and tell their stories. When they realized they were not getting anything out of it and that the Chinese government had already relinquished their personal rights to compensation because too much time had passed (which is what the Japanese courts ruled), Zhang said these women were very disappointed with the failed lawsuit. They fell into hopelessness and depression. They wanted justice and compensation money and recognition. Zhang was persecuted for being a spy for reasons he cannot understand. His wife lost her mind while pregnant with their second child because she was harassed by the police so much— as part of their intimidation tactics against Zhang. As punishment, he was posted as teacher in a region far from his home and with low pay. Zhang said that after working with lawyers and civil rights teams for many years and with the survivors, he now believes the elderly women need healing and spiritual support more than compensation."

For the most part, the women responded in heartfelt ways to the Japanese who repented on behalf of the Japanese government and military. It was especially powerful for these women to receive a weeping Japanese man repenting on behalf of his government and nation for what they had done to these women in their youth. Pastor Fujie, in July of 2008, was the first Japanese man to enter that region more than sixty years after the Imperial Japanese Military left in August of 1945. As the first Japanese man to offer an apology to these women, his apology held a particular weight.

"I feel that his apology is extremely important, critical, and effective because the decisions and implementation of these decisions in the war were all made by Japanese male leaders— the emperor, cabinet, and military," Chui Mai said.

Most of the women had no fear or inhibition in accepting his apologies. When he knelt down, wept, and embraced them, he asked the women to forgive the sins of his fellow Japanese. In return they also wept and embraced him.

The Japanese prepared a lot of small gifts and paid for their own travel expenses. What an incredible sacrifice of love that they would remember these elderly Chinese women who had suffered unimaginably in their tender youth. These Japanese sought them out and apologized and honored them. It is a true and beautiful act of faith.

Kneeling before two women, Pastor Fujie said, "When I was four years old, the war ended. When I grew up, I became a Christian. Later I learned the Japanese military committed a lot of atrocities in the war. We are the same human beings. In the past, we did not know, but now we know. We have to come to express our repentance and also share this love with you. I want to formally apologize as a representative of the Japanese people, especially men and soldiers, for the suffering you went through. We came here to repent. We need to continually apologize. I know that during the war, women and children were the victims," he trailed off as he teared up. "I have come because we would like to apologize."

One woman cried a lot. Another woman beside her said very graciously, crying, "It is all in the past. 'Mei guanxi,' no problem. Everything is in the past." A woman showed her wound on her arm from a knife stabbing of a soldier. Pastor Fujie hugged the survivor and she wept. It was the first time she had seen a Japanese man since she was held captive as a sex slave by the Imperial Japanese Military.

"The Japanese government has not paid compensation. We are Japanese Christians. The Japanese and Chinese are supposed to love one another and have harmony. Our ancestors had sin. We fought one another and had conflict. Men raped women because of sin... Jesus came down from his heavenly throne to take on sin and take on judgment on the cross and died on our behalf," he said.

At this point, the women kindly urged the pastor to stand up because he had been kneeling for so long and they were concerned that he was uncomfortable.

A local house church leader, called Brother Wang, then spoke to the women and said, "Their Japanese ancestors had raped and abused you and now their descendants have come to repent and apologize to you. This time with you is very critical."

Both of these women decided to accept the Christian faith, and Chui Mai made arrangements for them to be taken care of by a local church with the Chinese pastor who had joined this reconciliation time.

The elderly women asked the pastor, "Where are you from?" He explained he was from a nearby village. The

Chinese pastor laid hands on Chinese elderly survivors and prayed for them.

Over the decades, many Christians and church organizations have participated in the work of reconciliation with Chinese, Koreans, and other people groups affected by Japanese Imperialism. There have been Japanese Christians who contributed to the producing of films with a reconciliation message and many pastors who have repented and apologized on behalf of the government and military. The use of creative arts is one major way that distinguishes Chui Mai's reconciliation team from other works. Many on the team are dancers, musicians, calligraphers, and artists, as well as pastors.

In one dance, the women used brightly colored scarves and waved them around. One elderly woman beamed and clapped with a childlike joy. Another tambourine dance is based on the Jewish dance and every movement has spiritual significance. When the Japanese team performed their "healing river" dance and shared the words of repentance composed by Tomoko and written by a Japanese calligrapher named Fumiko to the Chinese, many Chinese on the streets or in house churches wept. Old men cried. At an official government church, the Three Self Church, in Beijing, the team danced and sang for five hours. The team repented and apologized for the atrocities the Japanese military committed; this apology came a week after anti-Japan protests erupted in Zhengzhou and Chengdu over China's territorial dispute with Japan over the Diaoyu islands. Some in the audience cried hearing the apology.

This issue of war wounds from the Japanese military touches something so deep in the heart of people. In China, whenever the Japanese reconciliation team repented for the atrocities committed by the Japanese in public places, young and old alike cried. Even with these crimes that took place generations ago, people identified with the pain their ancestors experienced. The Japanese team credits the power of prayer and their weekly prayer meetings in seeing visible receptivity to their apologies and repentance.

Some may say that collective responsibility for the sins of the previous generations should not be passed on to individuals who committed none of the sins. However, these modern day reconcilers, the Japanese Christians on Chui Mai's team, chose to stand in the gap and identify with the egregious human rights violations of the Imperial Japanese Military.

"An apology itself will not bring intensive healing. But the apology and repentance by the perpetrators or a representative group of the perpetrators will open the door and way for deep healing. This representative group of Japanese happen to be Christians. Their broken and contrite spirits touch the hearts of the women.

"The former military comfort women and the Chinese people need to reciprocate with acceptance, forgiveness, and repentance as they have been trapped by hatred, anger, bitterness, and unforgiveness," said Chui Mai. "Only the power of the unconditional love of Christ's death on the cross can set both the Japanese and the Chinese free from their spiritual bondages and release the healing grace to them and their future generations. Having broken down the walls of animosity and bondage, the cross is the bridge that draws, unites, and reconciles both the perpetrators and victims together."

Chui Mai and her team are addressing the spiritual issue of historical war crimes against women in sex slavery, and by looking at this historical root, they are taking steps towards national healing from present day racial barriers with the Japanese.[166]

The Japanese on her team have inherited the task of both honoring the righteousness of their ancestors while seeking forgiveness for ancestral sins. Embracing the guilt of their Japanese identity, they chose to humble themselves and repent even though they were not directly involved in committing any war crimes. Their genuine repentance and apology brought healing to the survivors. The elderly women are now filled with a hope they did not have before meeting the reconciliation team. They all, with a few exceptions, accepted the apologies from the Japanese and responded well.

Most Chinese referred to the Japanese soldiers as "Japanese devils" and voraciously expressed a desire for revenge. While some poor families sold their daughters to the Imperial Japanese Military, in these testimonies from elderly survivors it was reported that their relatives at times bribed Japanese military with gifts and food to release the girls from sexual violence and rape.

Tellingly, most of these women had bound feet. A stark picture that tells the tale of oppression women had to endure for centuries in China. Bound feet symbolize torture of women for men's pleasure.

These are the stories of the women from Shanxi who had been hidden and forgotten for almost seventy years. Some of these women have told their stories for the first time in more than sixty years and some were unwilling to refer directly to their sexual enslavement. Their voice was taken, now we give them a platform to be remembered for generations to come. We noted their ages at the time they gave testimony between 2006 and 2011. Their stories also reveal their felt needs.

Liu Haiyun (eighty-three years old)

In the spring of 1944, Japanese soldiers from "Jiaokou Fortress" captured me and another woman from my village. I was eighteen years old and I had just given birth to my first daughter who was one month old at that time. The soldiers beat and broke my hip bones and raped me repeatedly during my three months' imprisonment. My body and soul were subjected to harsh abuses, shame, and pain that have remained with me and tortured me throughout my entire life. I still have nightmares of Japanese soldiers chasing me even now.

Li Jinyu (eighty years old; passed away in January, 2010)

In February of 1944, Japanese soldiers from "Jiaokou Fortress" came to my village to detain members of the Communist Military but they caught none, so they took it out on the villagers. Some forty to fifty men and women were taken to "Jiaokou Fortress" and imprisoned. The soldiers took eight beehives, a basket of plates and bowls, some food, as well as some rough cloth from my house. My eldest uncle was beaten to death by clubs in his house. A neighbor's little girl was so terrified and started crying, and I held her in my arms. But the soldiers tore her away from me, threw her down on the floor and stabbed her stomach with their bayonets. There was blood all over the floor. We were placed into separate rooms, beaten and raped repeatedly. We were detained for three to four days. Some members of my village gave some gifts to the

Japanese to secure our release. After my release, I could not work in the fields for five months. More than sixty years have passed on and most of the women have died with hatred (for the Japanese) in their hearts. Now those who are still living include Li Fulan (passed away in March, 2008), my uncle's daughter Li Jine (passed away in June, 2007) and I.

Wang E-hai (eighty-one years old)

I was fourteen years old in 1943 when I was taken away by the Japanese soldiers while I was at my maternal grandmother's house. About forty-fifty soldiers from the "Jiaokou Nanshan" camp surrounded our village. They were led by informers and "traitors" and their purpose was to capture the local guerilla units of the Communist Military. Except for two men who managed to escape, the other fourteen men from the local guerilla unit were all killed. My father was working in the transportation department and he was beaten every day and after he passed out, the soldiers poured cold water on him to wake him up. I was detained with twelve men and more than ten women at Nanshan Fortress for two months. All the men were killed. I was interrogated regarding information on the Communist Military. Whether it be day or night, us women were beaten and raped. We were so afraid and we suffered tremendously. Each woman was raped by at least five to six soldiers, sometimes even more. And it did not stop. After one soldier left, another one would come in. The women were abused continuously. Later, my village and family gathered together a substantial amount of money as well as some millet, eggs, and chickens to give to the soldiers. Some members of the "Weichihui" brought these gifts to the Japanese captain to secure my father's and my release. The soldiers threw me out after two months. I was almost dead. A Chinese cook saved and brought me to my home. These traumatic experiences have caused me to lose control of my bowels and to this day, I have a great fear of people.

Liu Haiyu (ninety years old)

In March of 1944, Japanese soldiers from the "Baijiagou Fortress" came to my village while I was cooking breakfast. I did not have time to escape. The soldiers beat and interrogated me, and accused me of working for the Communist military. More than ten people from my village were captured. The Japanese officer was "Jitianmao". That afternoon, I was locked in a small room. A few Japanese "devils" (soldiers) came in and raped me repeatedly. My body and soul suffered severe damages as a result of the tortures by the Japanese "devils". I have not had a good day for the rest of my life and cannot forget those painful days for the past sixty years. I hate the Japanese soldiers to the bones and the only comfort that I could have in my lifetime is to have the Japanese government made a public apology for their past crimes.

Feng Nu-er (eight-four years old)

I was confined for about a month by the Japanese soldiers in 1939. I still have back pains now because I slept in the open fields to hide from the soldiers before they captured me. Over sixty years have passed and the Japanese "devils" had lost the war and they had admitted their wrongs in legal courts, but they have neglected us, the victims. I have counted the days that have passed by in more than sixty years, but I have not seen any Japanese that has expressed a little apology and compensation. They probably have forgotten the sin and evil of invasion committed by their forefathers. They are not willing to let us mention those things that they are unhappy about. But we have not forgotten and we cannot forget. We remember, and we will let our descendants remember. We want compensation from the Japanese government. We must remember this grievance and we must take revenge! Our future generations must not forget this national hatred and family revenge.

Feng's son did not allow Chui Mai and her team to visit her in 2010 because he did not want his mother's "shameful" past to be known.

Yuan Gailian (eighty-five years old)

On May 17, 1942—I will never forget this day—the Japanese "devils" came to my village, "Gucheng", and captured forty to fifty villagers. All of them were killed at "Xijinggou" in "Gucheng" that very day. When night came, my family went through terrible sufferings and we had no place to bring our grievances to. I was seventeen years old at that time. For more than twenty days, I was tortured and given very little food. I have suppressed all this pain and suffering within me for sixty-five years, and today, I want to voice out: I want the Japanese people to apologize to me, compensate for my losses, and provide for my living and medical expenses.

Guo Fengying (eighty-eight years old. She passed away in January, 2008)

In February of 1944, Japanese "devils" from the "Jiaokou Fortress" attacked my village, "Liangjiashancun". They captured a number of men and women including me. After returning home, even though I had sought medical treatments, I did not completely recover. This is because the conditions at that time were poor, medications were scarce, and to avoid the harassment of the Japanese "devils", I had to hide out in other villages and sometimes, in the mountains. My illness failed to totally heal even after the war ended. Now if given the opportunity to file a lawsuit against the

Japanese government, it is important that the Japanese government knows that it was their fault. They must make a public apology to the victims and give me one hundred fifty thousand US dollars as compensation.

Li Jine (seventy-seven years old; passed away in June, 2007)

On the morning of February of 1944, some Japanese soldiers came to our village, "Yangzhuangcun". I was only fourteen years old at that time. The soldiers captured me, Li Fulan, and my uncle's sister, Li Jinyu as well as more than thirty women and took us to "Jiaokoujudian". I have not fully recovered even after so many years. I still cannot see clearly and the greatest damage from the (sexual) torture was the loss of my childbearing ability. With no children, I have no source of income now, and there is no one to take care of me in my old age. There is no place where we can voice our sufferings and grievances.

Guo Maohai (eighty-five years old)

I was fourteen years old when I was captured by the Japanese soldiers in July 1939. The soldiers stole everything from my village including cooking pots. About ten women and girls were captured including my older sister and younger sister who was twelve years old. My younger sister died that very night after the soldiers raped her. My older sister and I were detained for about ten days and tortured inside a village house. All of my family homes were burned down and my older brother was murdered. My older sister and I escaped by running away and our father sent us to the mountains to rest and to avoid public attention.

Liu Fenghai (eighty-one years old)

The Japanese soldiers captured me, my aunt, and another girl from our village in the spring of 1943. The soldiers wanted to catch the Communists and to plunder food. I was fourteen years old at that time. We were detained for six days and released after the local people gave gifts to the soldiers. But my aunt and the girl died after returning home. After I came home, I could not move, and I had to see the doctor as well as take medications. It was only a month later that I was able to work in the fields and do some light work. Although this experience took place more than sixty years ago, whenever I think about it, it feels like it happened only recently. We must not forget, we must never forget!

Qin Aizhen (eighty-three years old. She passed away in November, 2009)

In the evening of May 16, 1941, the officials in the Communist Party held an emergency meeting in "Hedi village", but some traitors in the village informed the Japanese. Japanese soldiers came to my village soon after that. I was thirteen years old when I was taken away by the Japanese soldiers. My uncle was also detained but was killed two days later. I was released after a month. I went through unspeakable sufferings and pain that are buried deep in my heart for years. Who would be able to vindicate us, the victims, and give us an impartial verdict?

Hao Gaiying (eighty-nine years old; passed away in February, 2007)

My two younger sisters (Hao Juxiang and Hao Gaixiang) and I were captured by the Japanese soldiers on the morning of April 18, 1939. As I was going home from my mother-in-law's house, I came across three Japanese "devils" and they chased me down. I was detained for about forty days and beaten until I could not move. The soldiers poured petrol into my husband's mouth and my mouth, millstones were pressed on our bodies, and we were hanged upside down from the ceiling beam. My husband was finally killed and he was stabbed more than twenty times by bayonets. I was almost dead when I was released and I had to crawl my way home. I was already eight months pregnant when I was captured and my baby only lived for two days after birth. I remarried but I could not bear any child because of the endless torture by the Japanese soldiers.

Hao Juxiang (eighty-eight years old)

In April of 1939, Japanese "devils" came to my village, "Nangoucun" and plundered, looted all our homes, and chopped down many trees. They also killed many soldiers from the Communist military at

"Hetaogou". There were three girls in my family: my eldest sister was nineteen, I was seventeen, and my youngest sister was fifteen. In May of 1939, a few Japanese "devils" broke into our home. They had guns in their hands and we were terrified. We were taken away, but our parents were killed on the spot. Under the evil control of the Japanese "devils", we were brutally beaten, tortured, and wounded from head to toe. The three of us would embrace and weep everyday— weeping for our dead parents and for our unbearable sufferings. After we were taken away, some kind neighbors and relatives helped bury our parents. When we were released, we carried with us a huge burden of anger and grief when we paid respect to our parents at their graves. Then we went to stay at a relative's home in the mountains, and we dared not return to our village until the Japanese military had surrendered.

Although these painful times have passed, we will never be able to forget our parents' deaths and the hideous acts of the Japanese "devils". But we are ageing and we do not have many days left. We need to seize the hour to secure justice from the Japanese "devils". Even though we are in our seventies and eighties, we are still strong and we can go out and testify to the Japanese government regarding these evidences and truths. If the Japanese government does not respond to our demands for justice, we must continue to persevere. I have heard that the Japanese government is very cunning— why are both the older generation and the younger generation so similar? They are similar in their "robbery" and "controlling" acts and behaviors as well as not having any reason or principle at all!

Hao Gaixiang (eighty-seven years old)

My two older sisters and I were captured by the Japanese soldiers in 1939 and I was fifteen years old. I was detained for about one month and released with the help of the village members. I still have fear of the Japanese if I see them now on TV or in my dreams.

Bai Xiuying (seventy-seven years old; passed away in June, 2008)

On September 13 in 1943, Japanese soldiers passed by my village. My elder sister, younger brother, and I were preparing to escape from our house but we ran into some Japanese soldiers. I was detained for about three days. I was interrogated daily by the soldiers who were trying to find out the location of the Communist Military.

Hao Yuelian (eighty-three years old)

On June 13th in 1943, I was at home when the front door was kicked open. Two Japanese "devils" charged in and pointed their guns at me. I was so terrified that I dared not say anything. I was sixteen years old when I was abducted by the Japanese soldiers. I was detained for about eleven days. We will remember all the crimes committed by the Japanese "devils". As a result of their cruel torture, I lost the ability to bear a child. I have no son or daughter. After my husband passed away, I was left alone and life is very difficult as I do not have any source of income. The Japanese government must bear the responsibility. It was their forefathers who brutally abused us and caused me to become a handicapped person with no ability to take care of myself. Therefore, we are always waiting for justice and to settle with the

Japanese people their evil and sin that were committed by them.

Li Gailan (eighty-five years old)

In 1941, the Japanese soldiers detained me for about ten days. Six women including me were taken captive but two of them died early on. My husband was also captured, but he escaped and went home.

Li Fulan (eighty years old; passed away in March, 2008)

In the early morning of February 1944, the Japanese "devils" ransacked my village. As it was still dark, all of us were still sleeping and we were trapped in our homes. Had it been during the daytime, we would have been warned and able to escape into the mountains. I suffered terribly and almost lost my life to the Japanese military. The Japanese government should give me the compensation that I rightly deserve. They should compensate two hundred thousand US dollars for my emotional pain and suffering.

Li Ailian (eighty-two years old)

Both my husband and I were in the Communist military, and my husband was captured three times by the Japanese military and tortured. My second brother was killed by Japanese soldiers. I was captured in 1944 when I was seventeen years old, and I suffered a week of torture.

Ren Lan-E (eighty-one years old)

I was fourteen years old when I was taken by the Japanese soldiers in 1944 and detained for about a month. My father was burned to death in our house and my older brother also was slaughtered. The Japanese soldiers were like beasts: they would not allow me to rest at all throughout the long night, and if I resisted a little, they would hit me. I was afraid, yet I hated them so much! I was given very little rice and food to eat. One night about a month later, there were no Japanese soldiers around to abuse me and there was no guard watching over me because the Communist military was attacking their base. I seized this opportunity to run away and I ran all the way home and went into hiding. Over sixty years have passed and we should settle our accounts with the Japanese "devils". I want them to be accountable for what they did to me.

Zhao Zhilan (eighty years old; passed away)

I was captured for half a month in 1943 by the Japanese soldiers. I managed to escape on my own.

Zhao Lanying (eighty-eight years old)

In 1939, a guerilla military unit was set up in "Dongliangxiang", my village, and my husband was the unit leader. On May 19, 1941, my husband came home to see me but a (Chinese) traitor saw him and informed the Japanese soldiers. Both my husband and I were captured by the Japanese soldiers in 1941. My husband was forced to drink two large buckets of water (water torture). We were detained for about twenty days and released together. Although over sixty years have passed, I will remember the crimes committed by the Japanese "devils" in my heart. I want to discuss what happened with the Japanese people.

Fan Lianhua (eighty-eight years old)

In August of 1941, Japanese "devils" came to our village and took me captive. I was eighteen years old when the Japanese soldiers held me for ten days. My husband was a soldier in the Communist Military for four years and he was shot dead. Before he died in a farmer's house, I was able to see him for the last time.

Healing

In a city in northeast China in what's called the Garden of Peace, Chui Mai saw a surprising and prophetic stone statue sitting in the midst of trees and flowers. It was of a Japanese woman in a kimono embracing a Chinese lady wearing a traditional *cheongsam*[167] dress. Only in 2008, did Chui Mai see Chinese and Japanese Christians embracing one another just like the statute.

"Thank you for taking the time to travel to see them and all the sacrifices you've made. Your visits have sent them the message of 'you matter, your story matters' and helped restore their dignity," I said to Chui Mai at the end of our visit. I had tremendous respect for this woman from Singapore. She was short in stature, but underneath her cheery face was a steely determination. That's what has helped her pioneer a work of forgiveness and reconciliation in this very issue of Imperial Japanese Military sex slavery that is volatile and incendiary in a country that still despises and blames the present generation in Japan for the sins of their fathers. Her team is dealing with the generational cycles of pain and hatred.

Acknowledgment of the truth to promote reconciliation and trust again and spiritual reconciliation on the deepest level is urgently needed between Japan and China and Korea and other nations affected by Japanese war crimes. And for the women and children who were put through this, deep healing and restoration. Just as Auschwitz is an important political symbol and heart of the lesson of World War II, I hope the women who survived Imperial Japanese Military sex slavery will be the face and symbol for World War II in Asia. I pray that our children and future generations will not have to deal with the bitterness and alienating barriers that have marked the previous generations in China, Korea, and Japan because of strongholds of hate rooted in history.[168]

Let us expose the ancient wounds that were dealt to these women, without self-righteous accusations, dishonest cover-ups, and let us tell the raw truth. A sincere apology and contrition that the Japanese team members demonstrated, is proving to be one of the keys to opening doors that have been closed for decades. Chui Mai's Japanese team members have discovered the life changing power of forgiveness and confession. Until they came on the scene, no Japanese had gone to these Chinese survivors of Imperial Japanese Military sex slavery to identify with the Japanese military and government and confess, repent, and ask for forgiveness. A type of truth and reconciliation commission is required as well to mete out justice and accountability, then forgiveness and amnesty.

The issue of military sex slaves and their healing is relevant– their healing could ultimately affect and impact relationships between nations. We're not only calling for an apology to women but it should engage entire societies in Asia and beyond that have been affected by the Imperial Japanese Military invasion and human rights violations committed by their soldiers. We must remember and pray for the healing of survivors of sex slavery, victims of yesterday, and victims of today. An official memorial to victims, whether it is a physical one or even in the writing of their stories, gives great honor to them– dignity even in their death. How vital it is to learn from the evils of government enforced sex slavery and from the past. There is frightening potential in each of us to commit inhumane crimes against humanity. Ordinary people have the potential to do unimaginable evil.

Japanese government leaders have never apologised for the crimes against humanity and for systematically enslaving women from colonies they deemed inferior. The issue of military sex slavery is a social mirror for Japan, China and Korea and tells of how they treat and view women and how these people groups view each other. In Japan, the prime minister and government officials must stop their visits to Yasukuni Shrine—

instead of worshipping war criminals, they must bring these perpetrators to account and plainly expose their crimes against humanity.

For seventy years, the Japanese government has downplayed its role in the systemic enslavement of young women. But there has been too much evidence that confirms the direct involvement including evidence from the Japanese government and military archives and Japanese courts affirmed the abuses victims have suffered to the testimonies of victims themselves that have been verified through photographs and eyewitnesses. Japan must face one of its darkest periods in history, the military comfort women system, and in doing so, they are morally obligated to look in the face at current day sex trafficking, abuse and injustice against women and children.

China, Korea, and Japan are three nations at the crossroads, dealing with issues of national identity and rising nationalism. These nations need national identities that are not based on hating the Japanese or as victims or one that justifies its wartime atrocities and vilifies victims, but one that is full of peace. Racial healing is needed. The wound inflicted was never dealt with at the end of the war or any time thereafter. Teaching the truth of what happened in the Asia Pacific war and the plight of women in military sex slavery is vital in school textbooks. In Japan, China, Korea, and other nations, it is imperative to learn from history, but not to overemphasize the atrocities to spur racial hatred and nationalism. In East Asia, particularly in China, generations have been taught to hate Japan. A seven-year-old girl in a guesthouse said she was afraid of the Japanese when they came near her. The intensity of hatred for the Japanese is reflected in what should be friendly sports matches and the anti-Japan riots. Denials and distortions of war crimes and massacres by the Japanese government officials continually rip open a wound that was there all along. This must be resolved or else tensions could escalate.

Reconciliation brings together former enemies. Several activists I've spoken with have said the answer may lie in a grassroots reconciliation movement in Japan led by Japanese. One of the noble examples of forgiveness is from the communist military and managers of the Fushun concentration camp. They gave total amnesty to Japanese soldiers who had committed grave crimes including murder, torture, and rapes of civilians. In turn, these Japanese became indebted to China and were involved in a life-long campaign for the truth in textbooks, in Japanese society, and peace building and reconciliation with China, even when the two nations did not have diplomatic relations.

We have an opportunity to learn from historical injustices, and out of these ashes, birth a new justice movement to ensure the rights of all survivors and the freedom of modern day sex slaves alike. In our generation, we can help bring an end to modern day slavery and to the blocks to peace and unity between Japan and the nations in Asia and the nations affected by the Japanese military invasion. Racial reconciliation between Japan, China and Korea and a message of forgiveness is urgently needed so that:

1. The truth of Japan's unresolved war issues such as military sex slavery be known and taught in Japan (goal is for people to see truth and for justice to be realized).

2. Justice to happen on behalf of survivors of Imperial Japanese Military sex slavery and current day sex slaves.

3. Relationships with Japan rebuilt in Asia based upon an official apology and moral responsibility by the Japan government, radical forgiveness to flow between the nations.

Grassroots healing movement

"Darkness cannot drive out darkness; only light can do that. Hate cannot drive out hate; only love can do that." ~Martin Luther King, Jr.

We have seen the issue of military sex slavery through three different prisms: the survivor of military sex slavery, the perpetrator former Japanese soldier, and through generational racism. I became aware of the wounds of Asian history at a young age and how they were seeping into our present and debilitating our future.

This left a soft spot, a curiosity, to find out what was at the heart of the issue? Why couldn't Koreans and Chinese really get along with the Japanese? Why do they hate them even when they are Christian and supposed to love their enemies? I became interested in generational pain and generational racism. We need generational healing and reconciliation for the generational pain.

There is an urgent need for a grassroots healing and reconciliation process that will also deal with modern day systemic racism: in Japan, against ethnic Koreans and Chinese, who are treated like second-class citizens, and even generations later in China and Korea, hatred for the Japanese runs deep while the Japanese themselves cannot understand why they are hated and distrusted. Forgiving the Japanese will set the Koreans and Chinese free from bondage and self-rejection and self-hatred. It will set them free from the prison that has distorted their personality and identity, culture, and expression of faith.

There is a need for truth to be brought forth without ambiguity and a peace between the nations, a matter all the more pressing in light of North Korea's nuclear ambitions in the region and vitriolic hatred towards the

Japanese for colonizing the peninsula. North Korea has never forgotten the abuses that the Koreans had to endure and perhaps will never move on unless the Japanese government does something drastic and with loss of face, begs for forgiveness.

In the midst of the Japanese government's denials of its direct involvement in implementing military sex slavery and their unwillingness to repent and ask the surviving military sex slaves for forgiveness, there is also a group of courageous Japanese activists fighting on behalf of the victims and standing for the truth to be told about Japan's wartime atrocities. This is a beautiful aspect of this international human rights movement that does not get as much attention as the cover up by the government.

For years, activists, academics, and other stakeholders in the historical memory debate have wondered aloud about what it would take to have a breakthrough and move forward. Reconciliation has not been discussed in a formal way in East Asia. The most pressing matter is that these elderly surviving victims need healing. A debilitating sense of shame has prevented the victims from speaking out. Their families have not talked about it. Just as it is in North America and most of the world, it is considered shameful or a taboo to talk about rape or sexual violence openly in China and Korea. The women also felt it was their fault. They internalized the crimes committed against them and felt they could not speak out and hold their heads up high. By sharing these stories, we are breaking the shame. It is time that their stories are told to the world. It is time they know it wasn't their fault and that they are worthy of being honored.

Yet it is next to impossible to forgive when you have never heard an open acknowledgment of the injustices that have wounded you or your people. That is why the pain of the surviving Japanese military sex slaves is so heightened. The act of confession is particularly powerful in healing individuals and a nation's historical memory. It was in receiving forgiveness that compelled the Japanese soldiers, who had committed countless rapes against women, to testify of their grave crimes and become some of the more powerful voices for justice for military sex slaves. There is power in confession and in forgiveness.

On the spiritual side, forgiveness and reconciliation can heal the bitter historical divisions between the nations. On a grassroots level, healing has come when one person has humbly identified with the sins and injustices committed by her people against another people group and subsequently asked for forgiveness. Wars have started because of racism– the Japanese had their superior race theory that was kindred with Nazism. One does not need to look further than the Middle East to see how ethnic hatred, religious conflict and strife are causing wars. The Jewish Holocaust and the Asian forgotten war crimes are interestingly still at the center of political and ethnic conflict in their respective regions even seventy years after the end of World War II. That is why it is so urgent to heal these relations.

We need more voices that bring the message of forgiveness and healing on Imperial Japanese military sex slavery and other Japanese war crimes. Mike Honda has been a powerful spokesperson on racial reconciliation and healing for the survivors. While no one can force reconciliation to happen, those who know the truth can begin to pray and begin to dialogue with one person at a time.

The church was silent while these women were taken and forced into sex slavery. While it is difficult to prove whether they were aware of what was going on, what's clear now is that the church cannot be silent anymore. We can pray for healing for these victims and for nations. Prayer will erect change more than any humanly initiated action. I dream of seeing a movement of compassionate passion for social justice, healing, and reconciliation for these nations affected by Japanese military invasions and colonialism so that the next generation will have a fresh legacy of unity and a just peace in Asia.

The greatest lesson we can learn from military sex slavery is that we should prevent it from being repeated. But gender-based abuses such as sex trafficking and gender discrimination and the enslavement of girls and women in Syria and Iraq are still ongoing realities in Asia and around the world. There is a recurrent cycle of sex slavery that must be abolished. Human rights violations continue, as an extension of Japanese military sex slavery, in the modern day forms of sex trafficking and racial discrimination. We need to heal the wounds of the past in order to move on in the present and future with peace and freedom. Unresolved memories and traumas cause the culture to become diseased. Repercussions are real. We must pray that all barriers that divide ethnic groups and generations are removed and that this Imperial Japanese Military sex slavery issue will have a day of reckoning.

Afterword

I wrote this book to tell the world about one of the largest cases of human trafficking in the twentieth century—the comfort women system of sexual slavery for the Imperial Japanese Military—and to galvanize a movement to stand up against the oppression and enslavement of people. The comfort women system was a grave injustice that was never dealt with at the end of World War II. History infects the present and can determine our future if we do not take the time to analyze, understand the past, and change the course of history.

The suffering of women in Imperial Japanese Military sex slavery happened seventy years ago, yet today there are still 4.5 million women in forced prostitution and thousands of women being kidnapped, bought and sold like animals in the Middle East. In our living memory, women, men, and children continue to suffer from rape being used against them as a war weapon. Nearly thirty-six million people are suffering in silence as victims of human trafficking in either sex slavery or forced labor. For this slavery to end, we must care enough to get involved in fighting this scourge against humanity through contributing our time, skills and experience and our money (contribute to vetted organizations in underserved areas that are fighting human slavery).

Most of the Imperial Japanese Military sex slave survivors I have interviewed have died before receiving a sincere apology from the Japanese government that would have brought healing. I hope the voices of these elderly survivors will rouse people to identify with their sufferings. The breaking of their silence was a heroic act. They could have kept these secrets to their graves. But instead, to prevent it from happening again, they had the courage to speak up. Their stories needed to be told. As a way to honor these women, their legacies, and contributions to the prevention of sexual violence in global conflicts, we must reflect on their stories and ensure the world eradicates sexual slavery and exploitation of all forms.

I also wanted this book to offer a chance for true reconciliation. Unlike Germany, Japan has not come to terms with its wartime memories and carries a victim mentality due to the atomic bomb attacks. Closure of the war wounds is urgently needed. Reconciliation and healing needs to happen for the healing of both the victims and perpetrators alike, as well as for the nations involved.

When people see that this crime against humanity occurred, I hope they will understand the need to take responsibility. Indeed, the Japanese government needs to take moral responsibility. But it also goes beyond them. The entire world needs to take responsibility. If we don't, then we will be perpetuating the cycle of enslavement, abuse, and racism.

Seventy years after the end of World War II, the elderly survivors of Imperial Japanese Military sex slavery have left a legacy of moral courage and human rights activism. What happened to these women must be remembered. We must turn over and over again, like a burnished stone in our hands, the universal lessons from crimes against humanity. No one should ever be enslaved and exploited, thus let Imperial Japanese Military sex slavery or comfort women be remembered in history as something that is unequivocally unacceptable.

South China Morning Post article by Silenced No More author, Sylvia Yu

12 December, 2017

Wartime sex slaves still emerging in China, but some will take secret to the grave

Surviving 'comfort women' and their children pledge to continue fight for apology and compensation for suffering at hands of Japanese military

In the 12 months leading up to Wednesday's 80th anniversary of the start of the Nanking massacre, a researcher in the city discovered two previously unknown Chinese survivors of forced sexual slavery organised by the Japanese military.

Liu Guangjian, from the Memorial Hall for Victims in Nanjing Massacre by Japanese Invaders, has been researching the "comfort women" issue for the two-year-old, government-run Comfort Women Museum in Nanjing.

He said there were only 15 Chinese survivors left, the last of the comfort women who had testified publicly in China. He visited seven in Hainan last year, but two had since died.

Liu said two new survivors had come forward in the past year to testify of their suffering in Japanese military brothels.

"One was from Hunan, another one was in Zhejiang," he said. "The women didn't even know they were comfort women. When these women shared their suffering with the others, people passed on their stories to the researchers. After identification by specialists, they were confirmed as comfort women."

One survivor who testified 36 years ago, He Yuelian, still has traumatic flashbacks so intense she will scream "Get out! Get out!" day or night – 74 years after her terrifying ordeal in a Japanese military brothel.

In 1943, He, now 89, was 15 when Japanese soldiers invaded her village in Wuxiang county in Shanxi province. Two soldiers raped her. The soldiers ransacked her village and tortured and killed several men. They rounded up He and six girls and forced them to serve as sex slaves in a military brothel.

"I was bleeding [from the rapes] but that did not stop the raping and torture from the Japanese soldiers," she said, her leathery face contorted in an angry scowl.

The Japanese military used the euphemism comfort women to describe the girls and women rounded up or trafficked from all over the Asia-Pacific and forced into prostitution to comfort soldiers in military brothels called comfort stations. There were more than 1,000 comfort stations in China alone, mostly on the front lines of war. Scholars say up to 400,000 girls and women were trafficked in the highly organised military sexual slavery system.

The Japanese military set up the first comfort women stations in Shanghai in 1931 and went on to establish military brothels across China and East and Southeast Asia during the second world war.

Due to He's constant bleeding, she was sent home after new Chinese girls were forced into the comfort station. But she was captured again and forced to serve in another military brothel for two months.

She was raped continuously. Someone from her village spotted her one day and informed her family, which then gathered enough money to buy her back from the Japanese soldiers. After returning to her village, she remained depressed and in ill health. At 18, she married but due to the repeated rapes, she was unable to become pregnant.

"I suffered deeply. It cost me everything," she said. "I was pure, not aware of sex. It was a never-ending nightmare."

He said she would never stop fighting for an apology and compensation for her suffering at the hands of the Japanese soldiers.

"I remember all the devilish injustice the Japanese army committed against us," she said. "Shouldn't the Japanese government accept its unshirkable responsibility in committing these brutal acts? We were regular women but became handicapped. Because of this, we are waiting for the clearing of this debt by the Japanese people."

After the war, her younger sister had pity on He, who was depressed about her infertility, and gave her baby daughter to He and her husband to raise. "I survived because of my adopted daughter and the special love between us," He said. "Taking care of her kept me going."

He and her husband grew corn and grains and took on odd jobs to put food on the table for their daughter, Cheng Aixian.

"My mother did every kind of tough farming work," Cheng said. "She dug in the river, planted trees. She needed to survive. They were so poor."

In 1981, when she was 53, He testified publicly together with another woman from her village who had been forced into prostitution. She later joined a lawsuit to sue Japan for compensation and an apology for the severe pain she endured.

Why did she wait 38 years from the time she was forced into sex slavery before going public? "I was too ashamed to talk about it," she said, adding that she suffered because of her long silence.

She said there were other former comfort women sex slaves who would take their secret to the grave.

Liu, the researcher in Nanjing, said the Japanese military's comfort women system was "extremely inhumane and brought cruel destruction to the women".

"It was also a double trauma [physical and psychological] especially for the comfort woman survivors, because they also had to deal with the judgment from their families, friends and neighbours after the war," Liu said. "Living in a conservative culture and environment, [the survivors] had to live with immense pressure and trauma."

He's son-in-law, Bai Zengfa, said her trauma was "very intense".

"Every time she thinks about her experiences with the soldiers, she'll scream 'Get out!' Sometimes she doesn't know she's screaming," he said.

In 1981, the year she publicly testified that she had been a comfort woman, He also told her daughter, then 15, about her wartime trauma. Cheng said she sensed at the time that her mother's health was frail.

"I felt sad and angry," she said. "Her health is very poor due to the lifelong effects of sex slavery. Her pain is our pain. Even now I feel angry. I want justice."

Bai and Cheng said they had vowed to keep fighting for justice for He after "she leaves this world".

"We have to tell the world," Cheng said. "I will insist on chasing justice for my mother. I won't stop. The Japanese must apologise directly to my mother and all the elderly comfort women."

Seven years ago, He met some Japanese people for the first time since her enslavement at the comfort station. A Japanese Christian reconciliation team called Healing River-Rainbow Bridge made several trips to visit survivors and their families and apologised for their treatment at the hands of the Japanese military.

Tomoko Hasegawa, one of the leaders of Healing River-Rainbow Bridge, said she was inspired after hearing a former

Japanese soldier speak of his support for Wan Aihua, the first Chinese comfort women to go public about her experiences as a sex slave in Japanese military brothels.

Hasegawa said she hoped the team's reconciliation work would help reveal the historical truth and bring healing to the survivors of military sex slavery, their children and future generations in China, Japan and Korea. She said that although younger Chinese had not experienced the war, they "still hate the Japanese".

He, Cheng and Bai said the apologies had changed their view of ordinary Japanese people.

"We cried because we were touched by the apologies from the Japanese Christians ... before we felt hatred [for the Japanese] for the trauma done to our mother," Cheng said. "The feelings are so complex. I really hated the Japanese soldiers and what they did. But we don't hate the Japanese people any more."

In 1982, Zhang Shuangbing, 54, met an older woman in his village who told him she had been forced into being a comfort woman in Japanese military brothels. He was disturbed by her constant weeping. He met other women with the same experiences and volunteered to help them, making medical appointments for them and applying for medical subsidies from the government on their behalf.

He eventually resigned from his teaching job when the work of helping the traumatised women consumed his schedule.

Every month, he delivers a monthly stipend to the women. He said he had also helped survivors participate in 16 lawsuits in Japan since 1992 calling on the Japanese government to sincerely apologise. The last one was in 2007. But all the lawsuits failed to get the women the apology and compensation they demanded.

"The compensation amount that we asked for in 1992 was US$120,000 per woman," Zhang said. "Until now, 25 years have already passed. The Japanese government is still neglecting the sorrow and pain of the comfort women survivors and this shows their inhumanity."

He said they were now demanding compensation of US$1 million per survivor, and the fight would continue even after the last one died.

"I'll keep appealing and fighting for comfort women until I die," he said. "I really feel bad about the comfort women survivors as they pass away one by one. I feel sad.

"The Japanese recruited these women to be comfort women sex slaves. This is a fact. I believe one day the Japanese government will apologise. I have hope in this."

The apology from the Japanese government that would satisfy him would be directly given to the survivors but also in a "public way through media and television channels", he said.

He said that if the Japanese government did not apologise in a way that helped the women, generations of Chinese people would continue to have anger and unforgiveness in their hearts for Japanese military war crimes and human rights violations before and during the second world war.

"I definitely have intense hatred for them because I've heard so many stories of suffering comfort women," Zhang said.

Bryan Druzin, law professor at Chinese University of Hong Kong, said: "Unlike Germany, Japan has never fully come to terms with its past. It is yet to explicitly acknowledge the tens of thousands of comfort women who were raped by soldiers of the Imperial Japanese Army before and during the second world war."

Yoon Mee-hyang, co-chairwoman of the Korean Council for the Women Drafted for Military Sexual Slavery by Japan, said the 33 remaining survivors in South Korea – out of 237 who registered with the government – including some who were enslaved in China, wanted recognition of the Japanese government's legal responsibility for sexual slavery under the Japanese military, and a formal apology.

"Unless past histories across Korea, China, and Japan are properly cleared, it will be difficult to form a future-oriented relationship between China and Japan," she said. "The Japanese government's recognition of past crimes and the fulfilment of its responsibilities will take some time, but I think it will eventually happen."

In a speech two years ago, marking the 70th anniversary of Japan's surrender, Japanese Prime Minister Shinzo Abe reaffirmed the "heartfelt apology for its actions during the war" offered by his predecessors but stopped short of directly mentioning the plight of comfort women and the Nanking massacre.

China says Japanese soldiers killed more than 300,000 people in the six-week massacre, which started on December 13, 1937, the day the Japanese captured the city, now known as Nanjing.

The Japanese government says it issued a sufficient apology through a statement in 1993 by then chief cabinet secretary Yohei Kono that acknowledged the Japanese authorities' role in coercing the women.

Footnotes

[1] No definitive number of Imperial Japanese Military sex slaves exists, but researchers from The Republic of Korea suggest that two hundred thousand women were forced into the comfort women system. From my interview with Su Zhiliang, a Professor from Shanghai Normal University and Director of the China Comfort Women Research Centre, on August of 2004, he said the number is four hundred thousand. Of that number, he said, two hundred thousand women were from China.

[2] "Human Trafficking," http://www.unodc.org/southeastasiaandpacific/en/topics/illicit-trafficking/human-trafficking-definition.html, accessed July 2015 THE ORIGINAL S ITE IS NO LONGER WORKING.

[3] The United Nations estimates that twenty-one million people around the world are in slavery, but the Global Slavery Index states that the global figure is closer to 35.8 million people in forced labor and sex slavery.

[4] The Women's International War Crimes Tribunal for the Trial of Japan's Military Sexual Slavery. From henceforth I will refer to this as the Judgment, p. 83

[5] Yoshimi, Yoshiaki, *Comfort Women: Sexual Slavery in the Japanese Military During World War II* (New York: Columbia University Press, 2000), 37.

[6] Yoon, Mee-hyang, *The Korean Council for the Women Drafted for Military Sexual Slavery*, accessed August 30, 2006, http://www.womenandwar.net/english/menu_04.php.

[7] "Washington Coalition for Comfort Women Issues: Historical timeline of the Comfort Women system and redress movement," accessed May 2011, http://www.comfort-women.org/history.html

[8] "An Exhibit That Unites Faiths," *The Los Angeles Times*, October 14, 2000.

[9] The phenomena of a captive identifying and sympathizing with a captor.

[10] 'The Women's International War Crimes Tribunal for the Trial of Japan's Military Sexual Slavery' held in December 2000 was convened by non-governmental organizations throughout Asia because the Allies failed to prosecute Japanese officials for the crimes of military sexual slavery despite evidence of the 'comfort women' system. This crime against humanity has gone unpunished for more than sixty years. In a 'Peoples' Tribunal' setting, the NGOs wanted to give a platform for survivors of Japanese military sexual slavery to speak. The tribunal examined the evidence, developed a historical record and applied principles of international law to the evidence.

[11] "Taken Away," Asian Week, November 24, 2000.

[12] Kwon, Hee Soon. "The military sex slavery issue and Asian Peace," The Korean Council for the Women Drafted for the Military Sexual Slavery by Japan. Paper presented at "The First East Asian Women's Forum," Tokyo, Japan, October 20-22, 1994.

[13] Kwon. Ibid.

[14] This TVPA legislation created new federal crimes and enhanced penalties to fight sexual assault and domestic violence and new programs for law enforcement agencies, prosecution offices, and victim services organizations.

[15] The 1787 Alien Tort Claims Act is a law that allows foreigners to sue for violations of international law in American courts.

[16] The Peace Treaty of San Francisco or San Francisco Peace Treaty was signed between Japan and the Allied forces (forty-eight nations) on September 8, 1951 to not only end the war and Allied Occupation by returning the right to rule to Japan but to deal with war-related issues.

[17] Holocaust issues at the U.S. State Department can be found on the

website. http://www.state.gov/www/regions/eur/holocausthp.html

[18] Barry A. Fisher and Iris Chang, "With U.S. Collusion, Japan Shutters Its Past," *Los Angeles Times*, July 31, 2001.

18

[19] Ibid.

[20] The "Military Comfort Women" issue was never acknowledged in the 1965 Bilateral Treaty between Korea and Japan.

[21] McDougall, Gay J, "*Contemporary Forms of Slavery: Systematic rape, sexual slavery and slavery-like practices during armed conflict,*" At the 50th Session of the United Nations Commission on Human Rights, Sub-Commission on Prevention of Discrimination and Protection of Minorities, New York, 1998.

[22] The Treaty on Basic Relations between Japan and the Republic of Korea established diplomatic relations for the first time between the two countries and was signed on June 22, 1965.

[23] Totsuka, Etsuro, "*Postwar responsibilities of Japan: "Comfort Women", military sexual slavery — Non-fulfillment of obligations for apology, compensation, and punishment and the criticism of the treaty defense by Japan,*" Human Rights Council, Universal Periodic Review, New York, 2008.

[24] In a six-week rampage in China's capital Nanking in December 1937, the Imperial Japanese Military killed approximately three hundred thousand civilians and soldiers and raped at least twenty thousand women and girls. This atrocity became known as The Rape of Nanking.

[25] Unit 731 was a special unit of the Imperial Japanese military with a large budget authorized by the Japanese Emperor that specialized in creating biochemical weapons or weapons of mass destruction, and carrying out secret medical experiments on humans including captured Allied soldiers. The gruesome military-run experiments were regarded as some of the worst human rights violations in history.

[26] Rape of Nanjing Redress Coalition (RNRC) is an American organization founded by Asian-Americans to raise awareness of and bring redress to victims of the Rape of Nanjing. RNRC believes that if the Japanese government were to issue an apology and give reparations that it would bring healing to the Asian American communities in North America. http://rnrc-us.org/about.htm

[27] Ryan Kim, "Survivors protest anniversary / Testimony about Rape of Nanking," *San Francisco Chronicle,* September 07, 2001, http://articles.sfgate.com/2001-09-07/news/17620097_1_japanese-soldiers-japanese-imperial-military-japanese-military

[28] A Seoul-based NGO that advocates for survivors of imperial Japanese military sex slavery is called 'The Korean Council for the

Women Drafted for Military Sexual Slavery by Japan'. In addition to their international lobbying work, they provide shelter for the survivors and have established a museum to preserve historical records of the experience of these women. https://www.womenandwar.net/

29 The Hague Justice Portal: http://www.haguejusticeportal.net/eCache/DEF/12/015.html
30 "Memory and Reconciliation in the Asia Pacific," *George Washington University Project*, http://www.gwu.edu/~memory/data/judicial/comfortwomen_us/hwang%20geum%20joo.html
31 "Memory and Reconciliation in the Asia Pacific" *George Washington University Project*, http://www.gwu.edu/~memory/data/judicial/comfortwomen_us/hwang%20geum%20joo.html
32 Ibid.
33 Ibid.
34 "China refuses to apologise for wave of anti-Japan riots," *The Sunday Times*, April 18, 2005, http://www.timesonline.co.uk/tol/news/world/article382299.ece.
35 Stetz and Oh, *Legacies of the Comfort Women of World War II*. (UK: Routledge, 2000) 189..
36 Yoshiko Nozaki. The Asia-Pacific Journal: Japan Focus. The Comfort Women Controversy: History and Testimony
37 The March 1st Movement or Samil Movement was an impassioned protest for the liberty of the Korean people from the oppression and human rights violations under the brutal and extremely discriminatory policies of the Japanese colonial regime. The movement was a watershed marker of sorts, much like the catalytic Rosa Parks bus event, in the Korean peoples' struggle for independence and freedom.
38 Kazuko, Watanabe. Militarism, Colonialism, and the Trafficking of Women: Comfort Women Forced into Sexual Labor for Japanese Soldiers. Bulletin of Concerned Asian Scholars 26 (October-December 1994).
39 Connie Kang in her book, Home was the Land of Morning Calm, writes that Han is "this indescribable fate that Koreans feel in the depths of their hearts and deepest recesses of their souls . . . the Korean tenet of eternal woe, unrequited love, and unending hope and wishes" (298).
40 Stetz and Oh. *Legacies*, 189.
41 The Women's International War Crimes Tribunal For the Trial of Japan's Military Sexual Slavery: Judgment. Page 223. December 2001.
42 The tribunal was also known as the "Tokyo Trials, the Tokyo War Crimes Tribunal", and began April 29, 1946 to prosecute the leaders of Imperial Japan for war crimes.

[43] Judgment. Page 193. .
[44] "Comfort Women: Japan, Korean victims of the Asia-Pacific War (including Kim Hak-Soon)." Memory and Reconciliation in the Asia-Pacific. Dec. 1991. George Washington University. <http://www.gwu.edu/~memory/yang/new/data/judicial/comfortwome n_japan/haksun.html>.
[45] Judgment page 224.
[46] Ibid, 335.
[47] Yoshimi, *Comfort Women,* 33.
[48] Watanabe Kazuko, Militarism, Colonialism, and the Trafficking of Women," 7.
[49] Huffington Post. *Seeking Justice— Or at Least the Truth – For Comfort Women* June 25, 2014. http://www.huffingtonpost.com/christine-ahn/seeking-justiceor-at-comfort-women_b_5526919.html.
[50] The Asahi Shimbun. "Ex-'comfort women,' supporters submit new findings, demand Abe face past." June 3, 2014. <http://ajw.asahi.com/article/behind_news/social_affairs/AJ20140603 0013>.
[51] Hicks, George. *The Comfort Women: Japan's Brutal Regime of Enforced Prostitution in the Second World War.* (New York: W.W. Norton & Company, 1995), 176
[52] Hicks, *The Comfort Women,* 176.
[53] Yoshimi, *Comfort Women,* 193.
[54] The National Diet is Japan's legislature and is divided into two houses: a lower house called the House of Representatives, and the House of Councillors. The Diet is also responsible for selecting the Prime Minister.
[55] Yoshimi, *Comfort Women,* 34.
[56] Christine Chinkin, "Women's International Tribunal on Japanese Military Sexual Slavery," American Journal of International Law 95 (April 2001), 335.
[57] Ibid.
[58] Judgment page 225.
[59] Horsley, William. "Korean WWII sex slaves fight on." August 9, 2005. http://news.bbc.co.uk/2/hi/asia-pacific/4749467.stm
[60] Ibid.
[61] Kim Dae-jung was the 8th President of South Korea from 1998 to 2003, and the Nobel Peace Prize winner in 2000.
[62] Jeong is a special kind of Korean love or connection denoting affection, adoration for both people, enemies and even objects.
[63] Ibid.
[64] Ustinia Dolgopol, Women's Voices, Women's Pain, 21.
[65] Ibid, 29.
[66] Ibid, 28. Won-loy Chan, an interpreter who interviewed many of the

comfort women in Burma wrote a book on his experiences called "Burma—The Untold Story", (Presidio, Norato, California, 1986). In the book, he notes comfort women estimates were as high as 200,000 and they were daughters of farmers or peasants and most had come to Burma against their will.

[67] Ustinia Dolgopol and Snehal Paranjape, "Comfort Women: An Unfinished Ordeal. Report of a Mission", (Geneva, Switzerland: International Commission of Jurists, 1994), 53.

[68] "Japan's Mass Rape and Sexual Enslavement of Women and Girls from 1932-1945: The Comfort Women System," 3.

[69] Dower, John, "Embracing Defeat: Japan in the Wake of World War II", (New York: W.W. Norton & Company Inc., 1999) 124-126.

[70] "Japan's Mass Rape and Sexual Enslavement of Women and Girls from 1932-1945: The Comfort Women System," 3.

[71] "Japan's Mass Rape and Sexual Enslavement of Women and Girls from 1932-1945: The Comfort Women System," 3.

[72] Ibid, 3.

[73] Rita Nakashima Brock and Susan Brooks Thistlethwaite, "Casting Stones: Prostitution and Liberation in Asia and the United States," (Minneapolis: Fortress Press, 1996) 74.

[74] Ustinia Dolgopol, "Women's Voices, Women's Pain". (Human Rights Quarterly. 1995) 29.

[75] John R. Pritchard and Sonia M. Zaide and Donald Cameron Watt, The Tokyo war crimes trial: the complete transcripts of the proceedings of the International Military Tribunal for the Far East in twenty-two volumes. (New York: Garland Pub., 1981), 47, 233; 49, 638.

[76] Yoshiko Nozaki, "Feminism, Nationalism, and the Japanese Textbook Controversy over 'Comfort Women,'" in Feminism and Antiracism: International Struggles for Justice, France Winddance Twine et al., eds. (New York: New York University Press, 2001), 170.

[77] Soh, Sarah C., "Japan's Responsibility Toward Comfort Women Survivors," JPRI Working Paper No. 77, May 2001.

[78] Yoshimi, Comfort Women, 174.

[79] Judgment p. 221.

[80] The Netherlands, the U.S., Australia and France established its own War Crimes Section at the South East Asian Command (SEAC) headquarters in Singapore and there they maintained the "closest liaison" with its Allies so that everyone could achieve one aim. The Netherlands also formed its own team to investigate war crimes committed against Dutch nationals. Piccigallo, 178. But no such team was formed for the Koreans or other colonized countries by Japan for the Tokyo Trials.

[81] Dolgopol and Paranjape, Comfort Women,135.

[82] Chapkis, Wendy, Live Sex Acts: Women Performing Erotic Labour,

(New York: Routledge, 1997) 42-44. Chapter in Linda Shout, "Choice, Agency and Consent: Feminist Debates on Trafficking and Implications for Canadian Law and Policy Affecting Trafficked Women," (Women's Studies Honours Thesis, University of Victoria, 2001), 20.

83 Piccigallo, Philip R., *The Japanese on Trial: Allied War Crimes Operations in the East, 1945-1951* (Austin: University of Texas, 1979), 179.

84 Ibid, 179.

85 Dolgopol and Paranjape, *Comfort Women,* 135.

86 Ustinia Dolgopol, "Women's Voices, Women's Pain." (Human Rights Quarterly. 1995), 30.

87 The Netherlands-based Foundation of Japanese Honorary Debts is an organization that lobbies the Japanese government for redress on behalf of the Dutch citizens (or their living descendants) in the Netherlands East Indies (now Indonesia) who were prisoners-of-war and victims of war crimes committed by the Imperial Japanese military. It was established in 1990. http://www.japanse-ereschulden.nl/english/

88 The Second International Peace Conference in 1907 or known as the Hague Convention of 1907 is a treaty and declaration negotiated by several nations over the laws and customs of war on land. The First Hague Peace Conference was held in 1899.

89 Ranam is a district in Chongjin, North Hamgyong and Bangjin is in Chungam District.

90 Judgement, Page 49.

91 Taipei Women's Rescue Foundation's website: http://www.twrf.org.tw/eng/p3-service.asp?Class1=aBJLaB36

92 Taipei Times. PROFILE: Taiwanese former 'comfort woman' dies before apology. September 6, 2011. http://www.taipeitimes.com/News/taiwan/archives/2011/09/06/20035 12594/1

93 Ibid.

94 House Resolution 121 is a congressional resolution that urges Japan to formally apologize, and accept moral and historical responsibility for organising the system of Imperial military sex slavery otherwise known by the euphemism 'comfort women'.

95 Justice with Healing: An Anthology on the Lolas Kampanyera Survivors of WWII Japanese Military Sexual Slavery in the Philippines. 2007.

96 Amnesty International (2005). Still waiting after 60 years: Justice for survivors of Japan's military sexual slavery system. London: Amnesty International.

97 Families of the War Bereaved Society Office was founded by grieving families after World War II. The group is supportive of the

prime minister's visits to Yasukuni Shrine.

[98] Emperor Meiji of Japan was emperor from 1867 to 1912 and under his reign he helped to modernise Japan and established a powerful army and navy.

[99] Peoples' Daily, "Lawsuits launched against Japan's PM for shrine visit," November 1, 2001, http://english.peopledaily.com.cn/200111/01/eng20011101_83674.ht ml.

[100] Asahi Shimbun. October 17, 2014. 'Abe makes symbolic offering to Yasukuni, likely to forgo autumn festival visit'. http://ajw.asahi.com/article/behind_news/politics/AJ201410170029

[101] http://arts.cuhk.edu.hk/NanjingMassacre/NMB&J.html

[102] Saburo Ienaga (September 3, 1913 – November 29, 2002) was a Japanese historian and author. He was nominated for the Nobel Peace Prize in 1999 and 2001 for his decades long efforts to fight against censorship of war crimes in Japanese school textbooks.

[103] "Saburo Ienaga: One man's campaign against Japanese censorship," The Guardian, December 3, 2002. http://www.guardian.co.uk/news/2002/dec/03/guardianobituaries.japa n

[104] Yayori Matsui (April 12, 1934 - December 27, 2002) was a Japanese journalist and leading activist for sex slaves for the Imperial Japanese military. Yayori was the driving force behind the Violence Against Women in War Network, Japan (VAWW-NET Japan), and the Women's International War Crimes Tribunal on Japan's Military Sexual Slavery held in Tokyo in 2000.

[105] Talmadge, Eric, "Memoir of Japanese 'comfort woman' recounts 'this hell," AP News, July 9, 2007.

[106] Children and Textbooks Japan Network 21106 is an organization that documents cases of the Japanese government's use of school textbooks that glorify Japanese militarism before and during WWII and downplay and distort wartime atrocities of the Imperial Japanese military including war crimes such as military sex slavery and the gruesome military-run medical and biochemical weapons experiment program called "Unit 731". It also documents ultraconservatives (and ultranationalists) lobbying efforts for these whitewashed school textbooks.

[107] McDougall, Gay J. "Contemporary Forms of Slavery: Systematic rape, sexual slavery and slavery-like practices during armed conflict." At the 50th Session of the United Nations Commission on Human Rights, Sub-Commission on Prevention of Discrimination and Protection of Minorities, (New York, 1998). Radhika Coomaraswamy, "Report on the Mission to the Democratic People's Republic of Korea, the Republic of Korea and Japan on the Issues of Military Sexual Slavery in Wartime U.N. Commission on

Human Rights," 52nd Session, 1996.

108 Judgement, 26-29.

109 Paris, Erna. *Long Shadows: Truth, Lies and History,* (New York: Bloomsbury, 2000), 124.

110 The International Military Tribunals of the Far East (Tokyo) found that the state of Japan violated the 1907 Hague Convention Respecting the Laws and Customs of War on Land; and the Women's International War Crimes Tribunal for the Trial of Japan's Military Sexual Slavery found the state of Japan to have breached The 1921 International Convention for the Suppression of the Traffic in Women and Children and the 1929 Geneva Convention that prohibited the abuse of women and the 1930 International Labor Organisation Convention Concerning Forced Labor; and by the beginning of the 1900s , the prohibition against slavery and the slave trade was accepted as customary international law and therefore, the state of Japan is liable under international law for this violation of enslaving girls and women as sexual slaves for the Japanese military.

111 Japan Fellowship of Reconciliation <http://www.jfor.jp/>

112 Stetz and Oh, *Legacies*,15.

113 United Nations Commission on Human Rights: Written statement submitted by Japan Fellowship of Reconciliation, non-governmental organizations in special consultative status. http://www.unhchr.ch/Huridocda/Huridoca.nsf/TestFrame/6a8b8506c d17dd93c1256d78002bb245?Opendocument

114 Yoshimi, *Comfort Women*, 33.

115 The National Institute for Defense Studies (NIDS) is the Ministry of Defense's policy research division, focusing on security and military history and offering college-level education for high-ranking officers of Japan's Self-Defense Forces. The library of the NIDS is the leading military history research center and has military and naval documents and publications.

116 Yoshimi, *Comfort Women,*, 9.

117 Manchukuo means "State of Manchuria", a territory that encompasses northeast China and Inner Mongolia and was seized by Japan in 1931. A pro-Japanese "puppet government" was installed a year later with Puyi, the last Qing emperor as the emperor.

118 Nagasaki Prefecture is on the island of Kyushu, Japan. The capital of this prefecture is the city of Nagasaki.

119 Tokyo Tribunal Judgment

120 The Shanghai Expeditionary Army was a large military division of the Japanese army in the Second Sino-Japanese War (July 7, 1937 - September 2, 1945).

121 Judgment Page 39.

122 Onishi, Norimitsu, 'Historian documents Japan's role in sex slavery,' *New York Times,* March 30, 2007.

[123] Buerk, Roland, "Japan to boost aid to Afghanistan," *BBC News*, November 10, 2009.

[124] The Asian Women's Fund (AWF) was set up in 1995 by Prime Minister Tomiichi Murayama's government after he expressed "deep remorse" to its Asian neighbors for the suffering caused by Japan's wartime aggression and he apologized to the victims of sexual slavery by the Imperial Japanese military, the comfort women. The AWF was controversial and several leading activists in Korea, the Philippines and Taiwan denounced the funds because the money was from charity funds rather than state compensation and the apology letter was a personal one instead of an official government apology. These activists convinced more than half of the military sex slavery survivors to reject the money.

[125] Japan does not have a comprehensive counter-human trafficking law, but its amendment to the criminal code in 2005 prohibits the buying and selling of persons and could be used to prosecute trafficking offenses and punishment could range between one to 10 years in prison.

[126] The Yomiuri Shimbun is a Japanese newspaper, one of the five national newspapers, and is part of the Yomiuri Group, the largest media conglomerate in Japan. Its political views are conservative and sometimes seen as center-right.

[127] The Asahi Shimbun, a left-leaning publication, is one of the five national newspapers in Japan and has an alliance with the International Herald Tribune, which is owned by The New York Times. The Asahi considers the sexual slaves euphemistically referred to as 'comfort women' were forced into prostitution. However, the newspaper does not take into account the role of the Japanese military in forcibly recruiting women in Korea and Taiwan.

[128] The Gulag in the Soviet Union was a massive system of forced labor camps from the 1920s to 1950s and at one period, millions of people were imprisoned in the Gulag.

[129] The Chinese government prosecuted high-ranking Japanese military officials, but it repatriated war criminals of lower-ranking to Japan. The members of the Association of Returnees from China (Chūgoku Kikansha Renraku Kai), or often referred to as Chukiren, received such humane treatment and amnesty from the prison staff at the Fushun War Criminals Management Centre that they called it a "miracle", a miracle at Fushun.

[130] The Kuomintang of China (KMT) was the ruling party of China from 1928 to its defeat in the Chinese civil war by the Communist Party (CPC) in 1949. The KMT was established by Sun Yat-Sen and Song Jiaoren after the Xinhai Revolution of 1911. Later, military leader Chiang Kai-shek helped the KMT organize the National

Revolutionary Army which unified much of China in 1928. Chiang was the leader of the Republic of China from 1928 to 1975.

131 Mao Zedong, also referred to as Chairman Mao, was a Chinese Communist leader and the founder of the People's Republic of China. He led the Communist Party of China from its establishment in 1949 until his death in 1976.

132 Chiang Kai-shek was a military leader and helped the Kuomintang of China (KMT) organize the National Revolutionary Army and this army unified much of China in 1928. Chiang was the leader of the Nationalist government from 1928 to 1949, when he and many KMT and their families fled to Taiwan. He led this government in exile in Taiwan until his death in 1975.

133 The Potsdam Declaration called for the surrender of all Japanese military during World War II.

134 The Greater East Asia Co-Prosperity Sphere was an imperial propaganda concept to "free" Asia of colonial powers and was used by the Imperial Japanese military and government for occupied Asian nations in the 1930s until the end of WWII. The concept was used to justify Japanese aggression in East Asia before and during WWII and to manipulate local populations.

135 "Resource center on Japan's wartime aggression opens in Saitama," *Kyodo News,* November 6, 2006. http://goliath.ecnext.com/coms2/gi_0199-5973313/FEATURE-Resource-center-on-Japan.html

136 Cultural Revolution also known as the Great Proletarian Cultural Revolution was a 10-year political campaign that took place between 1966 to 1976 and was instigated by Mao Zedong and his wife Jiang Qing to re-establish Mao's authority over the government. This period was marked by extreme civil unrest and chaos as tens of thousands were executed. Young student 'Red Guards purged intellectuals and so-called counter-revolutionary elements, and millions were forced into manual labor. The Cultural Revolution officially ended with the arrest of the leading figures of the revolution called the Gang of Four, including Jiang Qing. They were arrested after Mao's death in September 1976.

137 Shinichiro, Kumagai, *"The Asia-Pacific Journal: Japan Focus. 'Fighting for Peace After War: Japanese War Veterans recall the war and their peace activism after repatriation.'"* November 18, 2008.

138 ABC TV show 'Australian Story.' An Uncomfortable Truth Transcript April 2, 2007 http://www.abc.net.au/austory/content/2007/s1886480.htm

139 Yoshimi, *Comfort Women,* 167.

140 "Australian Sex Slave Seeks Apology," *The Sydney Morning Herald,* http://www.smh.com.au/news/national/australian-sex-slave-seeks-

apology/2007/02/13/1171128950424.html
[141] Australian Broadcasting Corporation. Talking Heads with Peter Thompson. Transcript of interview with Jan Ruff-Ruff-O'Herne. February 23, 2009. http://www.abc.net.au/tv/talkingheads/txt/s2492804.htm
[142] Ibid.
[143] "Australian Sex Slave Seeks Apology," *The Sydney Morning Herald,* http://www.smh.com.au/news/national/australian-sex-slave-seeks-apology/2007/02/13/1171128950424.html
[144] "Australian Sex Slave Seeks Apology," *The Sydney Morning Herald* http://www.smh.com.au/news/national/australian-sex-slave-seeks-apology/2007/02/13/1171128950424.html
[145] "Australian Sex Slave Seeks Apology," *The Sydney Morning Herald,* http://www.smh.com.au/news/national/australian-sex-slave-seeks-apology/2007/02/13/1171128950424.html
[146] Subcommittee on Asia, the Pacific, and the Global Environment Committee on Foreign Affairs U.S. House of Representatives. Hearing on Protecting the Human Rights of "Comfort Women." http://foreignaffairs.house.gov/110/ohe021507.htm
[147] "Australian Sex Slave Seeks Apology," *The Sydney Morning Herald,* http://www.smh.com.au/news/national/australian-sex-slave-seeks-apology/2007/02/13/1171128950424.html
[148] Amnesty International. Open letter to the Prime Minister, Hatoyama Yukio. September 22, 2009. www.amnesty.org/en/library/asset/ASA22/013/.../asa220132009en.pdf
[149] Ibid.
[150] Ibid.
[151] Amnesty International. Open letter to the Prime Minister, Hatoyama Yukio. September 22, 2009. www.amnesty.org/en/library/asset/ASA22/013/.../asa220132009en.pdf
[152] Albert Speer was Hitler's chief architect and kept the war machine running and served as Minister of Armaments and War Production in World War II.
[153] http://www.global-alliance.net/SFPT/LegacyOfWarGermanyJapanAt50YearsEnd.htm
[154] Morris-Suzuki, Tessa, "Japan's 'Comfort Women': It's time for the truth (in the ordinary, everyday sense of the word)" http://www.japanfocus.org/-Tessa-Morris_Suzuki/2373
[155] Facing History and Ourselves: Willy Brandt's Silent Apology.

http://www2.facinghistory.org/Campus/Memorials.nsf/0/DC396F572 BD4D99F85256FA80055E9B1

[156] Dawson, John. *Reconciliation* (Sovereign World Limited, 1998) 9.

[157] The Diplomat. 'Shinzo Abe's Cabinet Reshuffle.' September 2, 2014. <http://thediplomat.com/2014/09/shinzo-abes-cabinet-reshuffle/>

[158] Citizenship and Immigration Canada website. http://www.cic.gc.ca/english/multiculturalism/asian/20years-jap.asp

[159] Citizenship and Immigration Canada website. http://www.cic.gc.ca/english/multiculturalism/asian/20years-jap.asp

[160] Ibid.

[161] The 1914 Komagata Maru incident was when hundreds of Indians, mostly Sikh immigrants, seeking a better life in Canada were turned away due to discriminatory immigration policies. The Komagata Maru steamship arrived at Vancouver harbour with 376 people, all British subjects, on May 23, 1914. But the government would not allow the passengers to disembark and the ship and people waited in limbo in the harbour for two months. Only 24 people were eventually admitted to land in Canada and the rest were forced to return to India where 20 people were killed by British soldiers when they arrived on land while others were jailed. On August 3, 2008, Prime Minister Stephen Harper apologized in B.C. for the incident.

[162] Citizenship and Immigration Canada: Canadian Multiculturalism. http://www.cic.gc.ca/english/multiculturalism/citizenship.asp

[163] Prime Minister Stephen Harper's official website: http://pm.gc.ca/eng/media.asp?id=2149

[164] "PM cites 'sad chapter' in apology for residential schools," *CBS News*, June 11, 2008, http://www.cbc.ca/news/canada/story/2008/06/11/aboriginal-apology.html

[165] "PM cites 'sad chapter' in apology for residential schools," *CBS News*, June 11, 2008, http://www.cbc.ca/news/canada/story/2008/06/11/aboriginal-apology.html

[166] Dawson, *Reconciliation*, 37.

[167] *Cheongsam* is a one-piece dress for Chinese women.

[168] Dawson, *Reconciliation*, 20.